EDITORIAL RESEARCH REPORTS
ON THE

GLOBAL
COMMUNITY

Published by Congressional Quarterly, Inc.
1735 K Street, N.W.
Washington, D.C. 20006

About the Cover

Editorial Research Reports art director
Howard Chapman is responsible for the de-
sign and execution of the cover.

Published January 1972

Library of Congress Catalogue Card Number 72-184858
International Standard Book Number 0-87187-028-2

Editorial Research Reports
Editor Emeritus, Richard M. Boeckel
Editor, William B. Dickinson, Jr.
Associate Editor for Reports, Hoyt Gimlin

Contents

FOREWORD

DESPITE all the talk about "Spaceship Earth" and "Global Village," mankind remains a victim of tribal instincts. Internationalism has appeal as a concept, but nationalism is the reality. There are signs all around us—from the troubles of foreign aid legislation on Capitol Hill to the hard line talk on world trade and monetary policy at the White House— that the United States may be moving toward a withdrawal into protectionism and isolationism. The combined trauma of Viet Nam and recession triggered a backlash that could carry the nation beyond introspection into introversion.

One cannot expect politicians to admit that they are suffering from a bad case of nationalism. Not only would it be old fashioned; it would be an admission of failure as well. U.S. policy since the end of World War II has been premised on expansion of America's role in the world. But too often we have seen our position as that of master rather than partner. It is this heavy-handed approach to the solution of world problems that has gained us more than our share of enmity.

Even if we should now wish to retreat to some kind of physical or pschological Fortress America, it is too late to dig a hole and climb in. The fragile structure of the U.S. economy would become more fragile still should we lose our world markets. The value of the dollar at home presupposes its continuing strength abroad. American citizens, both in and out of uniform, are spread throughout the globe. Finally, we can never forget the harsh imperatives of the atomic age, which decree that no spot in the world is exempt from potential destruction by thermonuclear missile.

America's problem in the 1970s will be to redefine its place in the world community. Leadership will have to flow out of respect rather than from fear. More U.S. aid will have to be channeled to the poor nations through multi-lateral agencies like the World Bank, even if it costs us leverage with recipient nations. The shattered world of 1945 has been rebuilt a generation later. It has grown up, and the old attitudes will not do. America's new task is to set an example that will keep peace and engender prosperity throughout the global community.

William B. Dickinson, Jr.
Editor

December 1971
Washington, D.C.

Presidential Diplomacy

by

Richard L. Worsnop

NIXON'S FORTHCOMING VISIT TO CHINA
Role of the U.S. President as 'Diplomat in Chief'
Probable Topics of Discussion in Peking Talks
Dealings With Chinese Communists Since 1953
Likelihood of Talks With Other Foreign Leaders

RISE AND FALL OF SUMMIT CONFERENCES
Dawn of Summit Era at Paris Peace Conference
Meetings of Allied Leaders During World War II
Controversy Over Secret Agreements at Yalta
Slow Ascent to the Geneva Summit Conference
Abortive Summit at Paris in 1960; Its Aftermath

CHARACTERISTICS OF SUMMIT DIPLOMACY
Secret Diplomacy Versus Negotiating in the Open
Sharply Opposing Views on Value of Summitry
Reliance of U.S. Presidents on Unofficial Envoys

1 9 7 1
Sept. 24

PRESIDENTIAL DIPLOMACY

THE PRESIDENT of the United States holds not one office but several. He is Chief Executive, Head of State, Commander in Chief of the armed forces, and head of his party. In the past three decades or so, still another function has been added to the list. To an ever-increasing extent, the President is the country's "Diplomat in Chief." It is in this capacity that President Nixon will travel to China sometime within the next several months for talks with Premier Chou En-lai and, presumably, Communist Party Chairman Mao Tse-tung.

Arrangements for the President's visit were worked out in talks between Chou and presidential assistant Henry A. Kissinger in Peking, July 9-11, 1971. Kissinger had flown secretly to the Chinese capital in the midst of an Asian fact-finding tour. His mission remained a secret until Nixon announced, in a July 15 nationwide telecast, that he would go to Peking before May 1972 "to seek the normalization of relations between the two countries and to exchange views on questions of concern to the two sides." There has been newspaper speculation that the visit might come as early as October 1971.

The President's announcement came as a stunning surprise to his countrymen and to the world. Mainland China and the United States have been bitter enemies since the Korean War (1950-53), when Chinese "volunteers" fought with the North Koreans against Americans. The first hint of a thaw in Sino-American relations came in April 1971, when an American table tennis team accepted an invitation to play in China.[1] At a reception in Peking, April 14, Chou told the Americans that they had "opened a new page in the relations of the Chinese and American people." No one would have guessed then that China would extend an invitation to President Nixon only three months later.

---

[1] See "Reconciliation With China," *E.R.R.*, 1971 Vol. I, pp. 451-470.

While reaction to the President's forthcoming visit has been overwhelmingly favorable, a number of Americans have expressed misgivings. Some opponents of the trip consider it immoral to deal with a government that actively supports this country's enemies in the Indochina War. Others feel that American Presidents tend to give much more than they get when they engage in personal diplomacy overseas. President Eisenhower, who took part in the only postwar summit conference of the Big Four,[2] shared this view. "This idea of the President of the United States going personally abroad to negotiate—it's just damn stupid," he once said. "Every time a President has gone abroad to get into the details of these things, he's lost his shirt."[3]

The Nixon administration has taken steps to reassure those who believe the China visit is ill-advised. "Because of previous experiences, there is in the minds of many Americans a lingering suspicion of summitry," Secretary of State William P. Rogers told the American Legion national convention on Aug. 31, in Houston, Texas. "But that should cause no concern in this case."

> In Richard Nixon [Rogers continued], the American people have a representative who is idealistic enough to believe that a generation of peace is possible, and who is realistic enough to know that the only way it can come about is for a strong America to take the lead in achieving it....If ever there was a man with an open mind and a tough mind, it is the man who now serves as President of the United States. He will protect your interests wherever he goes and whomever he sees.

The Constitution and the emergence of the United States as a great power made it inevitable that the President would become Diplomat in Chief. The Constitution gives him authority to appoint, with Senate concurrence, the nation's diplomats and to receive accredited foreign emissaries. From these functions flows the authority to conduct diplomatic communications. The President also is empowered to "make treaties" subject to the advice and consent of the Senate, although he has rarely conducted treaty negotiations in person. And since the Constitution says nothing about authority to make foreign policy, the President is free to act, in effect, as his own Secretary of State.

---

[2] The 1955 Geneva Conference of the United States, the Soviet Union, Great Britain and France *(see page 17).* A Geneva conference held the previous year (1954) dealt with Indochina; it was not attended by the President.

[3] Quoted by Emmet John Hughes, *The Ordeal of Power* (1963), p. 151.

"The President is the only officer who can speak officially for the United States to foreign governments," the constitutional scholars Edward S. Corwin and J. W. Peltason have written. "Conversely, foreign governments may speak to the United States only through the President, usually via his agent, the Secretary of State. The President's power to receive ambassadors includes the power to recognize new states or governments."[4]

In appraising the personal diplomacy of Presidents, Professor Elmer Plischke of the University of Maryland wrote: "Our forbears, including the framers of the constitutional system, can scarcely be imagined to have foreseen the global role that currently is exercisable by the President, both as Chief Executive of the United States and as an individual world leader." Plischke went on to assert that "personal presidential diplomacy is one of the most significant if not auspicious developments in the conduct of American diplomacy—as distinguished from substantive policy—in the mid-20th century."[5]

Probable Topics of Discussion in Peking Talks

While no agenda for Nixon's talks with Chinese leaders has been announced, a number of likely topics come to mind. The principal barrier to improved relations between China and the United States is the status of Taiwan, home of the Chinese Nationalist government of Generalissimo Chiang Kai-shek. Peking's position, as expressed by Chou En-lai in an interview with *New York Times* vice president James Reston, Aug. 5, is that "the liberation of Taiwan is China's internal affair which brooks no foreign interference." Chou added: "At the same time, I've said that the United States has commited aggression against and occupied China's Taiwan Province and the Taiwan Strait, so we are willing to sit down and enter negotiations with the U.S. government for a settlement of this question."

Washington's position with respect to Taiwan is more complex than Peking's. The United States and the Chiang Kai-shek government on Taiwan in 1955 ratified a mutual defense treaty pledging to meet an armed attack against American or Chinese Nationalist territories, including Taiwan, the Pescadores Islands and "such other territories as may be

---

[4] Edward S. Corwin and J. W. Peltason, *Understanding the Constitution* (4th ed., 1967), p. 81.

[5] Elmer Plischke, *Summit Diplomacy* (1958), p. 1.

determined by mutual agreement." Accordingly, the United States has often stated that before its military presence on Taiwan can be negotiated away, Peking must renounce the use of force. And this country is committed to continued Nationalist Chinese representation in the United Nations. In a statement Aug. 2, Secretary of State Rogers announced that the United States would, for the first time, "support action in the General Assembly this fall calling for seating the People's Republic of [Mainland] China." On the other hand, he said, this country would "oppose any action to expel the Republic of China [Taiwan] or otherwise deprive it representation in the United Nations."

His statement was denounced from Peking Aug. 4 by Hsinhua, the official Chinese news agency, which said the United States was continuing "to obstruct the restoration to the People's Republic of China of all of her legitimate rights in the U.N. and insists on being the enemy of the Chinese people." Diplomatic observers noted that although the Hsinhua statement was sharply critical of U.S. policy it did not imply that the Rogers text had fallen short of Peking's expectations or that it in any way jeopardized Nixon's projected visit.

The New Republic suggested, Aug. 7, that "Peking's objective, at a minimum, is the removal of all U.S. military presence, materiel and personnel from the islands under Chiang Kai-shek's rule, including the offshore islands." It added:

> Next in order of importance to Peking is cessation of all clandestine operations directed against the mainland from Chinese Nationalist bases with U.S. assistance, whether mounted in this area or elsewhere. Third, less burning, is an end to intelligence collection (reconnaissance flights, infiltration teams).[6]

> Fourth, and perhaps not foreseen by Peking as achievable in this round of talks, is U.S. renunciation of its mutual defense agreement with the Nationalist Chinese. Finally, Peking would like Mr. Nixon to terminate diplomatic relations with the Republic of China. Since the Chinese are not obtuse, they could not expect this to happen before the November 1972 election.

O. Edmund Clubb, a retired U.S. Foreign Service officer, recently expressed doubt that U.S.-Chinese differences on Taiwan could be settled. "When the President asserted, in his July 15 announcement, that the search for a new relationship

---

[6] Administration officials announced on July 28 that the United States had suspended flights over Communist China by manned SR-71 spy planes and unmanned reconnaissance drones to avoid any incident that might interfere with President Nixon's visit to Peking. In 1960, Soviet Premier Nikita S. Khrushchev called off a conference with President Eisenhower after an American U-2 spy plane was shot down over Soviet territory. *See page 18.*

with China would not be at the expense of 'our old friends,' he confirmed once more that existing ties with Taipei and Saigon would be maintained," Clubb wrote. "By the evidence, the administration remains bound to the strategy and goals laid down previously....The President thus approaches the bargaining table with much to ask but little to offer." Clubb concluded: "The period of greatest danger in Sino-American relations is thus not past, but probably still lies ahead."[7]

Other issues that may well be discussed in Peking include U.S.-Chinese trade relations, reunification of Korea, settlement of the Indochina War and, in particular, the future role of Japan in Asia. Chou indicated several times in his interview with Reston that Peking was deeply disturbed by what it regarded as nascent Japanese "militarism." At one point, the Premier said: "Japan has ambitious designs on Taiwan. Japan wants to control Taiwan in her hands." Later in the conversation, he asserted that "the Korean question is also linked up with the problem of Japanese militarism." Chou explained that "if things do not go well, Japan may use the treaty it has concluded with South Korea...to get into South Korea immediately upon the withdrawal of the U.S. forces."[8]

Dealings With Chinese Communists Since 1953

Although their relations with each other have been frozen for more than two decades, the United States and China "have dealt with each other far more frequently and much more extensively than is generally known," according to Kenneth T. Young, a former ambassador to Thailand.[9] Washington and Peking representatives have met at three international conferences—one at Panmunjom, North Korea (1951-53), and two at Geneva (1954 and 1961-62).[10] But the primary diplomatic contact between the two countries has taken place in their ambassadorial talks held off and on since Aug. 1, 1955, in Geneva and (since 1958) in Warsaw. To date, there have been 136 such meetings. The most recent one was held Feb. 20, 1970. A State Department spokesman told *Editorial Research Reports* she could not comment on the current status of the talks.

---

[7] O. Edmund Clubb, "China and the United States: Beyond Ping-Pong," *Current History,* September 1971, pp. 131, 180.

[8] Japan and South Korea in 1965 signed and ratified a treaty on basic relations and related agreements designed to normalize relations between the two countries.

[9] Kenneth T. Young, *Diplomacy and Power in Washington-Peking Dealings: 1953-1967* (1967), p. 9.

[10] The Panmunjom talks resulted in an armistice in the Korean War; the 1954 Geneva conferences provided for a truce in the 7 1/2-year [French] Indochina war; the 1961-62 Geneva conference guaranteed the neutrality of Laos.

PRESIDENT NIXON'S VISITS ABROAD

1969.

Feb. 23-March 2. Belgium, England, West Germany, West Berlin, Italy, the Vatican, France.

July 26-Aug. 3. Philippines, Indonesia, Thailand, South Viet Nam, India, Pakistan, Romania, and England.

1970.

Aug. 20-21. Mexico.

Sept. 27-Oct. 5. Italy, the Vatican, Yugoslavia, Spain, England, Ireland.

The sole agreement reached in the ambassadorial talks came only six weeks after they had begun. That accord provided for the release of approximately 70 American military and civilian prisoners held in China; only a handful currently remain in captivity. Otherwise, the talks have consisted of each party's reading policy statements to the other on such issues as Viet Nam, nuclear arms control, Taiwan, and U.S.-Chinese bilateral relations.

"The Chinese Communists have a monopoly on patience and a conviction of inevitability" in diplomatic relations, Young wrote. "However, they take nothing for granted and leave nothing to chance. They come prepared after painstaking planning for each meeting. There is nothing too trivial for them to overlook. They come with a position paper and a ready reference for everything." They know, in addition, "how to manipulate the short, impulsive time sense of the Americans" and to "extract concessions out of our 'instant diplomacy' because the Americans watch the clock to end the game, [and] often give up strong bargaining positions to conclude an agreement."

Likelihood of Talks With Other Foreign Leaders

Nixon's trip to Peking may presage other presidential visits abroad to meet foreign leaders. White House Press Secretary Ronald L. Ziegler announced in San Clemente, Calif., Aug. 30, that the President would travel to Canada in the spring of 1972 and that he "would like to go to Japan."[11] The two countries are the largest trading partners of the United States and hence the two most severely affected by Nixon's New Economic Policy, which included a temporary surcharge on imports and a *de facto* devaluation of the

---

[11] It was announced earlier that the President planned to fly to Anchorage, Alaska, on Sept. 26 to welcome Emperor Hirohito and Empress Nagako when their plane stops there for refueling on its way to Europe.

dollar.[12] Nixon has made previous trips abroad as President *(see opposite page),* including a visit to Romania in 1969—the first to a Communist country by an American President since Franklin D. Roosevelt went to Russia for the Yalta Conference in 1945. The Romanian visit was seen as a step toward easing U.S. relations with Soviet-dominated Eastern Europe.

The shift in U.S. policy toward China provides another pressing reason for a presidential diplomatic mission to Tokyo. Edwin O. Reischauer, a former U.S. ambassador to Japan, believes that a trip to Tokyo should precede the one to Peking. "To see the United States now making a spectacular step forward in its relations with China without even notifying Japan in advance, much less consulting with her," he wrote, "is a humiliation and a politically dangerous blow to the [Eisaku] Sato administration."

> The argument that secrecy was necessary to the success of the Kissinger mission is no excuse, because it merely shows that the United States gives little thought to its relations with Japan when it turns its attention to the more fascinating China question. This is exactly what the Japanese fear....Any meaningful Sino-American rapprochement must be paralleled by a rapprochement between China and Japan. It should be unthinkable that President Nixon would confer with the Chinese leaders in Peking before he has first gone to Tokyo and quite openly reached an understanding with the Japanese leaders on our mutual relations with China.[13]

Meanwhile, the Soviet Union has launched a diplomatic offensive of its own to which Nixon may have to respond. Soviet Premier Alexei N. Kosygin will visit Canada for a week beginning Oct. 18, 1971. West German Chancellor Willy Brandt went to Russia Sept. 16. In addition, the three top Soviet leaders—Kosygin, Communist Party General Secretary Leonid I. Brezhnev and President Nikolai V. Podgorny—are planning trips that will take one or another of them to France, Yugoslavia, Algeria, Iran, Norway, Denmark and North Viet Nam in the next several months. Commenting on these and related developments, Sept. 8, Reston wrote: "The clearest trend among the nations today is toward some kind of new world order none of them can define. In the words of the old song, they don't know where they're going, but they're on their way."

---

[12] See "World Monetary Crisis," *E.R.R.,* 1971 Vol. II, pp. 693-713.

[13] Edwin O. Reischauer, "Yes to China Must Not Be No to Japan," *Life,* Sept. 10, 1971, p. 4.

Rise and Fall of Summit Conferences

PRESIDENTIAL DIPLOMACY—indeed, diplomacy at any level—was slow to develop in the United States. George Washington, in his Farewell Address, advised against close relations with the leading powers of the day. Freedom from contact with foreign countries did not go so far as some members of the First Congress had anticipated; they felt that after the country had made treaties of commerce and friendship with the leading nations it would not need representation abroad except through consuls, and that there would not be enough work for a Department of Foreign Affairs. That is why other duties of a domestic character were added and the name of the first department was changed to Department of State.

As late as 1801, President Jefferson continued to hope for some such situation. Writing to William Short in Paris, he said: "We wish to let every treaty we have drop off without renewal. We call in our diplomatic missions, barely keeping up those to the most important nations." America's physical isolation from the center of world power enabled it to pursue such a course well into the 19th century. Thus, by 1835 Alexis de Tocqueville could describe the position of the country in these terms: "The United States is a nation without neighbors. Separated from the rest of the world by the ocean, and too weak as yet to aim at dominion of the seas, it has no enemies, and its interests rarely come into contact with those of any other nation of the globe."

Later in the century when vital American interests were at stake, as in the Civil War, diplomacy was conducted almost solely by diplomats—not by the President. Charles Francis Adams, American minister to the Court of St. James's, was instrumental in achieving a paramount Union aim, that of dissuading the British government from taking up the cause of the Confederacy. But Adams was wont to complain he had met President Lincoln once, briefly, before being assigned to London and did not then or later receive presidential guidance.

The leading example of presidential diplomacy in the 19th century may have been Grover Cleveland's intervention in the British-Venezuelan boundary dispute of the 1890s. In response to an appeal from Venezuela, the United States asked

Britain a number of times to arbitrate the matter, only to be turned down on every occasion. Cleveland, in a message to Congress in December 1895, asked for authorization to appoint a commission to determine the true boundary between Venezuela and British Guiana. Congress immediately approved the request; the British agreed to arbitration shortly thereafter.

The first President to engage in personal diplomacy between great powers was Theodore Roosevelt. In 1905, he extended a formal offer of good offices to Japan and Russia during their Far Eastern war. Roosevelt's initiative resulted in the conclusion of a peace treaty by the two belligerents at Portsmouth, N.H. Roosevelt also intervened in the Moroccan crisis of the same year. He did so by playing a key role in bringing British, French and German representatives together in the Algeciras Conference of 1906, at which their differences were peaceably composed.

Dawn of Summit Era at Paris Peace Conference

President Wilson was deeply involved in European diplomacy both before and after American entry into World War I. On Dec. 18, 1916, shortly after his re-election, he asked the belligerents to state the terms on which they would be willing to stop fighting. Through his special envoy, Col. Edward M. House,[14] Wilson also began secret negotiations with the British and German governments. The British apparently were ready for serious discussions, but the Germans did not trust Wilson and decided to make one last bid for victory through unrestricted submarine warfare. An American declaration of war against Germany followed April 6, 1917.

Over the next 19 months, Wilson became the key figure in various exchanges regarding the termination of hostilities. He turned down a peace appeal by Pope Benedict XV in August 1917. However, he exchanged notes with Emperor Karl of Austria for nearly a year before the Armistice. And it was Wilson to whom the German government eventually transmitted a request for the cessation of hostilities. Wilson persuaded the Germans to accept terms that meant virtual surrender—though with the promise that the settlement would be based on the Fourteen Points[15]—and the Armistice was signed on Nov. 11, 1918.

---

[14] The title of colonel was bestowed on House by Gov. James S. Hogg of Texas when House was a member of the governor's staff.

[15] The Fourteen Points, set forth by Wilson in a message to Congress on Jan. 8, 1918, were designed as a peace appeal to liberal elements in the Central Powers and as a warning to the Allies that the United States would not be a party to a selfish peace.

Less than a month later, on Dec. 4, Wilson and a large group of advisers embarked for Europe to take part in the Paris Peace Conference. Wilson's decision to go to Paris represented a sharp break with the tradition that a President should not leave American territory during his incumbency.[16] However, his stature as moral leader of the Allies left him little choice. As it turned out, Wilson's wish to negotiate a peace settlement in public view proved impossible to realize. The European Allies had made secret commitments during the war which complicated the President's peace aims. The Council of Ten, which initially directed the work of the conference, eventually gave way to the Council of Four, not only because the larger group's numbers impeded progress but also because its deliberations, conducted in secret, did not remain secret.

The Treaty of Versailles thus was drawn up behind closed doors by four heads of government—Wilson, David Lloyd George of England, Georges Clemenceau of France and Vittorio Orlando of Italy. Their solutions did not get much beyond the "old methods of bartering the destinies of small and weak peoples, which had been used by the Congresses of Vienna and Berlin with disastrous results."[17] In its final form, the treaty was a compromise that vindicated some of the Fourteen Points and violated others. Wilson, as one of its architects, was committed to its ratification. But the Senate refused to ratify it because of opposition to the League of Nations. The league's covenant was written into the treaty.

It has since been suggested that Wilson's long sojourn in Europe made him lose contact with American opinion and that he thus overestimated domestic support for the Versailles Treaty. But even before the President left for Paris, he had been forewarned of the dangers of personal diplomacy. Frank I. Cobb, editor-in-chief of the *New York World,* on Nov. 4, 1918, gave Col. House a memorandum that was passed on to the President. It said:

> The moment President Wilson sits at the council table with these Prime Ministers and Foreign Secretaries he has lost all the power that comes from distance and detachment....He becomes merely a negotiator dealing with other negotiators. He is... bound to abide by the will of the majority or disrupt its proceedings....Any public protest to which the President gave utterance would thus be only the complaint of a thwarted and disappointed negotiator....

---

[16] Actually, Theodore Roosevelt was the first to depart from this tradition. In 1906 TR traveled to Panama and Puerto Rico.

[17] Paul S. Reinsch, *Secret Diplomacy* (1922), p. 201.

In Washington President Wilson has the ear of the whole world....If his representatives are balked by the representatives of the other powers,...he can go before Congress and appeal to the conscience and hope of mankind....This is a mighty weapon, but if the President were to participate personally in the proceedings, it would be a broken stick.[18]

In any event, rejection of the Treaty of Versailles by the Senate marked a return to isolationism for the United States. From that time until Pearl Harbor, this country sought for the most part to avoid close involvement in the concerns of other nations. The 1938 Munich Conference, which led to Germany's takeover of Czechoslovakia, deepened American distrust of diplomacy at the summit. The conference came to symbolize weakness and surrender in the face of aggression. British Prime Minister Neville Chamberlain, who came home from Munich bearing his famous umbrella and raising the prospect of "peace in our time," won momentary popularity but soon afterward was considered to have been badly outwitted by German Chancellor Adolf Hitler.

Meetings of Allied Leaders During World War II

During the negotiations with Japan that preceded the Dec. 7, 1941, attack on Pearl Harbor, the United States was repeatedly pressed to agree to a conference somewhere in the Pacific between President Franklin D. Roosevelt and Premier Fumimaro Konoye. Roosevelt was attracted to the idea and tentatively proposed a meeting at Juneau, Alaska. The Japanese sought to pin Washington down to an early date and insisted that actual negotiations for settlement of outstanding differences could be left until later. Cordell Hull, then Secretary of State, wrote after the war that the United States hesitated because "a meeting with Konoye, without an advance agreement, could only result in another Munich or in nothing at all."[19]

After this country entered World War II, conferences of Allied heads of government played a vital role in coordinating planning for both war and peace. Roosevelt and Winston Churchill, the British Prime Minister, had already met on a warship off Newfoundland in August 1941, four months before Pearl Harbor, and drawn up the Atlantic Charter—a statement of "common principles...on which they based their hopes for a better future for the world." The two

---

[18] Quoted by Dean Acheson, *Meetings at the Summit: A Study in Diplomatic Method* (1958), pp. 23-24.

[19] *The Memoirs of Cordell Hull* (1948), pp. 1024-1025.

leaders met five more times in the next two years; their Washington meeting of June 19-25, 1942, was notable for the decision to go ahead with development of the atomic bomb.

The first summit meeting attended by Soviet Premier Josef Stalin took place at Teheran in late 1943. It was there in the Iranian capital that the decision was made to open a second front in Europe. The Teheran conference was preceded and followed by two meetings at Cairo involving Roosevelt, Churchill and Chiang Kai-shek. The most controversial of the wartime Big Three conferences opened in Yalta on Feb. 4, 1945, two months before Roosevelt's death and three months before Germany's surrender. In a week of secret deliberations at the Russian resort city on the Black Sea, the Allies took far-reaching decisions affecting the future of Europe. They left Russia the dominant power in the newly occupied countries of Eastern Europe.

Yalta agreements also reached into the Far East. Stalin promised to enter the war against Japan within three months of the end of hostilities in Europe. In return, the Soviet Union was to regain territory and rights lost in the Russo-Japanese War of 1904-05: the southern half of Sakhalin Island; predominant control of the Chinese Eastern Railway; a Russian naval base at Port Arthur, and the port city of Dairen. It was agreed to perpetuate the status of Outer Mongolia, which had long been a Soviet protectorate. Finally, the Soviet Union was to acquire the Kurile Islands immediately north of Japan.

Russia agreed to participate in the United Nations Conference on International Organization, scheduled to open the following April in San Francisco. To counter-balance the multiple votes of the British Commonwealth countries, and of American allies in the Western Hemisphere, Russia was given three seats in the world organization—one each for the Soviet Union, Byelorussia and the Ukraine. The Big Three agreed that the most important body of the United Nations would be a Security Council whose decisions would require unanimous approval of its five permanent members: China (now Taiwan), Britain, France, Soviet Union, and the United States.

The final Big Three conference was held at Potsdam, near occupied Berlin, in the summer of 1945 to cover many issues discussed five months earlier at Yalta. By now there were unmistakable signs of strain among the leaders. Stalin's

MAJOR SUMMIT CONFERENCES ABROAD
ATTENDED BY U.S. PRESIDENTS

Place	Time	Participants
Paris	Jan. 12-June 28, 1919	Wilson, Lloyd George, Clemenceau, Orlando
Casablanca	Jan. 14-24, 1943	Roosevelt, Churchill*
Cairo	Nov. 22-26, 1943	Roosevelt, Churchill, Chiang Kai-shek
Teheran	Nov. 28-Dec. 1, 1943	Roosevelt, Churchill, Stalin
Yalta	Feb. 4-11, 1945	Roosevelt, Churchill, Stalin
Potsdam	July 17-Aug. 2, 1945	Truman, Stalin, Churchill-Attlee†
Geneva	July 18-23, 1955	Eisenhower, Bulganin, Faure, Eden
Paris	May 16-17, 1960	Eisenhower, Khrushchev, DeGaulle, Macmillan

* Stalin was invited but was unable to attend.
† Clement R. Attlee succeeded Churchill as Prime Minister as the result of a general parliamentary election held while the conference was in session.

behavior led President Truman, at his first summit conference, to observe that "force is the only thing the Russians understand." He concluded that the Soviet Union was "planning world conquest."[20]

Controversy Over Secret Agreements at Yalta

The Yalta agreements were bitterly criticized as East-West differences became more pronounced after the war. Some Republicans went so far as to describe the conference as a Democratic "sellout" of Poland and China to the Communists. Comparisons were drawn between Yalta and Munich. But Keith Eubank contends that, in retrospect, the Teheran Conference "was the most important meeting of those held during the war, including Yalta and Potsdam." He explained: "By agreeing to the plan for Overlord [code name for the D-Day invasion of Normandy], with Russian forces coming from the East, Roosevelt, Churchill and Stalin had shaped the future of Europe. Regardless of future conferences and agreements, Russian armies would control Eastern Europe and the other allies the West. Russian armies would pass over lands once held or coveted by the czars."[21] The Yalta Conference, in his view, did little more than ratify the decisions taken at Teheran.

By the time the Yalta Conference opened, Soviet troops had swept through almost all of Poland and East Prussia, had at some points reached the Oder River in Germany, and had captured most of Hungary. Yugoslav partisans had retaken Belgrade. Meanwhile, British and American troops were still recovering from their setback in the Battle of the Bulge, and had not yet crossed the Rhine. Given these circum-

---

[20] *Memoirs of Harry S Truman* (1955), p. 412.
[21] Keith Eubank, *The Summit Conferences, 1919-1960* (1966), p. 75.

stances, George F. Kennan wrote, "There was nothing the Western democracies could have done to prevent the Russians from entering those areas except to get there first, and this they were not in a position to do."

Nevertheless, Republicans made Yalta a leading political issue of the late 1940s and early 1950s, just as they had done in the case of the Treaty of Versailles in 1919-20. The late John Foster Dulles charged in 1950 that Roosevelt had surrendered "great moral principles at Yalta" and that his concessions had given Moscow a springboard for "further aggressive expansion." The 1952 GOP platform promised that a Republican administration would "repudiate all commitments...in secret understandings, such as those of Yalta, which aid Communist enslavements." Subsequently, the Eisenhower administration did no such thing—although it did release a large part of the previously secret official record of the Yalta Conference on March 16, 1955.[22]

Slow Ascent to the Geneva Summit Conference

The death of Stalin in March 1953 offered some hope that East-West tensions might be eased. During a foreign policy debate in the House of Commons, May 11, 1953, Churchill, again Prime Minister, called for a "conference on the highest level...between the leading powers without delay." He asserted that "at the worst, the participants in the meeting could...[establish] more intimate contacts, and at best we might have a generation of peace."[23]

Although Washington praised Churchill's proposal, President Eisenhower insisted that the Soviet Union must prove its good faith before a summit meeting was convened. That proof was slow in coming. An armistice was signed in Korea in July 1953, but a Berlin foreign ministers' conference in January-February 1954 made no progress on the question of divided Germany or on that of still-occupied Austria. East-West tensions increased soon afterward when the Western powers agreed to terminate the remnants of the occupation of West Germany and to admit that country to the North Atlantic Treaty Organization.

Apparently fearing that the Western powers were aiming also to bring the Western-occupied part of Austria into NATO, Soviet leaders invited Austrian Chancellor Julius Raab to

---

[22] See "Secrecy in Government," *E.R.R.*, 1971 Vol. II, p. 650.

[23] In the same speech, Churchill coined the term "summit" conference. *See box.*

Origin of Phrase "Summit Conference"

Winston Churchill, the British Prime Minister, coined the phrase "summit conference" during a foreign policy debate in the House of Commons, May 11, 1953. Calling for a "conference at the highest level...between the leading powers," he asserted: "If there is not at the summit of the nations the will to win the greatest prize and the greatest honor ever offered to mankind [that of peace], doom-laden responsibility will fall upon those who now possess the power to decide."

Moscow in March 1955. Raab and his hosts quickly agreed on terms for neutralization of Austria. The way was thus opened to a long-delayed signing of an Austrian state treaty by the four occupying powers and to the withdrawal of foreign troops. Meanwhile, hints that a similar over-all settlement for Germany might be acceptable to the Kremlin had come from Moscow, along with apparent Soviet concessions on disarmament.

These indications of a softening of the Soviet position raised Western hopes that a summit conference might be fruitful. The United States, Britain and France accordingly proposed to the Soviet Union, five days before the Austrian treaty was signed on May 15, 1955, that the heads of the Big Four governments hold an early meeting to "remove the sources of conflict between us." Moscow agreed and the summit session opened at Geneva on July 18—almost 10 years to the day after the opening of the last previous summit conference at Potsdam.

A four-point agenda drawn up on the second day of the Geneva Conference listed four subjects: German reunification, European security, disarmament, and improvement of East-West relations. There was no attempt to reach detailed agreements on any question. However, it was announced that "Settlement of the German question and the reunification of Germany by means of free elections shall be carried out in conformity with the national interest of European security." In addition, there was said to be tacit agreement among the heads of government that nuclear war would be so devastating that it must be avoided at any cost.

"Throughout the conference," Eubank wrote, "United States leaders were fearful of the ghosts of summit conferences past, which had been used for political ammunition in Eisenhower's presidential election campaign, and these fears prevented more definite accomplishments. Feeling that too

17

much had been decided in the past, nothing must be decided now. When Eisenhower returned to the United States, Vice President Richard M. Nixon was so frightened of the comparison with the Munich Conference of 1938 that he banned umbrellas at the airport reception. To quiet the ghosts of Munich, Eisenhower made his arrival speech standing in the rain." To further allay suspicion, the State Department issued an official report on the Geneva Conference only two months after it ended.

Abortive Summit at Paris in 1960; Its Aftermath

One month after Russia's launching of Sputnik I on Oct. 4, 1957, Soviet Communist Party Secretary Nikita S. Krushchev announced that the Kremlin was ready for a new high-level meeting of Soviet and Western leaders. Almost two years of Soviet pressure for such a conference followed. Finally, after three days of talks with Khrushchev at Camp David, Md., Sept. 25-27, 1959, Eisenhower announced that the Soviet leader had "removed many of the objections that I have heretofore held" to a summit meeting. An agreement to convene a top-level parley in Paris the following spring was reached in an exchange of notes among the Big Four at the end of December.

The "spirit of Camp David," like the 1955 "spirit of Geneva," evaporated within a matter of months. It was apparent long before the summit meeting was to open, May 16, 1960, that the negotiating positions of both East and West had stiffened. An American U-2 spy plane, shot down over Russia on May 1, gave Khrushchev an excuse to scuttle the conference. At the first session in Paris, he demanded that Eisenhower apologize for having sent reconnaissance aircraft over Soviet territory. When the President declined to do so, Khrushchev refused to go on with the meeting. At a tumultuous news conference, May 18, he denounced Eisenhower in vitriolic terms and declared he was "convinced that persons will come to power in the United States who will [be]...in favor of reaching mutually acceptable agreements."

John F. Kennedy's election as President was hailed by Khrushchev at a Jan. 1, 1961, reception in the Kremlin. He recalled a "statement made by Mr. Kennedy...that, if he were President, he would express his regret to the Soviet government over the U-2 plane flight." Asserting that the American people had in effect voted for "condemnation of...

the cold war," Khrushchev expressed hope that a "fresh wind will begin to blow with the coming of the new President."

Kennedy and Khrushchev met at Vienna, June 3-4, 1961, for talks that were described as generally unproductive. A joint communique issued at the end of the meeting affirmed support of a "neutral and independent Laos under a government chosen by the Laotians themselves" and stated that Kennedy and Khrushchev had agreed to "maintain contact on all questions of interest to the two countries and...the whole world." The President reported to the nation, in a broadcast on his return home, that the Vienna meeting had been a "very sober two days." He added: "No advantage or concession was either gained or given. No major decision was either planned or taken. No spectacular progress was... achieved."

Some observers, however, later speculated that Khrushchev had mistaken Kennedy's inexperience at Vienna for weakness, and that this assessment of the President's character led the Premier to instigate the Berlin crisis of 1961 and to order the installation of missiles in Cuba the following year. The Cuban missile crisis, which brought the world to the brink of nuclear warfare, was put on the way to settlement by what amounted to a summit conference by correspondence. Hans J. Morgenthau pointed out that Kennedy and Khrushchev "resorted successfully to a device which neither belongs to the traditional diplomatic procedures nor is a summit meeting proper: a kind of long-distance summit in the exchange of personal letters."[24]

President Johnson's one venture in East-West summitry came in June 1967, when he met with Soviet Premier Alexei N. Kosygin at Glassboro, N.J.[25] In two separate meetings on June 23 and June 25, Johnson and Kosygin discussed the Middle East crisis, the Viet Nam War, efforts to halt the proliferation of nuclear weapons, limitations on anti-ballistic missile systems, and U.S.-Soviet relations. Although the talks failed to resolve any outstanding U.S.-Soviet differences, both sides agreed to continue their efforts at the ministerial level.

---

[24] Hans J. Morgenthau, "Dilemma of the Summit," *The New York Times Magazine,* Nov. 11, 1962, p. 118. For other details of the missile-crisis diplomacy, see "Heads-of-State Diplomacy," *E.R.R.,* 1962 Vol. II, pp. 875-878.

[25] Kosygin had come to the United States June 17 to address the U.N. General Assembly on the Middle East crisis. Glassboro was chosen as the site of his talks with Johnson because it is roughly halfway between New York and Washington.

Characteristics of Summit Diplomacy

ADVANCES IN TRANSPORTATION and communication have had profound effects on the conduct of diplomacy. A century ago, meetings of heads of government or even of foreign ministers were reserved for only the most momentous decisions. With the coming of intercontinental air travel, such meetings have become commonplace. Radio, television and telegraph, moreover, have intruded on the secrecy that formerly characterized diplomatic negotiation. Accordingly, "The masses are expected to take an interest in foreign affairs, to know the details of current controversies, to come to their own conclusions, and to render these conclusions effective through press and parliament."[26]

Whether these developments are bad or good is debatable. Professional diplomats tend to look with disfavor upon negotiation carried out at the highest level and in public view. Sisley Huddleston wrote that a President "should remember...that he is a lofty and lonely figure, a final court of appeal placed by his office above the dusty arena of personal contacts, personal prepossessions, personal prejudices, personal sentiments of any kind."[27]

On the other hand, it is argued that heads-of-government diplomacy, conducted more or less in the open, is an inevitable result of the present world power structure. As recently as the 1930s, there were half a dozen great powers; today there are two "superpowers"—the United States and the Soviet Union. Hence, as Prime Minister Harold Macmillan told the House of Commons in 1960, there is "general acceptance of the view that, in addition to what can be done by diplomats and foreign ministers, there may be circumstances in which conclusions cannot be reached, especially when dealing with the Soviet government, except by the heads of government themselves." The Chinese Communists evidently share this view. Chou En-lai told James Reston that "if these questions [of interest to the United States and China] are to be solved, they can only be solved when the President himself comes."

---

[26] Harold Nicolson, "Diplomacy Then and Now," *Foreign Affairs,* October 1961, p. 39.
[27] Sisley Huddleston, *Popular Diplomacy and War* (1954), p. 230.

In many instances, however, presidential diplomacy can be conducted electronically. Kennedy and Khrushchev agreed, in the aftermath of the Cuban missile crisis, that the White House and Kremlin needed fast and direct communication. Thus, on Aug. 30, 1963, a "hot line" was installed, linking the two centers of world power with a 4,823-mile cable and radio circuit. The hot line may soon be updated. *The Washington Post* reported on Sept. 9, 1971, that the United States and the Soviet Union had agreed in August to establish a communications satellite hot line to provide virtually instantaneous communication in event of a crisis.

Sharply Opposing Views on Value of Summitry

Opinion is sharply divided on the value of summitry. On the one hand, it is asserted that traditional methods of diplomacy are dangerously time-consuming in an age of push-button warfare. Furthermore, summit meetings, by giving leaders of the great powers personal knowledge of one another, may enable the leaders to make more accurate judgments of intentions and probable reactions, and thus reduce the danger of war by miscalculation. Moreover, because a head of government speaks with maximum authority, he may be able to deal with important matters more expeditiously than is otherwise possible and to speedily resolve any impasse at the traditional diplomatic level.

Opponents of summitry assert that the postwar top-level meetings have been notably unproductive and tend to create rather than dissipate ill will. The public nature of summit meetings, it is further argued, is not conducive to effective negotiation; more lasting, if not more satisfactory, results may be obtained by using diplomatic channels. Still another drawback is that summit meetings arouse great popular expectations as to results, which often prove disappointing.

Few Presidents have had prior diplomatic experience, hence "the possibility of being outmaneuvered and unwisely committed is great," according to Dean Acheson. "Or," he added, "pride and stubbornness may combine to deflect cool and detached judgment." The personality of a President therefore plays a greater role in diplomacy than would be the case when negotiations are carried out at a lower level. Wilson, for example, arrived at the Paris Peace Conference brimming with idealism. "He believed sincerely that he had come to the Old World bringing the newfound wisdom of the United States. Often he could not refrain from delivering a short sermon on the principles of justice that should govern the world henceforth. Neither Lloyd George nor Clemenceau really wanted him at the conference."[28]

During World War II, Roosevelt was convinced he "had a way with Stalin." To Churchill he wrote: "I know you will not mind my being brutally frank when I tell you that I think I can personally handle Stalin better than either your Foreign Office or my State Department. Stalin hates the guts of all your top people. He thinks he likes me better, and I hope he will continue to do so."[29] In the end, no special Roosevelt-Stalin relationship seems to have developed.

Sometimes the full import of a summit meeting does not make itself known until many years later. The 1955 Geneva summit offers a case in point. Dean Acheson wrote in 1958: "Geneva was not merely a failure; it was a fraud and positive harm. It brought relaxation to the West just when the need was for endurance."[30] Robert J. Donovan, associate editor of the *Los Angeles Times,* offered quite a different appraisal in the year 1971. At Geneva, he asserted, "Eisenhower in fact had helped bring about a new era in Soviet-American relations, whose first great landmark was the nuclear test-ban treaty signed by President Kennedy and whose consequences are still unfolding."[31]

Reliance of U.S. Presidents on Unofficial Envoys

The manifold demands of the office force a President to reserve his diplomatic efforts for only the most important matters. In January 1957, Eisenhower indicated that he was "always obliged" when foreign dignitaries visited him because his "peculiar constitutional position" as head of both state and government[32] made it difficult for him to be absent from the United States for any length of time. He added that high-ranking visitors, appreciating his difficulty, willingly came to Washington without expecting him to return the visit out of courtesy. Eisenhower entrusted Vice President Nixon with the task of making routine ceremonial visits abroad.[33] Vice Presidents Johnson, Humphrey and Agnew performed similar duties.

---

[28] Keith Eubank, *op. cit.,* p. 15.

[29] Quoted by Winston Churchill in *The Hinge of Fate* (1951), p. 201.

[30] Dean Acheson, *op. cit.,* p. 19.

[31] *Los Angeles Times,* July 18, 1971.

[32] In many countries, the head of state is not the head of government. In Britain, for instance, the Queen is the head of state and the Prime Minister is the head of government.

[33] Nixon traveled to 54 countries in his eight years as Vice President. See "Vice Presidency," *E.R.R.,* 1970 Vol. II, pp. 851-852.

To ease the President's diplomatic burden still further, Eubank proposed the appointment of an "ambassador-at-large as the personal representative of the President with full negotiating powers." He added: "Modern communications would enable the President to maintain contact with his personal representative. Once the agreement was completed, the President could attend a summit conference for the purpose of signing the instrument and conferring with other heads of government."

Several Presidents have employed special, unappointed envoys to conduct important diplomatic business for them. One of the most prominent was Col. House, Wilson's confidant, who played a leading role in negotiations to end World War I and at the Paris Peace Conference. House traveled to Europe on peace missions in 1915 and 1916, helped to draft the Fourteen Points, and was Wilson's representative at the meeting of Allied leaders that drew up the pre-Armistice agreement ending the war with Germany. Wilson's faith in House was shattered at the peace conference. The President fell ill with flu on April 5, 1919, and House took his place in the negotiations. Improperly briefed, House agreed to the omission from the peace treaty of any time limit on the payment of reparations. Wilson became convinced that he had been betrayed, and the two men never again were close.

President Franklin D. Roosevelt employed numerous personal representatives on diplomatic missions. For example, he sent William C. Bullitt to the Soviet Union in advance of U.S. diplomatic recognition; Col. William Donovan to Yugoslavia in 1941 to assess the country's ability to withstand German diplomatic and military pressure; Gen. Patrick J. Hurley to China in 1944; and Judge Samuel I. Rosenman to Europe in 1945 to assess the food needs of the liberated countries.

But FDR's best known special agent was Harry L. Hopkins, who served as the President's personal confidant and emissary. On many of the issues on which the President tended to become his own Secretary of State, Hopkins served as his deputy. "The State Department was bypassed, and it provided inadequate balm to [Secretary of State Cordell] Hull's pride to receive occasional polite notes from Hopkins enclosing copies of cables 'for your information'."[34] Elmer

---

[34] Robert E. Sherwood, *Roosevelt and Hopkins* (1948), pp. 269-270.

Plischke wrote that both Stalin and Churchill came to regard Hopkins as Roosevelt's alter ego; "they appeared to have had confidence in him, and they felt that in dealing with him they were communicating with Roosevelt in a way which channels of conventional diplomacy could scarcely parallel."

Henry A. Kissinger, President Nixon's adviser on national security, appears to occupy a position similar to that held by House and Hopkins in previous administrations. It was Kissinger, not Secretary of State Rogers, who was given the sensitive task of arranging President Nixon's visit to China. Even before Kissinger's trip to Peking was disclosed, however, he had come under fire for allegedly having usurped the authority of Secretary of State Rogers. Sen. Stuart Symington (D Mo.) told the Senate on March 2, 1971, that Kissinger had become "Secretary of State in everything but name" and that Rogers was being "laughed at" in Washington circles.

Symington went on to note that Kissinger had refused to testify before Congress under the protection of executive privilege. As a result, Congress and the public were "being increasingly denied access to pertinent facts about major foreign policy decisions" and lacked "any real knowledge, let alone a voice, in the formulation of policy decisions which could well determine the nation's future."

President Nixon, like his predecessors, faces difficulties both at home and abroad when engaging in personal diplomacy. A Chief Executive is expected to achieve more at the bargaining table than a professional diplomat can, but there also is fear that he may lose more. In addition, second-guessers stand ready to criticize the President's advisers. All these hazards, however, are part and parcel of top-level negotiation, and no President can afford to abdicate his responsibilities as Diplomat in Chief.

WORLD MONEY CRISIS

by

Ralph C. Deans

1971
Sept. 8

WORLD MONEY CRISIS

P RESIDENT NIXON'S decision to suspend the convertibility of the dollar into gold has launched the
world monetary system on uncharted waters. For a quarter-
century, the American dollar—which foreign governments
could exchange for gold at $35 an ounce—had been the yard-
stick against which all free world currencies had been measured. Suddenly, it was as if that yardstick had turned to
rubber, capable of being expanded or contracted at will.
Nixon made it clear that his intention was to prompt "an
urgently needed reform" of the rules governing international
payments. The President's timing was appropriate. His
announcement of the gold embargo on Aug. 15 came just 45
days before the 118-nation International Monetary Fund was
scheduled to meet in Washington on Sept. 27. The meeting
is being billed as the most important monetary conference
since the IMF was created in Bretton Woods, N.H., in 1944.
Other important meetings to discuss international monetary
problems were scheduled to precede the Washington conference.[1]

Nixon's suspension of the gold-dollar link, as well as his
imposition of a temporary 10 per cent surcharge on imports,
came as a stunning blow to America's trading partners. The
moves prompted complaints that the United States had
violated two international treaties—the Bretton Woods
Agreement and the General Agreement on Tariffs and
Trade.[2] At home, the reaction was generally favorable. Aside
from the monetary and trade aspects of the new economic
policy announced on national television Aug. 15, Nixon instituted a wage-price freeze and took other actions *(see page
28)* to combat inflation, speed recovery from the 1970 reces-

---

[1] These included a cabinet-level meeting of American and Japanese officials in
Washington, Sept. 9; the Council of Ministers of the European Common Market in Brus-
sels, Sept. 13; and the so-called Group of Ten leading member-nations of the IMF in
London, Sept. 15.

[2] The GATT Agreement of 1947 consists of a complex set of principles and rules dedi-
cated to the removal of barriers to trade. It is subscribed to by 77 countries, including
the United States.

President Nixon's Economic Package

Wages and prices. Invoked 90-day freeze on wages and prices, until Nov. 13.

Dollar. Temporarily suspended convertibility of the dollar into gold.

Imports. Imposed temporary 10 per cent surcharge on most imports.

Foreign aid. Reduced foreign economic aid by 10 per cent.

Budget. Ordered fiscal 1972 budget cut $4.7 billion by
—a 5 per cent reduction in federal employment.
—deferral for six months of a federal pay increase due Jan. 1, 1972.
—postponement of revenue sharing plan for three months and of welfare law changes for one year.

Excise tax. Asked Congress to repeal 7 per cent excise tax on automobiles.

Jobs. Requested Congress to pass a Job Development Act, including an accelerated job investment tax credit of 10 per cent for one year and a 5 per cent writeoff after that.

Income tax. Asked Congress to permit income tax reductions to begin one year ahead of their scheduled starting date, Jan. 1, 1973.

Cost of Living Council. Appointed the council to plan for price and wage stability after the 90-day freeze ends.

Dividends. Requested that corporations freeze dividends for 90 days.

sion and reduce unemployment—hovering around 6 per cent of the labor force.

Even before Nixon acted, a series of monetary crises, especially since the 1967 devaluation of the British pound, convinced many economists that the system of fixed parities agreed to at Bretton Woods had to be changed. Under that agreement, every currency is "pegged" to the American dollar and can fluctuate only 1 per cent on either side of its fixed value. Experts said the system had now become incapable of responding to gains and losses of economic strength between industrial nations—gains and losses which were reflected in the value of one currency in terms of another. Moreover, maintaining the system required interventions in the money markets by central banks—which frequently had to sell or buy their national currencies in huge amounts to preserve the pegged values. The fact that three major currencies—the German mark, the Dutch guilder and the Canadian dollar— were "floating" without a fixed par value at the time of

Chronology of Crisis

1967	*Nov. 18*	British pound devalued by 14.3 per cent.
1968	*March 18*	Two-tier gold system announced.
1969	*Aug. 8*	French franc devalued by 11.1 per cent.
	Sept. 28	German mark floated without par value.
	Oct. 24	German mark revalued by 9.3 per cent.
1970	*June 1*	Canadian dollar floated.
1971	*May 5*	Main European exchanges closed under onslaught of American dollars.
	May 10	German mark and Dutch guilder floated; Swiss franc revalued 7.1 per cent; Austrian schilling revalued 5.05 per cent.
	Aug. 15	President Nixon suspended convertibility of dollar into gold.
	Aug. 16	Foreign exchange windows in Europe shut down for a week; Japan announced it would maintain parity of yen at 360 to the dollar.
	Aug. 19	Common Market Council of Ministers met in Brussels to discuss monetary crisis—failed to evolve a common policy.
	Aug. 27	Japanese yen floated.

Nixon's Aug. 15 announcement was evidence that the fixed-parity system was already breaking down.

Canadian, German Decisions to Float Currencies

A monetary crisis had been brewing for more than a year *(see chronology)*. The first sign of it was Ottawa's decision of June 1, 1970, to allow the Canadian dollar to float. Canada had amassed large foreign reserve balances, chiefly from trade. A run on the Canadian dollar had developed and the Bank of Canada was forced to sell its currency to all comers at the fixed rate of 92.5 cents American. In effect, the bank had to flood the market with its currency to ensure that the demand for it did not raise its value. Canadian dollars were draining away from the country and foreign reserves, for which Canada had no immediate use, were building up.[3]

A sharp favorable shift in the balance of trade of any country usually indicates that it is producing goods and services more efficiently than its trading partners. The money managers of large international corporations see it as evidence of currency strength and arrange to hold large percentages of their funds in that currency. This is regarded as a prudent hedge in business circles. But its effect in the money market is a flight from

---

[3] See "Canada's Troubled Economy," *E.R.R.*, 1970 Vol. II, pp. 926-927.

weaker currencies to stronger ones. This creates "disequilibrium"—economic unbalance—at both ends: Countries with strong currencies have to maintain large and, for them, useless foreign reserve balances while countries with weaker currencies must pay out foreign reserves which they need.

The International Monetary Fund, a pool of all currencies, provides funds which central bankers can borrow to fend off a raid on their currencies. If even this does not quench the demand for a strong currency, the country can revalue the currency in terms of the American dollar. Instead of doing that, however, Canada cut its dollar loose from the parity system altogether. Finance Minister Edgar Benson of Canada pointed up a basic weakness of the parity system when he explained his actions at the International Monetary Fund meeting in Copenhagen on Sept. 22, 1970.

> We could, of course, have sought the concurrence of the Fund in a new and higher par value [he said], but what par value would we have proposed? If we had chosen a new rate which was too low, we would not have dealt adequately with our difficulties and their attendant risks for the international payments situation. If we had chosen a new rate which was too high, the Canadian economy would have been adversely affected.... We therefore chose to let the rate find its own level and to seek in that way an exchange rate that could be sustained over a protracted period of time.

Canada's decision to float its dollar was preceded, in 1969, by the French devaluation of the franc by 11.1 per cent and

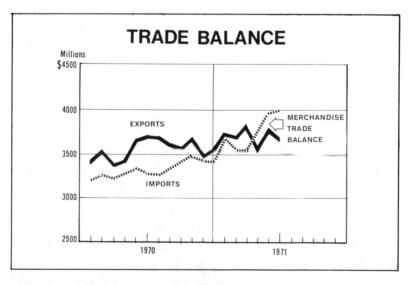

TRADE BALANCE

TRADE WITH AMERICA'S LEADING PARTNERS, 1970

(in millions of dollars)

	U.S. exports to	U.S. imports from	Balance
Canada	9,137	11,091	—1,954
Japan	4,652	5,875	—1,223
W. Germany	2,740	3,129	— 389

SOURCE: Department of Commerce

---

the West German revaluation of the mark by 9.3 per cent. It was followed in the spring of 1971 by the shock of world recognition that the U.S. economy was not performing well in relation to the rest of the world. The U.S. balance-of-payments deficit reached a record $5.53 billion in the first quarter of the year—a record surpassed in the second quarter by a deficit of $5.77 billion.[4] Far more worrisome was the growing likelihood that the United States would end the year with its first trade deficit since 1893. While American exports continued to grow, imports grew faster. There was a $676 million trade deficit for the first seven months of 1971, compared with a $2 billion surplus in the same period of 1970.[5]

As details of this economic picture became known, it stimulated a flight from the dollar to stronger European currencies. All European central banks were called on to exchange dollars but the West German Bundesbank was under the heaviest pressure. It was estimated that the bank absorbed nearly $3 billion in the two days before it shut down its foreign-exchange window on May 5. On May 10, the West German government floated the mark. Other European countries took immediate action to deflect a flow of U.S. dollars away from their central banks. The Netherlands followed Germany and floated the guilder; Belgium set up a free market for its franc for international monetary purposes but not for commercial transactions; Austria revalued its schilling by 5 per cent and Switzerland its franc by 7 per cent.

There was wide agreement among monetary experts that the reason so many dollars began to pile up in Europe early in 1971 was that its interest rates were higher than America's. Lawrence A. Mayer of *Fortune* magazine explained that the

---

[4] On the "official settlements" basis, which measures the dollars held in foreign central banks. By the "current-account" measurement, a record of all commercial transactions, the second-quarter deficit was $5.85 billion.

[5] See "Competition for World Markets," *E.R.R.*, 1970 Vol. II, pp. 589-594.

spread in interest rates "made it profitable for foreigners to shift funds into marks."

> By early May the flow became a torrent as corporations and banks saw that by moving into marks they could bet on revaluation while enjoying an interest-rate advantage with no downside risk. This flow stopped not only because of the monetary actions taken by Germany and some of its neighbors, but also because U.S. interest rates have been converging with those abroad, and may converge further.[6]

Mayer added that some European officials believed that "if the chronic deficit in the U.S. balance of payments had not undermined confidence in the dollar, far fewer dollars would have moved into Germany."

Dollar's Weakness Abroad; Indirect Devaluation

The floating mark and revaluations of other European currencies resulted in a *de facto* devaluation of the American dollar in Europe by 2 to 3 per cent. This situation was still far from stable. The Federal Reserve Board announced that in June U.S. gold stocks—backing for the dollar—were down to $10.5 billion, the lowest total since 1936. Dollar holdings by foreign central banks had in April climbed to more than $31 billion; private liabilities inflated that total to $47 billion *(see chart)*. It was obvious that the United States could not redeem those dollars for gold unless it raised the price of gold.[7]

Succeeding administrations have been saying that the price of gold is "immutable" ever since President Roosevelt increased its value to $35 an ounce in 1934. As recently as May 28, 1971, Treasury Secretary John B. Connally affirmed, "We are not going to devalue. We are not going to change the price of gold."[8] Its changeless value has been the foundation of the monetary system since the end of World War II. Nevertheless, speculators were betting that the United States would have to raise the price of gold and they drove the open-market price to a peak of $44 an ounce by early August.

Clyde H. Farnsworth of *The New York Times* reported from Paris Aug. 2 that a devaluation of the dollar was a matter of "not whether but when" in European newspapers. The conviction was shared by many Americans. The congressional Sub-

---

[6] Lawrence A. Mayer, "Into a Time of Stagflation," *Fortune*, August 1971. p. 146.

[7] Doubling the price of gold to $70 an ounce, for instance, would increase the value of the gold hoard to $21 billion.

[8] Speech to the American Bankers Association, Munich, Germany.

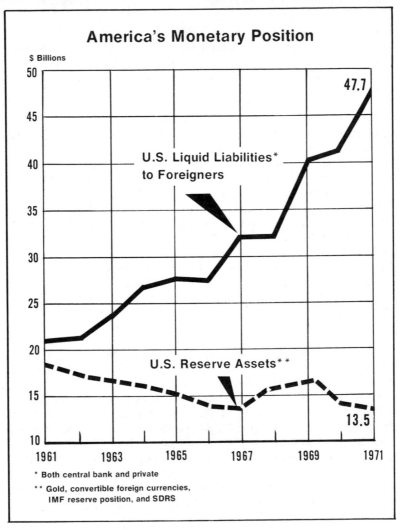

America's Monetary Position

$ Billions

U.S. Liquid Liabilities*
to Foreigners

47.7

U.S. Reserve Assets**

13.5

1961 1963 1965 1967 1969 1971

* Both central bank and private
** Gold, convertible foreign currencies,
   IMF reserve position, and SDRS

committee on International Exchange and Payments, a unit of the Joint Economic Committee, issued a report on Aug. 6 stating that the dollar was "clearly overvalued." The Treasury Department quickly retorted that the report reflected the opinion of the subcommittee chairman, Henry S. Reuss (D Wis.), and not "any wide body of congressional opinion."

The subcommittee urged the IMF to apply firm pressure on other countries to revalue their currencies—since this would have almost the same effect as a U.S. devaluation. But if this did not work, the subcommittee suggested the United States "promptly consider a unilateral initiative to achieve this same

result, perhaps by floating the dollar within specified limits."
Prophetically, the report noted that such a step would require
the United States formally to abandon its commitment to buy
and sell gold at $35 an ounce in transactions with foreign
central banks.

Nine days after the report was released, President Nixon
announced that he had instructed Connally "to suspend
temporarily the convertibility of the dollar into gold or other
reserve assets, except in amounts and conditions determined
to be in the interest of monetary stability and in the best
interests of the United States." Nixon blamed "speculators"
for the dollar's problems—a claim that was widely disputed.
The London *Economist* of Aug. 27 described it as "old-
fashioned political bunk." As a further step to protect the
dollar, Nixon said: "I am today imposing an additional tax of
10 per cent on goods imported into the United States."[9] His
authority for imposing the import surcharge was contained in
the Trade Expansion Act of 1962. The Gold Reserve Act of
1934 empowered the Treasury Secretary to buy or sell gold on
terms he deemed to be in the public interest.

With the notable exception of organized labor[10] and many
Democrats in Congress, the President's economic package was
favorably received in the United States. The Gallup organization announced Aug. 21 that 68 per cent of the American
adults it polled approved of the new program. The Dow Jones
Industrial Average leaped 32.93 points on Aug. 16, the greatest
one-day bull market in the history of the New York Stock Exchange. American tourists abroad, however, ran into problems
as many European central banks put limits on the amount of
dollars they could exchange. In view of the uncertainty of the
dollar at that point, some hotels, banks and shops refused to
accept dollars at all.

Among foreigners, the reaction was mixed but generally un-
favorable. The *Frankfurter Allgemeine*, for instance, editori-
alized on Aug. 17 that the Nixon program "with certainty will
not go down in American economic history as a stroke of genius:
It documents a relapse of the world's strongest economic power
into nationalism and protectionism." A prevalent feeling

---

[9] For text of Nixon's statement, see *Congressional Quarterly Weekly Report*, Aug. 21, 1971, pp. 1769-1770.

[10] AFL-CIO President George Meany at first described the package as "pro-business" and vowed to challenge the administration's plans in the courts and in Congress. Labor's opposition was modified, however, when Labor Secretary James Hodgson agreed to consult labor leaders on any post-freeze policy.

expressed in the European press was that the role of the dollar as the world's leading currency was at an end. The London *Sunday Times* on Aug. 22 said that Nixon "certainly acted with commendable boldness and realism. It was time an American President did something about the weakness of the dollar; high time. But that does not alter, it emphasizes, the historical importance of what has happened. An era is over."

Japanese Revaluation as Chief Aim of U.S. Action

Monetary officials in Europe were so uncertain what effect the dollar "float" would have that they closed their foreign-exchange windows for a week. When the windows reopened on Aug. 23, the dollar drifted lower in value. The pound sterling, for instance, was quoted at $2.4725 when the market closed on Aug. 26, up from the previously fixed rate of $2.40. This represented a 2.9 per cent devaluation of the American dollar in terms of the pound. In terms of the German mark, the devaluation was 7 per cent. According to Treasury officials in Washington, this was exactly what the United States intended to accomplish—a devaluation of the dollar by means of a revaluation of other currencies.

The European Economic Community, unable to reach a common position on monetary exchange rates because of differences between France and West Germany, was united in opposition to the U.S. import surcharge. Ralf Dahrendorf, the Common Market trade commissioner, described the surcharge as "unacceptable" on Aug. 24 and urged its repeal. Other U.S. trading partners joined in denouncing the surcharge during a two-day meeting (Aug. 24-25) in Geneva of the General Agreement on Tariffs and Trade. Economic writer Edwin L. Dale Jr. quoted "top-level officials" in the Treasury Department as saying the import surcharge was "a form of leverage that can be retained until other countries—above all Japan—make upward changes in their currencies' exchange rates."[11]

From a surplus of over $200 million in 1964, the American balance of trade with Japan plunged to a deficit of $1.38 billion in the first half of 1971. The United States had long urged Japan—its No. 2 trading partner (after Canada)—to dismantle barriers against imports and investment. Japan, in fact, had been moving in that direction but the progress was judged too slow by U.S. businessmen.[12] At first, Japan rejected any suggestion of revaluing the yen. Mikio Mizuta, the Finance

[11] *The New York Times*, Aug. 18, 1971.
[12] See "Emergent Japan," *E.R.R.*, 1970 Vol. I, pp. 178-180.

Minister, told journalists after a cabinet meeting on Aug. 17, 1971, that the government was determined to maintain the parity of 360 yen to the dollar, in spite of panic selling on the Tokyo stock exchange and a flood of American dollars.[13] Ten days later, on Aug. 27, Mizuta reluctantly announced that the yen would be floated to find its own level in world markets. In the meantime, the Bank of Japan had been forced to absorb as much as $1.1 billion in foreign currencies in a single day, a record amount, in defense of the yen.

Paul A. Samuelson, the economist and former critic of the Nixon administration, praised the new economic moves. Samuelson said the coming readjustment of parities would heavily affect Japan:

> No longer can Japanese industries count upon flooding the American market with an increasing volume of exports. I am afraid that the Japanese government is itself much to blame. Economists like myself have been advising it for years now to appreciate the yen in an orderly way at its own volition.... I know that 28 of Japan's best economists have publicly called upon the Japanese government to make this move toward economic sanity.[14]

Samuelson added that the depreciation of the dollar in terms of the yen would undoubtedly help the U.S. trade balance since it would make American exports less expensive in Japan and Japanese exports more expensive in the United States. In the long run, however, Japan would benefit because it was "foolish of Japan to give away goods without being repaid for them in equivalent goods."

Development of World Monetary System

GOLD HAS BEEN USED from time immemorial as a metal of exchange but its use as a standard of value is comparatively recent. Silver was the historic metal of exchange and the principal medium of payment between countries until 1821 when Britain became the first nation in the world to use gold as the standard. Other countries gradually turned to gold in the 1870s but only from about 1895 to 1914 did it prevail through most of the world. In the United States a bimetallic

---

[13] The Dow Jones Index of the Tokyo market plummeted a record 210.50 yen the day following Nixon's statement. To support the yen's parity, the Bank of Japan had to exchange yen for $690 million on Aug. 16.

[14] Article written for *The New York Times*, Aug. 18, 1971.

standard—gold and silver—prevailed from 1792 to the Civil War. This system broke down in the early days of the Civil War and from 1861 to 1879 the country used paper money—greenbacks—without either gold or silver to guarantee their value. The Resumption Act of 1875 made all American currency exchangeable for gold as of Jan. 1, 1879.

Under the "gold coin" standard as it then operated, a gold dollar contained 23.22 grains of pure gold, making an ounce of gold (480 grains) worth $22.67. Citizens were allowed to, and often did, melt coins into bullion and turn bullion into coins. British sovereigns—or any other gold currency—could be melted down and minted into American dollars for a modest fee. The pure-gold standard worked well enough as long as gold production kept pace with the production of real goods. But when gold production faltered, as it did in the last third of the 19th century, there was not enough money in circulation. "Tight" money led to unemployment, strikes and social unrest—giving rise in the United States to the era of populism between 1875 and 1895. Faced with crop failures and scarcity of ready cash, western farmers flocked to the cry of populism for "free coinage of silver." Democrats stole the thunder of the Populist Party in 1896 when they came out for bimetalism and nominated William Jennings Bryan for President; Bryan warned against "crucifying mankind on a cross of gold."

By and large, however, the gold standard "worked" throughout the world until World War I. Economic conditions were relatively stable from country to country, a fact that contributed to the stability of the gold standard. After the war, pent-up demand led to an upsurge in world trade. Moreover, the need to rebuild a shattered Europe put heavy strains on the full-gold standard. Most countries on the standard found they did not need to keep 100 per cent gold reserves to back up the coins and paper currency they issued. Modern banks held only fractional reserves. Finally, many countries, particularly small ones, held no gold at all. Instead, they built up reserves of stronger currencies—usually the dollar and the pound—which they used to finance imports and settle international accounts. Fractional reserves, the "gold-exchange standard" and new methods of extracting gold all enabled the world to stay on the gold standard and stave off deflation up to the onset of the world depression in the 1930s.

Britain devalued the pound sterling on Sept. 21, 1931, sounding the death knell of the gold standard. The United

States held on until March 16, 1933, when President Roosevelt, who had taken office 12 days earlier in the midst of a domestic banking crisis, proclaimed an embargo on the export of gold.[15] The domestic gold standard was abandoned a few months later, when all gold and gold certificates in private hands were ordered returned to the Treasury or Federal Reserve banks for replacement by currency not redeemable in gold.

Interestingly enough, President Roosevelt devalued the dollar in terms of gold in a haphazard way, without knowing precisely what effect the action would have. Through a reluctant Treasury Department, the administration steadily increased the value of gold by purchasing it at ever-greater prices. According to Arthur M. Schlesinger Jr., the new values were decided almost arbitrarily in Roosevelt's bedroom each morning. One day Henry Morgenthau Jr., who would later become Treasury Secretary, came in "more worried than usual" and suggested a per ounce increase in the gold price by 19 to 22 cents.

> Roosevelt took one look at Morgenthau's anxious face [Schlesinger added] and proposed 21 cents. 'It's a lucky number,' he said with a laugh, 'because it's three times seven.' Morgenthau, never sure when his leg was being pulled, later made the literal-minded notation in his diary, 'If anybody ever knew how we really set the gold price through a combination of lucky numbers, etc., I think they would really be frightened.'[16]

As soon as the United States began buying gold at inflated prices from other countries, it cheapened the American dollar, contributing to a revival of world trade as well as to an improvement in American prices. Congress passed the Gold Reserve Act of 1934 on Jan. 30 and Roosevelt immediately fixed by proclamation the value of the dollar at 59.06 per cent of its last official gold value. He established the price of gold at $35 an ounce—a standard that has remained in force since then.

Bretton Woods Conference and Creation of IMF

The modern international monetary system began to take shape toward the end of World War II at the Bretton Woods Conference. The finance ministers and economists who met at the resort town of Bretton Woods in June 1944 wanted to prevent a recurrence of the disasters of the 1930s when there was a chain reaction of devaluation, deflation and depression.

---

[15] See "World Monetary Reform," *E.R.R.*, 1965 Vol. I, pp. 190-191, and "Gold Policies and Production," *E.R.R.*, 1968 Vol. I, pp. 101-120.

[16] See Arthur M. Schlesinger Jr., *The Coming of the New Deal* (1958), p. 241.

The basic principle adopted at Bretton Woods was that national currencies could be exchanged for dollars at essentially fixed rates. The International Monetary Fund was created to regulate the flow of international payments. Any change in parity, such as the 1967 devaluation of the British pound, was to be made only to meet a fundamental payments disequilibrium and upon prior consultation with the IMF.

Because demands for a nation's currency vary from time to time, a nation needs monetary reserves to support the value of its currency in a system of fixed exchange rates. These reserves are held both in gold and in certain foreign currencies, principally in U.S. dollars and British pounds. All countries except the United States meet their IMF obligations by buying and selling other currencies—mostly dollars. The United States, up to Aug. 15, 1971, met its basic commitment under IMF rules by freely buying and selling gold to foreign monetary authorities at $35 an ounce.

The Bretton Woods agreement, signed by 25 nations, went into effect in 1946. Since then, 19 of the 25 have had to devalue their national currencies once or more for a total of 38 devaluations. Britain devalued the pound twice, in 1949 and again in 1967, from $4.03 to $2.40; France changed the franc's value—now about 18 cents—a total of five times; and West Germany lowered the mark's value once and raised it twice for a net loss of 10 per cent. If the mark, now floating, is revalued the percentage of loss will be reduced.

The Japanese yen was set at a value of $0.0028—about one-fourth of a cent—in 1949 and remained there until it was floated in the aftermath of President Nixon's action in 1971. In the first day of trading after it was floated Aug. 27 the yen increased in value by 5.2 per cent in relation to the dollar and continued to edge slightly upward almost daily, confirming the belief of most western economists who contended that it had been vastly undervalued.

One of the greatest challenges to the Bretton Woods agreement was posed by the late President Charles de Gaulle of France who advocated a return to the full gold standard. He explained at a press conference Feb. 4, 1965:

> Yes, gold, which does not change in nature, which can be made either into bars, ingots or coins, which has no nationality, which is considered, in all places and at all times, the immutable and fiduciary value *par excellence.*

It is a fact that even today no currency has any value except by direct or indirect relation to gold, real or supposed.

De Gaulle's pronouncement was met within hours by a U.S. Treasury statement asserting that the full gold standard collapsed in 1931 and "proved incapable of financing the huge increase of world trade that has marked the 20th century." French officials, undeterred, disclosed that France would cash in for gold all new inflows of foreign currencies.

Recurring Gold Crises and Britain's Devaluation

De Gaulle's "raid" on the U.S. gold hoard failed to return the world to the full gold standard. However, it helped to change the U.S. gold policies and led to a gold crisis of 1968 *(see page 42)*. Although the U.S. gold stock exceeded $15 billion at the end of 1964, most of it—$13.7 billion—was earmarked by law as backing for the nation's currency and for certain bank deposits held by the Federal Reserve System.[17] The remaining $1.3 billion was considered insufficient to convince foreign nations that the United States would stand by its pledge to redeem their dollars for gold at $35 an ounce. Any likelihood that the United States might increase the value of gold—and thereby decrease the value of dollars held abroad—tempted foreign nations to exchange their dollars while the price remained the same.

To alleviate this situation, Congress in 1965 removed the gold-backing requirement for bank deposits held by the Federal Reserve and thus made available an additional $4.9 billion in gold to redeem foreign-owned dollars. Congress removed the remaining gold backing from U.S. currency in 1968 by eliminating the requirement that each Federal Reserve Bank maintain reserves in gold certificates of not less than 25 per cent of the face value of its Federal Reserve notes (currency) in circulation. At that time, the gold stock was about $12 billion but $10.7 billion was earmarked to meet the 25 per cent requirement.

In the meantime—1967—came Britain's devaluation after a long fight waged by Prime Minister Harold Wilson to avert it. Britain had, like the United States today, run up a string of deficits in its international trade and balance of payments. Despite a 14.3 per cent devaluation of the pound, from $2.80 to $2.40, and a deflationary budget aimed at cutting consumer

---

[17] For workings of the Federal Reserve, see "Money Supply in Inflation," *E.R.R.*, 1969 Vol. I, pp. 152-158.

spending, the country's economic picture did not improve quickly.[18] Expected benefits were undercut by a persistent demand for imports even though import prices rose between 10 and 12 per cent.

British devaluation sent shock waves through the world monetary system. The United States, fearing that the pound's devaluation might bring down the dollar also, was instrumental in arranging several multi-national loans to help Britain meet the challenge to its currency. The fact that most other countries maintained their existing exchange rates helped to stop the raid on the pound. In 1949, by contrast, nearly all of the countries of Europe and the Commonwealth devalued at the same time as Britain, negating the benefits that the British otherwise would have reaped from devaluation.

Although the United States in 1933 forbade its citizens to hold gold—except for artistic or industrial uses—the metal continued to be freely traded in several European centers and the price fluctuated wildly in times of an exchange crisis. To stabilize the market price of gold, the United States and seven other countries[19] formed in November 1961 what was known as the London Gold Pool. The theory of the arrangement was that the eight governments could flood the private gold markets when necessary to stabilize prices. The London market was the key one because the main supply of new gold in the western world—the output of South African mines—was sold there. Thus all other gold markets tend to replenish their supplies through London.

The Gold Pool worked reasonably well until the mid-1960s. Then came De Gaulle's attack on the dollar, stimulating gold speculation, followed the next year, 1966, by two other unwelcome developments: the Soviet Union stopped selling gold and South Africa's output began to level off. And in June 1967, France withdrew from the pool arrangement, removing $5.2 billion of its gold reserves. Balance-of-payments deficits being incurred by America and Britain ate into the gold stocks available to the pool and Britain's devaluation depleted them further.[20]

---

[18] See "British Economy Since Devaluation," *E.R.R.*, 1968 Vol. II, pp. 781-802.

[19] Britain, Belgium, France, West Germany, Italy, The Netherlands, and Switzerland.

[20] In all, gold reserves of the nations participating in the gold pool dropped from $34.2 billion at the beginning of 1966 to about $26.5 billion at the beginning of 1968. See *Congress and the Nation* Vol. II (1969, publication of Congressional Quarterly Inc.), pp. 272-273.

A round of speculative buying on the London gold market was touched off after the U.S. Treasury announced on Feb. 28, 1968, that the U.S. gold stock totaled only $12 billion, its lowest point since 1936. On March 10, the governors of the seven central banks contributing to the Gold Pool, including the U.S. Federal Reserve, issued a statement reaffirming their determination "to continue their support to the pool based on the fixed price of $35 an ounce."

The announcement stopped speculation but only briefly. The price of gold in London soon pushed through the $35.20 ceiling. Seven days after affirming their support of the Gold Pool, the pool nations announced on March 17 that they would no longer supply gold to private buyers as they had been doing. In effect, the decision established a two-tier system for gold: the price for official transactions between governments was to remain at $35 an ounce; the price for all other transactions was to be allowed to fluctuate freely based on the normal supply of gold and the demand for it.

Use of 'Paper Gold' to Alleviate Liquidity Problems

At least in part, the 1968 gold crisis was a problem of liquidity—that is, of having a readily available medium of exchange in sufficient quantity. It had long been recognized that the production of gold could not meet indefinitely the monetary demands imposed by growth in industrial production. John Maynard Keynes, the British financial expert, told the Bretton Woods Conference that gold was a "barbarous metal." He suggested that a new kind of international currency, which he chose to call "bancor," be created and accorded equivalent status with gold. His theory was that the new money would be based on the liquidity needs of the world, not on the physical availability of a metal. Bancor was rejected at the time but when the IMF in 1967 agreed to a plan for the creation of Special Drawing Rights (SDRs) it was patterned on the Keynesian model.

Special Drawing Rights are popularly referred to as "paper gold"—partly because they are intended to take the place of gold in the monetary system and partly because they are assigned a value in terms of gold.[21] They are not backed by gold, however. In effect, SDRs are a bookkeeping device of the International Monetary Fund. When the original allocation of $3.414 billion in SDRs was made on Jan. 1, 1970, the IMF

---

[21] Each SDR is equal in value to 1/35 of an ounce of gold—the same value accorded the dollar until Aug. 15, 1971.

entered in the "Special Drawing Account" of every participating nation[22] an amount of SDRs equal to 16.8 per cent
of each nation's deposit with the bank. When a country decides
to activate its SDRs, the IMF selects one or a number of
countries with satisfactory balance-of-payments surpluses
to provide the applicant with "currency convertible in fact."[23]
At the same time, the Fund debits SDRs from the applicant
country and places them in the accounts of the countries that
have provided the currency. During 1970, a total of $857 mil-
lion in SDRs was activated by all participants in the Special
Drawing Account.

The basic purpose of SDRs is to create liquidity—to make
available enough funds to satisfy the uses to which they can
be put. The creation of wealth, however, must be carefully
controlled since too great a supply causes inflation and too
small a supply brings on deflation. Some economists believe
that too many SDRs were created and that they contributed
to the current monetary crisis. According to one argument, at
the time it was decided to activate the first SDRs "it was
already clear that some important facts indicated a surplus
rather than a shortage of international liquidity." Moreover,
the deficit in the U.S. balance of payments was rising and
"this meant an increase in the worldwide availability of
dollars."[24]

U.S. View Versus European on Current Disorder

American and European officials agree that at least one
cause of the monetary crisis was America's balance-of-payments
deficit—at least in the sense that there was a plethora of dollars piling up in Europe. But there is a wide divergence of views
as to what caused the deficit in the first place. Treasury Secretary Connally and other administration officials argue that the
deficit was caused by American investment abroad, heavy
outlays for defense costs in Europe and Asia and the shoul-
dering of a disproportionate share of foreign aid.[25] America's
worsening performance in international trade, meanwhile, has
been attributed to trade barriers in foreign countries.

The European view is much different. The European Common Market denies that it has placed unfair restrictions on

---

[22] Seven member-nations of the IMF did not take part in the Special Drawing
Account allocation—Ethiopia, Kuwait, Lebanon, Libya, Portugal, Saudi Arabia and
Singapore.

[23] These are U.S. dollars, Belgian francs, West German marks, French francs,
British pounds, Italian lire, Mexican pesos or Dutch guilders.

[4] Heinz Portmann and W. Linder, "A Test for Paper Gold," *Swiss Review of
World Affairs*, June 1971, p. 11.

[25] See "American Investments In European Industry," *E.R.R.*, 1968 Vol. I, pp. 61-78.

American trade. *Fortune* magazine agrees: "It is not the unfair trading practices of our competitors that have been damaging the U.S. trade surplus but differing rates of inflation and economic growth among trading nations..."[26] Europeans also contend that they have been forced indirectly to finance a portion of the Viet Nam war: Instead of reducing private consumption in order to prosecute the war, the Americans kept domestic consumption high with imports.

To purchase imports, the argument continues, America inflated its money supply far beyond the point where it could redeem the dollars for gold. European newspapers frequently suggest that the Nixon administration reduce domestic consumption by raising taxes so that the war costs fall entirely on the American people. The American rejoinder is that European countries should have been bearing a greater share of defense costs in Europe.

On another level, the growth of the Eurodollar market has helped to bring on the monetary crisis. "Eurodollars" designate American dollars held in Europe either by Europeans or Americans doing business in Europe, but not by European governments. Since 1964, these funds have increased almost fivefold—from $11 billion to $52 billion. Some of this growth is seen as a result of America's continuing balance-of-payments deficit and some of it as the result of continual relending. Not every dollar in the pool represents a claim on the United States.

The Eurodollar market adds an element of uncertainty to the monetary system because much of it is "hot money"—speculative capital moved by its owners from country to country to benefit from higher interest rates or as a hedge against an expected devaluation. The United States frequently sells securities in the Euromarket specifically to withdraw American dollars from Europe before they end up in European central banks. In a speech to American bankers in Munich, West Germany, on May 28, 1971, Connally urged that foreign governments bring this market under supervision and control.

---

[26] "U.S. Foreign Trade: There's No Need to Panic," *Fortune*, August 1971, p. 2.

Future of Dollar in International Trade

THE AMERICAN DOLLAR, after financing the postwar recoveries of Europe and Japan and serving as the chief engine of worldwide economic development since then, now appears to be at a crossroads. For some time, monetary scholars have been suggesting that the international monetary system faces a fundamental decision: either the dollar will continue to be the reserve currency of the world—in which case foreign countries will have to accept the need for disruptive parity changes—or the system must be changed so that the dollar is relegated to a parity role with other currencies.

There is no clear-cut consensus. Harry G. Johnson, a professor of economics at both the University of Chicago and the London School of Economics, writes that in the long run "the chief problem facing the international monetary system is whether Special Drawing Rights will take over the role of the dollar as a substitute for gold."[27] Johnson points out that the Federal Reserve Board, which regulates the American money supply, has become the world's real, but not its constitutional, central banker. If the dollar is to remain the world's reserve currency, Johnson writes, the problem is "how to make American monetary policy responsive to the needs of the world economy, especially when those needs conflicted with the domestic needs of the United States."

But if SDRs are to become the reserve currency of the world, many experts believe, they must be modified and their issuance and use must be carefully controlled. Developing countries are discovering that the SDR can be used as a means of development financing, despite IMF rules which expressly forbid their use for this purpose. It is feared that if this practice spreads it could have inflationary consequences on a worldwide scale.

Proposals for Flexibility in Rates of Exchange

Many observers believe that the rise of the dollar to the status of a reserve currency was inevitable, comparable to

---

[27] Harry G. Johnson, "International Questions Facing Britain, the United States, and Canada in the 70s," *Looking Ahead* (a publication of the National Planning Association), March 1971, p. 2.

the spread of English as the basic international language. "It is hard to imagine any system using something other than the dollar as a base," *The Wall Street Journal* has said editorially. "What most likely will emerge [from the present crisis] is something very much resembling what has existed in the past, with the dollar remaining as the base with some new parities for major currencies but without a link to gold, which was partly a fiction anyway."

A less likely option is a return to the full gold standard with its strict monetary discipline. If that happened, the official price of gold would have to be increased and every country would have to settle surpluses and debts quickly and adjust internal economic policy to the availability of gold. This idea meets vigorous opposition in the United States and many other countries. In response to growing Japanese and European demands for an increase in the price of gold, Paul Volcker, Under Secretary of the Treasury, told a news conference Sept. 4 that the United States would not change the price of gold and expected to return to a price of $35 an ounce when the gold suspension ended.

Regardless of whether currencies are pegged to the American dollar, to the SDR or to any other medium or reserve asset, it will not obviate the necessity to modify the system of exchange rates. National economies will continue to gain and lose competitive strength and, as a consequence, their currencies will gain or lose real buying power. The basic problem is how to make necessary parity changes gradually so that they do not disrupt the entire system. An idealistic solution is to give the IMF or some other supranational body the power to assign currency values, based on economic performance indicators from each country. The complexity of such a system and the loss of sovereignty involved probably make it unacceptable to all governments.

A frequently suggested reform is the broadening of parity "bands" within which a country is committed to maintain the value of its currency. Under present IMF rules, a currency must be maintained within 1 per cent of its assigned value. The argument is that if the bands were wider—2 or 3 per cent—it would negate speculative rushes of "hot money" and ease the pressure on central banks to buy or sell their currencies to maintain the par value. Other suggestions include "crawling" and "sliding" pegs which would allow governments to revalue or devalue their currencies by small amounts as frequently as necessary.

The creation of a European Common Market currency, as proposed, could have a profound effect on the future of the monetary system. Heads of state of the six Common Market countries agreed at a meeting at The Hague in December 1969 to attempt full monetary integration by 1980. A committee headed by Premier Pierre Werner of Luxembourg was appointed to devise and implement such a plan by gradual steps. The first step was to have been a narrowing of the range of price variation between each of the six currencies and the dollar via joint purchases or sales of dollars in the foreign exchange market.

Likely Challenge to Dollar from Common Market

This first step was knocked askew when the monetary crisis of 1971 forced floats and revaluations of several European currencies. Differences between France and West Germany prevented the Common Market from acting as a bloc in response to the suspension of the convertibility of the dollar into gold. Nevertheless, the Common Market is still committed to an eventual monetary union. Later steps outlined by the Werner committee envisioned the creation of an institution for the management of the community monetary policy—including money supply, interest rates and control of the financial market. Ultimately, the proposed system would operate like the U.S. Federal Reserve System; existing central banks would act as Reserve Banks do in the U.S. system, and a new executive group would formulate community-wide policy in much the same way the Federal Reserve Board does.

A separate start was made through the issuance in January 1971 of EMUs, or European Monetary Units, [28] by the European Coal and Steel Community. The EMU is defined in terms of gold at the same value as the U.S. dollar at par. Robert Prinsky reported that the unit "could be an important first step towards the use of a common currency within the Common Market and could help unify the capital markets of the six."[29] The Coal and Steel Community started the project by floating a 15-year, $50 million bond issue denominated in EMUs.

For the United States, the creation of a strong European currency could have several important repercussions. Norman N. Mintz, economics professor at Columbia University,

---

[28] The unit is symbolized by a capital E with a slash through it.
[29] Robert Prinsky, "A European Monetary Unit," *The Atlantic Community Quarterly,* Spring 1971, p. 85.

wrote that a more unified European community would be able to "challenge the hegemony of the United States in international economic and monetary relations."

> The EEC [he wrote] is acutely aware of its subservience to the dollar. European countries, charged with keeping their currencies in line with the dollar have had to absorb, against their inclinations, large quantities of dollars. The Community, acting as an entity, would be able to revalue its common monetary unit against an overvalued dollar, an action that none of the countries individually would feel strong enough to take.[30]

Mintz added that the existence of a strong currency would force the United States to limit any additional outflow of dollars, and it probably would result in the United States opening up trade with Communist countries.[31] Finally, he suggested that since the United States could no longer create liquidity in the face of a European currency, the United States would have to examine its economic and political priorities more carefully.

It does not seem likely that a common European currency will evolve for another decade, however. For the present, the world's monetary officials are faced with the task of either patching up a system that is badly battered, or striking off in a bold new direction. The negotiators will be trying to build a system that is at once rigid enough to provide a fundamental stability and at the same time is flexible enough to accommodate parity changes without touching off a new series of crises. It will take the best efforts of politicans and economists to find this elusive middle ground.

---

[30] Norman N. Mintz, "Toward a Common European Currency," *Columbia Journal of World Business,* January-February, 1971, p. 20.

[31] See "Reconciliation with China," *E.R.R.,* 1971 Vol. I, pp.454-455, 469-470.

Nuclear Balance of Terror: 25 Years After Alamogordo

by

Helen B. Shaffer

1 9 7 0
July 1

NUCLEAR BALANCE OF TERROR:
25 YEARS AFTER ALAMOGORDO

THE AGE OF NUCLEAR WEAPONS will soon be 25 years old. It was on July 16, 1945, that the first atomic bomb—a pygmy compared with its descendants—was successfully tested on a remote stretch of desert near Alamogordo, New Mexico. The first fire-blast to be caused by the splitting of atoms marked far more than the birth of a superior weapon. So much was changed in that instant of atomic energy release that the years immediately preceding it seem to belong to a totally different era. A few weeks after the triumph at Alamogordo, the bomb proved, at Hiroshima and Nagasaki, its unique power to terrorize a powerful enemy into surrender. But though the bomb ended the war, the euphoria of peace was tempered, for victor and vanquished alike, by the existence of so destructive a weapon and the fear that it would someday bring about the doom of man.

Changes wrought by the bomb soon became apparent: It forced an overhaul of strategic planning for national defense, injected a radically new factor into the old game of power politics between nations, initiated an era of "grand alliance" between the scientific community and the military establishment, and inaugurated a new kind of open-end arms race of astronomic cost to the taxpayer. The bomb had other pervasive effects: it created a new stimulus for pacifism, thrust a number of once politically indifferent scientists into the unaccustomed role of political activists, and contributed markedly to an element of nervous distemper in the psychological climate that infected an entire generation of youth the world over. Ultimately it brought the two leading military powers of the world—the United States and the Soviet Union—into a shaky state of equilibrium popularly known as the "balance of terror," a state in which each has more than enough arms on the ready to demolish the other within a few hours.

Over the quarter-century since Alamogordo, both nations have pressed forward in a competitive arms race. They have not only increased their stockpiles of deadly weapons, but have

51

engaged in a continuing effort to improve their firepower and to refine their delivery systems. So today we have not simply a supply of bombs to be airlifted to drop points, but elaborate systems of nuclear defense and offense of a complexity and sophistication beyond the dreams of 25 years ago.

Dual Policy of Nuclear Escalation and Limitation

For most of the years of the atomic age, there has been a continuing debate on whether to continue the nuclear weapon build-up or seek agreement with the major competitor to halt the arms race. As policy, both courses may be said to have been followed by both super-powers. But the record shows that, despite a few limited successes for de-escalation, the primary commitment over the years has been to escalation. Like the super-powers themselves, the opposing policies of nuclear arms escalation and nuclear disarmament have learned to co-exist. The Nixon administration is now pressing Congress for funds to extend deployment of the latest refinements in the nuclear arsenal—the Safeguard ABM and the multiple-warhead Minuteman III missile. At the same time U.S. representatives and their Soviet counterparts have been negotiating strategic arms limitation at the SALT talks in Vienna. Previous administrations have similarly followed the dual course, as have the Russians.

In a curious way, fear of the bomb seems to have lessened or at least taken a less panicky form than in the early years of atomic age shock.[1] Either man has learned to live under what President Kennedy called the "nuclear sword of Damocles,"[2] or the failure to use nuclear weapons in the wars of the 1950s and 1960s has eased the sense of imminent doom. After atomic bombs were dropped on two Japanese cities in the last week of World War II, many people believed that only total abolition of war could prevent unthinkable destruction of life on this planet. Yet the United States suffered 157,000 casualties in the Korean War and 330,000 to date in the Vietnamese War without threatening to use even tactical nuclear weapons.[3]

---

[1] Cassandra-like warnings are far from absent. The title of a new book, *A Time for Hysteria* (1969), offered as a "citizen's guide to disarmament," by Mortimer Lipsky, suggests the desperation of those who seek to arouse the public to a sharper appreciation of the nuclear threat.

[2] "Every man, woman and child lives under a nuclear sword of Damocles, hanging by the slenderest threads, capable of being cut off at any moment by accident or miscalculation or by madness."—Address to the United Nations General Assembly, Sept. 25, 1961.

[3] Gen. Douglas MacArthur told interviewer Bob Considine in 1964 that he had favored "dropping from 30 to 50 atomic bombs on air bases and other sensitive points" in Manchuria as part of a proposed offensive during the Korean War. President Truman gave the proposal no consideration.—*New York Journal-American*, April 8, 1964.

ABM. Anti-ballistic missile, designed to intercept and destroy an approaching missile.

BMEWS. Ballistic missile early warning system (radar).

GALOSH. Soviet ABM deployed around Moscow.

Hardened silo. Reinforced concrete-protected underground site for missile launchers.

ICBM. Intercontinental ballistic missile.

Kiloton. Explosive power equal to 1,000 tons of TNT.

Megaton. Explosive power equal to one million tons of TNT.

Minuteman. Solid-fueled ICBM deployed in underground silos.

MIRV. Multiple Independently Targeted Re-entry Vehicles, for use on Minuteman III and Poseidon.

MRV. Multiple Re-entry Vehicle, not individually targeted, on a single ICBM, giving a spraying effect.

Polaris. U.S. submarine carrying ballistic missiles.

Poseidon. Later version of Polaris, carrying MIRV warheads.

Safeguard. Version of ABM system, designed primarily to protect missile silos.

SALT. Strategic Arms Limitation Talks, between the United States and the Soviet Union.

SCAD. Subsonic Cruise Armed Decoy, for use on bombers to penetrate defenses against attack from the air.

SLBM. Submarine Launched Ballistic Missile.

SRAM. Short-Range Attack Missile, air-to-ground weapon designed to penetrate defenses against bombers, now in final stage of development.

SS-9. Heavy Soviet strategic missile.

SS-11. Light Soviet strategic missile.

Titan II. Heavy U.S. strategic ICBM.

Warhead. Nuclear explosive on missile.

The balance of terror undoubtedly played a major role in restraining the use of nuclear weapons. On the other hand, it seems to have had little influence in preventing non-nuclear wars. No one can guarantee how long the balance of terror can continue to function as a deterrent to a nuclear holocaust —or whether it might someday help to deter all forms of warfare. The two super-powers are at a standoff, each equipped with overkill. But there are three other lesser members of the atomic club—Britain, France and China—and possibly a dozen other countries capable of gaining admittance if they

NUCLEAR WEAPONS CAPABILITY

Status	Countries
Possess nuclear weapons today . .	United States, Britain, China, France, Soviet Union.
Capable of developing nuclear weapons	Canada, West Germany, Japan, Israel.
Could achieve necessary technical and financial capability in near future	Australia, Belgium, Czechoslovakia, East Germany, Netherlands, Poland, Switzerland.

decide to throw their resources in that direction. China has begun to cause the Big Two to worry. Both have justified certain extensions of their nuclear arms systems on the basis of a present or future threat from China.

The more nations that join the nuclear arms race, even in junior status, the more complicated the arms control problem becomes and the less secure the fate of man. Even a minor nuclear power can initiate the chain reaction of response and counter-response that could involve the might of the major powers. Conventional wars carry with them the threat of eventual use of small tactical nuclear weapons, leading to unleashing the big ones. And there is always the possibility that a major power will misinterpret an accident or misjudge the source of a wildcat thrust by a minor nuclear power.

On the other hand, the years have shown that the world's most powerful nations can hold back their super-weapons out of self-interest. The nuclear dilemma has thus changed little since J. Robert Oppenheimer, "father of the A-bomb," told fellow scientists at Los Alamos, N.M., in November 1945, that the new field of atomic energy development held "not only a great peril but a great hope."[4] Twenty-five years later these same choices remain.

Deterrence as Rationale of Nuclear Arms Race

From the beginning, the impetus to develop the most ominous weapon in the history of warfare has been competition with an actual or potential enemy. The first bomb was produced in a crash project during World War II in the belief that

---

[4] Cited by Alice Kimball Smith, *A Peril and a Hope—The Scientists' Movement in America: 1945-46* (1965), p.x. Oppenheimer was called "father of the A-bomb" because he was scientific director of the wartime project that produced the bomb.

Nazi Germany was working on a similar project and that the nation that got the bomb first would win the war.[5] The continuing effort to enlarge and improve atomic weaponry has been the result primarily of competition between the two most powerful contenders in the Cold War, the United States and the Soviet Union.

The nuclear arms race between these two has been governed primarily by the principle of deterrence. The idea of each contender is that it must have an arsenal of nuclear weapons and a capability for delivering them on target so powerful and so well protected that even if the nation sustains a nuclear attack, it will still retain sufficient capability to retaliate with devastating effect on the other. Thus, no matter how much destruction one nation can wreak on another, it would be a fool to strike first because of the certainty and severity of the counter-strike.

Nuclear deterrence thus functions as a psychological weapon. Its effectiveness depends on what strategists call "credibility." This means that a nuclear power must convince its opponents that it has not only the ability but the will and determination to deliver a devastating strike if attacked or intolerably threatened. Like the gold in Ft. Knox, nuclear warheads can remain safely stashed away in their shelters so long as everyone believes in their existence and their usability.

Two major keys to effectiveness of the nuclear deterrent are "first-strike capability" and "assured-destruction capability." The former means not merely the ability to deliver a strong first punch, but to deliver one so effective it will destroy the enemy's ability to strike back. In a practical sense, then, a "first-strike capability" means not merely an ability to demolish the enemy's cities and industries but the ability to zero in on its missile sites and carriers. "Assured-destruction capability" is the ability of a nation, even after undergoing a nuclear attack, to devastate the attacking nation. This is something a nation could do only if its control centers and nuclear weapon delivery systems were still operative, even though millions of its people were dead and its major cities and industries in ruins.

---

[5] Germany was working on a top-priority atomic energy project during World War II but had made little progress and finally abandoned hope of making a bomb for that war. Two German scientists—one of them the discoverer of uranium fission, a key discovery leading to production of the A-bomb—were reported to have attempted suicide after learning of American success in producing the bomb.—William Laurence, *Dawn Over Zero: The Story of the Atomic Bomb* (1946), pp. 114-115.

The rationale of the strategic arms race is thus plainly exposed: the opposing nations must have a near-equal balance of power for destroying each other. If either nation ever attains a superiority so great that it can actually achieve a first-strike capability, the nuclear deterrent will no longer exist.

Much depends on what strategists believe to be the opponent's concept of the limit of acceptable damage. A nuclear power might be willing to deliver a first punch in full expectation of a retaliatory strike if it believed the damage from the latter would not rise above an acceptable level. Strategists of national defense mull over such questions, though no one knows what an acceptable level of damage would be. Robert S. McNamara suggested in early 1968, shortly before leaving office as Secretary of Defense, that the Soviet Union might consider 'the loss of one-fifth to one-fourth its population and one-half its industry too high a price to pay. As few as 400 warheads of one megaton each on target would be enough to kill one-third of its population and three-fourths of its industry, he said. At the time, the United States had 4,206 deliverable nuclear warheads and the Soviets 1,200, according to the annual defense "posture" statement to Congress.

Defense Planning for 'Worst Possible' Condition

Theoretically, parity of power serves as a deterrent to nuclear war. In actuality, the fear of each contender that the other will gain that first-strike capability at some future date causes it to seek safety in an extra margin of strength. This is the nuclear nightmare that keeps the arms race going. McNamara observed that "mutual capability" in destroying each other "is precisely...[what] provides us both with the strongest possible motive to avoid a nuclear war." But he also took note of an "action-reaction phenomenon that fuels an arms race." What one super-power does about building up its nuclear forces inevitably triggers a reaction by the other.[6]

The equation of escalation goes even beyond the action-reaction formula. One super-power reacts not only to acts of the other but to what it *thinks* the other *might* do at some future date. This follows the so-called "worst case" principle in strategic defense planning. In effect, it means that the defense planner, when considering possible situations in the future on which to base decisions about developing and deploying its forces, "must prepare for the worst plausible case and

---

[6] Robert S. McNamara, *The Essence of Security* (an edited compilation of policy statements during his tenure, 1961-1968, as Secretary of Defense), pp. 55-56.

not be content to hope and prepare merely for the most probable."[7]

Sometimes this leads to needless escalation. McNamara candidly described an instance during his time in office. Because Russia was believed in 1961 to possess the capability for building up a strong force of intercontinental missiles which might conceivably knock out a large part of the American carrier fleet, the new Kennedy administration ordered a major build-up of strategic missiles. "We had no evidence that the Soviets did plan, in fact, fully to use that capability," McNamara said later. But he felt that the decision was justified because they *might* have been planning to do so. As it turned out, they did not begin to build up their missile force until the United States, under impetus of this fear, had built up a massive system. "Clearly the Soviet build-up [of missiles] is in part a reaction to our own build-up since the beginning of this decade," McNamara said in a speech six years later.

Nixon's Call for Build-Up To Meet Soviet Gains

Basic strategic policy in this regard has changed little over the years of the nuclear arms race. Deterrence of nuclear attack is still the prime goal of strategic defense and decisions on developing and deploying nuclear weapons are still made on the "worst case" basis. President Nixon said in a foreign policy report to Congress, Feb. 18, 1970:

> The overriding purpose of our strategic posture is political and defensive: to deny other countries the ability to impose their will on the United States and its allies under the weight of a strategic military superiority. We must insure that all potential aggressors see unacceptable risks in contemplating a nuclear attack, or nuclear blackmail, or acts which could escalate to strategic nuclear war, such as a Soviet conventional attack on Europe.

Secretary of Defense Melvin R. Laird has referred to a "new strategy" for national defense, but this does not change the underlying objective. The "new strategy" applies rather to decisions on the specifics of what to do to maintain the effectiveness of the nuclear deterrent in the light of changing conditions. Both the President's foreign policy message and the Defense Department's annual "posture statement,"[8] called for a new build-up of nuclear arms in response to gains the Soviet Union had made in its effort to catch up with—and possibly overtake—the United States. "The growth of Soviet

---

[7] *Ibid*, p. 58.
[8] Presented to the House Appropriations Subcommittee on the Department of Defense, Feb. 25, 1970.

U.S. AND SOVIET NUCLEAR OFFENSIVE FORCES

	United States	Soviet Union
Deliverable warheads*	4,200	1,350
Launchers:		
Land-based ICBMs**	1,054	1,290
Sea-launched missiles**	656	300
Intercontinental bombers*	581	140-145

  * As of Sept. 1, 1969; figures cited by Secretary of Defense Melvin R. Laird in annual "defense posture" statement to Congress, Feb. 25, 1970.

  ** Projected for year-end 1970; figures cited in President Nixon's report to Congress on U.S. foreign policy for the 1970s, Feb. 18, 1970.

---

strategic capabilities" had raised new hazards, the President said. The main questions were the familiar ones: "Why might a nuclear war start or be threatened?" and "What U.S. strategic capabilities are needed for deterrence?"

"An inescapable reality of the 1970s," Nixon said, "is the Soviet Union's possession of powerful and sophisticated strategic forces approaching and, in some categories, exceeding ours in numbers and capability." The Soviets had developed "more accurate warhead and perhaps penetration aids" for their ICBMs, were continuing to test a multiple warhead for their SS-9 missile, and were carrying on research and development activities to improve their ABM system.

Though the Russians had gained appreciably in the past few years, the United States was still ahead. Secretary Laird told the Senate Armed Services Committee on May 12, 1970: "We believe that today we do have sufficient forces for deterrence. However, we are very much disturbed by what we have observed about the character and rate of build-up of Soviet strategic forces. Thus, our concern is not about today, or even next year...[but] what the future may bring." The following were among examples he cited of Soviet gains in nuclear strategic weaponry over the five years since 1965:

> Small IBM launchers comparable to U.S. Minuteman: increased in numbers from zero to 800, with the possibility of 1,000 by 1972.
>
> Operational launchers for the large SS-9 missile for which the United States has no counterpart: from zero to 220 in operation, and at least 60 under construction.
>
> Nuclear-propelled ballistic missile submarine force: from 25 missile launchers to more than 200; expected to increase to 400-500 by 1972 and 656 in 1974-75.

"What these factors show," Laird testified, "is that the Soviet Union, in the last five years, has multiplied its strategic offensive missile launchers from 300 to about 1,500, a five-fold increase.... The United States, by contrast, has made no increase in the force level that was established around 1965 for strategic offensive missile launchers—1,710—and has actually reduced its heavy bomber force in this period...from 780 to about 550." The rapid Russian build-up gave "reason to wonder what the Soviet goal is."

What worried Laird most was that "the momentum behind Soviet deployments and developments in major strategic systems...could carry them well beyond the crossover point [in strategic balance] in a short period of time, unless we take major offsetting actions." In other words, the United States had to stay ahead.

Quarter-Century of Atomic Development

IT IS A SAD COMMENTARY on man's fate that the first practical product of so great a leap forward in knowledge as the discovery of atomic fission should have been a device to terrorize the world. The well-known story of the birth of the bomb has many of the qualities of myth: the wise men pleading with the leader to let them seek a magic weapon of superlative power, the secret undertaking itself racing against time lest the enemy learn to make the weapon first, the triumphant explosion with "the radiance of a thousand suns,"[9] and then the aftermath—the gods outraged at the discovery of their secret, banishing the hero of the undertaking, physicist J. Robert Oppenheimer, and placing on all mankind the curse of the "nuclear sword of Damocles."

The famous letter from Albert Einstein to President Roosevelt, dated Aug. 2, 1939, was actually drafted by Leo Szilard, Hungarian-born physicist, and personally delivered a month later by Alexander Sachs, a businessman, economist, and in-

---

[9] J. Robert Oppenheimer, who became known as "the father of the A-bomb" because of his leading role in its development, said that at the instant of the flash of the first bomb at Alamogordo, the following lines from the sacred Hindu epic, Bhagavad-Gita, came to his mind:
> If the radiance of a thousand suns
> Were to burst at once into the sky
> That would be like the splendor of the Mighty One....
> I am become Death,
> The Shatterer of Worlds.

formal adviser to the President. The letter informed Roosevelt of recent work by Szilard and others showing it was possible to initiate a nuclear chain reaction in a large mass of uranium: "This new phenomenon would...lead to the construction of bombs and it is conceivable—though much less certain—that powerful bombs of a new type may thus be constructed." The bomb might prove too heavy for air transport, but carried by boat and exploded in a port, "it might very well destroy the whole port together with some of the surrounding territory."

The selling point of the short letter was in its last paragraph: "I understand that Germany has actually stopped the sale of uranium [key element needed for atomic fission] from the Czechoslovakian mines." Roosevelt got the point. "What you are after," he said to Sachs after reading the letter and attached memoranda, "is to see that the Nazis don't blow us up," and Sachs replied: "Precisely."[10] The President immediately assigned government scientists and military experts to look into the matter.

Birth of the Bomb in Wartime Manhattan Project

A second Einstein letter to Roosevelt, dated March 7, 1940, also taken to him by Sachs, was intended to speed up sluggish government support, for the atomic project had encountered skepticism in military circles and only $6,000 had been allotted to it from Army and Navy budgets. Einstein, the most prestigious scientist of his day and a refugee from Nazi Germany, wrote that new information from the scientists' international grapevine showed that Germany had intensified secret research on uranium.[11] Meanwhile Britain, already at war, had assigned high priority to atomic research and in October 1941 American, British and Canadian scientists pooled their atomic research.

Two months later, on Dec. 6, 1941, the day before the Japanese attack on Pearl Harbor, Roosevelt appointed a special

---

[10] Quoted by William Laurence, *Dawn Over Zero: The Story of the Atomic Bomb* (1946), p. 85.

[11] When France fell to the Nazis in June 1940, Frederic Joliot, who had been directing major research on uranium, sent two co-workers to England with instructions to seek British government cooperation in carrying out a crucial experiment involving heavy water (water in which the hydrogen has an atomic mass of two, needed to slow down neutrons exploding out of atomic nuclei). Joliot remained in France to serve in the underground. The two scientist-emissaries took with them some 40 gallons of heavy water, nearly the entire world stock at the time, just purchased from Norway. After the Germans occupied Norway, they ordered an increase of heavy water production at the Norwegian plant, but the plant was incapacitated by allied attack and underground sabotage.

July 16, 1945. First atomic bomb exploded on test site in desert near Alamogordo, N.M.

Aug. 6, 1945. Air Force dropped atomic bomb on Hiroshima and followed three days later by dropping a second atomic bomb on Nagasaki.

Jan. 1, 1947. Atomic Energy Commission officially came into existence, as created by Congress under terms of the Atomic Energy Act of 1946 to administer the government's atomic energy programs for civilian and military use.

Sept. 23, 1949. President Truman disclosed that Russia had successfully built and tested an atomic bomb.

Jan. 31, 1950. President Truman announced that he had directed the AEC to build a hydrogen bomb.

Nov. 1, 1952. United States tested its first hydrogen bomb at Eniwetok in the Pacific. Some 23 atomic and nuclear explosions were set off underwater, in air or on land between 1946 and 1958 in the Pacific test area on or around the atoll of Bikini.

Aug. 20, 1953. Radio Moscow announced the explosion of Russia's first nuclear bomb.

Aug. 5, 1963. United States, Russia and Britain signed, in Moscow, a Nuclear Test Ban Treaty in which they pledged to discontinue above-ground and underwater testing of atomic and nuclear explosives.

June 17, 1967. China set off its first hydrogen bomb.

July 1, 1968. Sixty nations, including the United States and Russia, signed the Nuclear Non-Proliferation Treaty to prevent the spread of nuclear weapons. Treaty went into effect March 5, 1970.

Nov. 17, 1969. Strategic Arms Limitation Talks opened in Helsinki, Finland, between Russia and the United States.

June 19, 1970. United States announced it had deployed multiple warheads on some intercontinental missiles.

---

committee of scientists, headed by Vannevar Bush, director of the Carnegie Institution, to determine whether a bomb could actually be made and how much it was likely to cost. The committee reported back that if a true crash program were mounted, it might produce a bomb at a cost of at least $100 million by mid-1944. The Atomic Bomb Project—known by its camouflage name of Manhattan Project—was officially launched on Aug. 16, 1942, and placed under Army command. The confidence of the Bush group proved well-founded, though its time and cost schedules were off. It took nearly three years and $2 billion to produce the bomb.

The go-ahead signal marked the beginning of an extraordinary period of cooperation between government and abstruse science for a military goal, an alliance which has left its mark to this day. A vast effort was made to recruit the nation's best scientific brains and engineering skills for the mystery project. Brilliant theoretical physicists were induced to leave their classrooms and laboratories to take up residence in Los Alamos, a newly created barracks town, high on a remote New Mexico mesa, where they would work and live under strictest military surveillance. To the great men of science who had escaped political persecution in Europe, the place had an ominous resemblance to a concentration camp. Nevertheless, despite the empathy gap between "the long hairs" (academic scientists) and "the plumbers" (army engineers)[12] morale was extraordinarily high for the life of the project.

Los Alamos was one of four "hidden cities"[13] built within a few months to house the thousands who worked under strictest secrecy—many of them without knowledge of the goal—to produce the atomic bomb. Los Alamos was the research and development center where the bomb was fashioned; its peak wartime population of 5,800 "included so many world-famous scientists that it no doubt had the highest average I. Q. of any city in the world."[14]

Atomic Bombs at Alamogordo, Hiroshima, Nagasaki

Until zero hour of the first A-bomb test, no one could be certain the bomb would go off. Scientists and engineers had been working night and day to meet the July 16 deadline, for the Army had denied Oppenheimer's plea for more time. The Potsdam Conference was due to begin on July 17 and President Truman wanted a successful A-bomb "in his pocket" when he met Stalin.[15]

The bomb set off at Alamogordo had a potential explosive power of 20 kilotons (20,000 tons) of TNT. The few who watched from assigned vantage points, 10 to 20 miles from the explosion site –Trinity Site—saw an unearthly light change colors

---

[12] Lansing Lamont, *Day of Trinity* (1965), p. 50.

[13] Others were Oak Ridge, Tenn.; Hanford and Richland, Wash.

[14] Laurence, *op. cit.,* p. 127.

[15] Churchill was privy to the project secrets, but Stalin, third member of the allied triumvirate, had been told nothing. Truman informed him at Potsdam on July 24 of the successful test at Alamogordo. Stalin took the news coolly; the project was known to him through espionage. The Soviet Union was then secretly working on its own A-bomb project.

and expand while a great cloud rose and mushroomed out to a height of 40,000 feet. A minute later came a thunderous roar. "It was as though the earth had opened and the skies had split," recalled *New York Times* science editor William Laurence—one of the few non-project workers allowed on the scene. "One felt as though one were present at the moment of creation when God said: 'Let there be light'."[16] All present were awe-struck. Brig. Gen. T.F. Farrell, the project's second in command, floundered for words in his report to the War Department. The sight was "magnificent, beautiful, stupendous and terrifying," he wrote. "....It was that beauty the great poets dream about....Words are inadequate tools for the job of acquainting those not present with the physical, mental and psychological effects."

Destructive effects exceeded expectations. The explosion carved a hole in the earth 400 yards wide to a depth of 10 to 25 feet, vaporized the steel tower on which the bomb had been mounted 100 feet above the ground, and destroyed all animals and vegetable life within one mile. Three weeks later, on Aug. 6, the Air Force dropped a sister bomb on Hiroshima, destroying or damaging nearly two-thirds of its buildings and killing or injuring possibly one-half of its 350,000 population.[17] Three days later, Aug. 9, another and even more destructive A-bomb was dropped over Nagasaki. The next day Japan sued for peace and on Aug. 14 hostilities ended.

Creation of Hydrogen Bombs in America, Russia

Production of atomic bombs and efforts to build up their punch did not cease with the war's end. Nearly a year after Alamogordo, the 20-kiloton bomb proved its mettle in a sea test—one bomb exploding underwater, another in the air over target ships—off the Pacific atoll of Bikini, which had been cleared of its 150 natives.[18] By the end of the 1940s, the ex-

---

[16] Laurence, *op. cit.,* p. 11.

[17] The Atomic Bomb Casualty Commission, a joint U.S.-Japanese government research agency, has been studying the effects of the Hiroshima-Nagasaki bombing since 1947. There is much disagreement on findings. Estimates of the number of deaths in Hiroshima alone range from 64,000 to 240,000. Determining genetic effects is even more difficult. Some scientists report a higher incidence of fetal death and mentally retarded infants due to radiation effects on pregnant women. Experts say it may take at least 20 more years for a full understanding of long-range effects. See "Hiroshima/Nagasaki," *Science,* May 8, 1970, p. 679, and Ernest J. Sternglass, "Infant Mortality and Nuclear Tests," *Bulletin of the Atomic Scientists,* April 1969, p. 18.

[18] Bikini sustained 23 atomic and thermonuclear tests between 1946 and 1958. The atoll has now been determined safe for habitation and the U.S. government is helping the natives to return. See James Cameron, "23 Explosions Later," *New York Times Magazine,* March 1, 1970, pp. 24, 26.

plosive capability of the A-bomb had inched up to 150 kilotons. But scientists already knew that if they could utilize fusion rather than fission of atoms as the explosive factor they could create a bomb one thousand times more powerful than the ones that devastated Hiroshima and Nagasaki.

Knowledge that atoms of hydrogen, the lightest element, would fuse under conditions of tremendous heat and pressure existed even before it was discovered that the atoms of the heaviest element, uranium, could be split. The problem was how to produce the intensity of heat required to trigger the fusion. The successful development of the atomic bomb, which produced a heat level of 50 million degrees centigrade, solved that problem.

Theoretical work on fusion of hydrogen atoms had been going on at Los Alamos even during the war. But scientists disagreed on the feasibility of a hydrogen bomb and their dispute spread to policy makers on the Atomic Energy Commission,[19] in the defense establishment, and in Congress. The main question was whether to divert resources to the task of developing a hydrogen bomb or whether to concentrate on improving the bomb already in hand. Opponents of what began to be known as the "hell-bomb" included those who thought it wouldn't work, those who feared it would work too well and set the world on fire, those who believed its overkill power would be a waste, and those who believed it would be immoral to try to develop so frightful an instrument of destruction.

Russia's detonation of an A-bomb, disclosed to the world by President Truman on Sept. 23, 1949, put an end to the debate. American leaders were shocked by the unexpected speed with which the Soviet Union had been able to build the bomb. If Russia had the science, the technology and the will to produce an A-bomb, they argued, there was little reason to believe it would not move on quickly to the next level of atomic achievement. President Truman announced Jan. 31, 1950, that he had directed the AEC to work "on all forms of atomic weapons, including the so-called super-bomb."[20]

---

[19] A civilian agency created by the Atomic Energy Act of 1946 to administer the government's atomic energy program, including development, production and testing of nuclear weapons.

[20] Truman's announcement followed a sensation-causing security leak: the disclosure on television on Nov. 1, 1949, by Sen. Edwin Johnson (D Colo., 1937-54), that the United States was in fact working on a "super-bomb" 1,000 times more powerful than the atomic bomb.

The United States tested its first hydrogen "device" on Nov. 1, 1952, at Eniwetok in the Pacific. Nearly 10 months later, Aug. 20, 1953, Radio Moscow announced the explosion of Russia's first thermonuclear device. Full appreciation of the dimensions of the new weapon did not hit the average citizen, however, until the United States exploded its second thermonuclear bomb on March 1, 1954, at Bikini. The destructive effect of this larger bomb took even its developers by surprise. It raised a nuclear cloud 17 miles high, scattered radioactive debris over hundreds of miles and contaminated 7,000 square miles downwind from the burst point. Twenty-three Japanese fishermen on the boat *Fortunate Dragon,* nearly 100 miles from the explosion site, suffered serious radiation burns.

There appears to be no reasonable limit to the amount of explosive power that can be built into an H-bomb. As early as Oct. 30, 1961, the Soviet Union detonated a bomb with the power of 58 megatons. If not for its casing of lead, used to reduce radioactive fallout, this bomb would have had twice its actual blast power. "There was no mistaking the fact," wrote Dr. Ralph E. Lapp, atomic physicist, author, and unofficial watchdog over U.S. nuclear policy, "that if the Soviets replaced lead with uranium they had in their possession a 100+ megaton weapon of fantastic kill-power."[21]

Diversification of Sources of Nuclear Attacks

In the early years of the atomic age, U.S. strategic planning depended solely on its bomber force for delivering the new weapon. Dropping an A-bomb over a Japanese city conformed with strategic bombing policy of World War II except that instead of sending a force of 1,000 or more bombers loaded with "block-busters" to devastate a city, a single bomber with a single bomb could do as much damage. After the war, superiority in air power continued to be relied on, particularly in view of the Russian's much larger ground forces. The effort to maintain a superior strategic posture *vis-à-vis* Russia therefore emphasized not only nuclear weapons but long-range bombers.

The emergence of the missile changed, or rather enlarged, the strategic picture. By the mid-1950s, both the United States and Russia were committed to developing an intercontinental ballistic missile that could carry nuclear warheads half way around the world.[22] Missile technology developed rapidly.

---

[21] Ralph E. Lapp, *The Weapons Culture* (1968), pp. 47-48. In his latest book, *Arms Beyond Doubt: The Tyranny of Weapons Technology* (1970), Lapp contends that technological advances give momentum to the arms race.

[22] See "Anti-Missile Defense Systems," *E.R.R.*, 1967 Vol. I, pp. 123-139.

By the end of the 1950s the early missiles—Jupiter, Thor, Atlas, Titan I—had been replaced by the more powerful and accurately targeted Minuteman missiles. A similar technological advance converted the submarine into a wide-ranging undersea carrier of nuclear missiles.

A major refinement of weapon design has diminished the significance of sheer size of a single warhead. This is the development of the multiple-warhead missile, at first providing a cluster of shots at a single target area, now capable of providing a sequential volley with each warhead aimed and timed to strike a separate target. Dr. John S. Foster Jr., Director of Defense Research and Engineering, has described the latter, known as MIRV, as a "space bus." He explained in a speech in Dallas, Dec. 13, 1967: "After the main booster has cut off, the bus keeps making minute adjustments to its speed and direction and after each adjustment it ejects another warhead. Thus each warhead is delivered on a trajectory to a different city or, if desired, all can be delivered within one city."

The Defense Department disclosed on May 26, 1970, that deployment of Minuteman III missiles, built to "space bus" specifications, began on April 18 in silos near Minot, N.D. The schedule called for 100 Minuteman III devices to become operative during 1970. Ultimately more than one-half of the existing 1,000 single-warhead Minuteman missiles will be replaced with the new MIRV version.

MIRV is also the main feature of the nuclear-powered Poseidon submarine. The Defense Department plans to convert 31 of the nation's 41 Polaris submarines to Poseidon specifications. Funds for conversion were first authorized in 1968; the schedule calls for 14 conversions to be completed by June 30, 1971. Meanwhile, a new undersea missile system called ULMS is in a research-and-development stage. This system would make it possible for submarines based in the United States to maintain their weapons in "on target" status throughout their deployment, Secretary Laird told the House Subcommittee on Department of Defense Appropriations, Feb. 25, 1970.

The manned bomber has not been neglected in the nuclear procession. The B-52, capable of carrying two 20-megaton bombs—or 2,000 times the explosive power of the bombs dropped on Hiroshima and Nagasaki—is still a major part of the strategic system. The B-1, an intercontinental jet bomber still on the drawing board but slated for early production, would carry a greater payload than the B-52. A new air-to-ground missile (SRAM) is ready for installation and a nuclear-tipped decoy weapon (SCAD) is under development. These will provide bombers with greater power to penetrate enemy air defenses. The nuclear deterrent has thus grown from a relatively simple single bomb to a complex and multiple system involving airborne, seaborne, undersea and land-based delivery fleets.

Effort to Restrain Nuclear Arms Race

THE NUCLEAR ARMS RACE has had a continuing minor theme: the effort to stop the escalation. This effort began among scientists in the Manhattan Project before the first atomic bomb was produced. The renowned Danish physicist Niels Bohr sought without success to win Churchill and Roosevelt to his view that a generous offer to share control with Stalin would forestall "a fateful competition about the formidable weapon."[23] Szilard quickly foresaw the dangers of an atomic arms race and urged that steps be taken to develop an international control system even before the weapon was ready to detonate. Szilard was among 69 scientists who petitioned President Truman not to use the bomb on Japan, at least not without prior warning.

Aim of Scientists' Lobby in 1946 to Ban Bomb

Younger scientists on the Manhattan Project shared these concerns but lacked access to high places and were hampered by security restraints on their activities. But as soon as the war was over they flocked to Washington and voiced their concerns. The ensuing period, lasting hardly more than a year, was unique in the annals of science or government. Young physicists from a milieu normally indifferent to public affairs were suddenly transformed into a corps of lobbyists determined to "educate" the lawmakers and influence their decisions on major policy issues. The scientists wanted an "open science," with no rule of secrecy to bar the free exchange of ideas and findings among scientists of different nations. They tried to convince authorities that the United States could not hope to

---

[23] Quoted by Alice Kimball Smith, *A Peril and a Hope—the Scientists' Movement in America: 1945-47* (1965), p. 9.

maintain a monopoly on the knowledge that produced the bomb. There was no true defense against atomic attack, the scientists said, and the United States, with its large cities and industrial concentrations, was particularly vulnerable. The only hope lay in civilian control of atomic energy development at home and a universal ban on the bomb.

Their youth and brilliance, the intensity of their crusading spirit, and the glamor of their recent association with the A-bomb project entranced Washington society, while Capitol Hill received their testimony with respect. The passage of the Atomic Energy Act, which established civilian control over the nation's atomic energy program through the Atomic Energy Commission, may be chalked up as their greatest victory.[24] But by the time Truman signed the act, in August 1946, the scientists' period of political activism was already on the decline. According to one study of the movement, the lobbying fervor of the scientists was probably neutralized by the widening of opportunities for their employment in government. "At a high cost to their political activism, attention shifted to the management of this delicate new partnership [science and government]."[25] The spirit of the movement continues today in the Federation of American Scientists and in the *Bulletin of the Atomic Scientists*, founded in 1945 and now published by the Educational Foundation for Nuclear Science.

Not all scientists agreed with the scientists' lobby of 1945-46. Differences among them have been marked on nearly every issue pertaining to nuclear arms development. Their argument over developing the H-bomb had much to do with events leading to the ouster of Dr. Oppenheimer from advisory posts in the government.[26] Scientists are divided today over issues involving development and deployment of ABM and MIRV.

---

[24] Even this victory has been tainted because the AEC, especially in its early years, devoted itself to building bombs for the Department of Defense. Peaceful uses of atomic energy, the other task of the AEC, have been slower in coming about. Atomic energy has yet to fulfill its earlier expectations. See Richard Karp, "The Marginal Nuclear Utilities," *The Washington Monthly*, July 1970, pp. 15-22, and "Electric Power Problems," *E.R.R.*, 1969 Vol. II, pp. 939-955.

[25] Donald A. Strickland, *Scientists in Politics* (1968), pp. 140-141. For review of Atomic Energy Act and events leading up to it, see also Congressional Quarterly's *Congress and the Nation, 1945-64* (1965), pp. 242-246, and "Atomic Proliferation," *E.R.R.*, 1965 Vol. I, pp. 461-477.

[26] After a lengthy hearing before a security board, Oppenheimer was found in June 1954 to be a "loyal" citizen though his conduct reflected "disregard for the requirements of the security system." He was therefore barred from access to atomic secrets. Oppenheimer had opposed development of the H-bomb. In 1963, President Johnson presented Oppenheimer the Enrico Fermi award for achievement in nuclear physics. The White House ceremony was widely regarded as a symbolic erasure of government disapproval of the "father of the A-bomb." Oppenheimer died in 1967.

Efforts to restrain the nuclear arms race by international agreement have moved slowly. Over the 25 years only few agreements of consequence were consummated. The Nuclear Test Ban Treaty of 1963 and the Non-Proliferation of Nuclear Weapons Treaty, which went into force on March 5, 1970, were the major ones.[27] Both took years from the earliest decision to negotiate until validation of a formal treaty. The first prohibited atmospheric testing of nuclear weapons but not underground testing. So while it may have relieved the atmosphere of radioactive contamination, it did little to stem the proliferation of new and mightier nuclear weapons. Under the Non-Proliferation Treaty, three nuclear powers—United States, United Kingdom and the Soviet Union—agreed not to furnish nuclear weapons to non-nuclear countries. Notably absent from the long list of signatories—around 100 nations for each of the treaties—are two minor nuclear powers (China and France), countries with a nuclear capability potential, and certain nations in tinderbox situations where acquisition of a few nuclear weapons could be exceedingly dangerous.

Treaties on Nuclear Testing and Arms Control

Still another arms control agreement was contained in the treaty governing the peaceful exploration and use of outer space. The signatory nations, including the United States and Russia, pledged in a key provision of the 1967 treaty not to station in space or place in orbit any object carrying nuclear weapons or other weapons of mass destruction. That treaty was patterned after a 1960 treaty dealing with Antarctica, in which the two major powers and other signatory nations pledged not to test nuclear weapons or dispose of radioactive wastes on the frozen continent. The United States and Russia further have helped to draft a treaty to prohibit the emplacement of nuclear weapons on the ocean floor beyond the 12-mile offshore territorial limits. A revised draft, the product of more than one year's negotiations, was placed before the United Nations Disarmament Conference on April 23, 1970, for study prior to submission to the U.N. General Assembly.

Disarmament hope now centers on the SALT talks. It took three years from the signing of the Non-Proliferation Treaty before the two most powerful signatories sat down to negotiate, as called for by Article IV of the treaty, "on effective measures relating to cessation of the nuclear arms race and to nuclear

---

[27] See "Prospects for Arms Control," *E.R.R.*, 1969 Vol. I, pp. 269-286.

disarmament, and on a treaty on general and complete disarmament under strict and effective international control." After a 10-week preliminary session in Helsinki, Nov. 17-Dec. 22, 1969, substantive talks began on April 16, 1970, in Vienna and will continue until summer recess probably in July, to be resumed in Helsinki in the fall. No official reports of progress at the closed sessions are made. That they have continued without interruption and without evidence of frayed nerves despite tensions on other cold war fronts is taken as a good omen. Secretary of State William P. Rogers told a news conference June 25, 1970, that "there is prospect of an agreement." He did not elaborate. Optimists believe both sides are sufficiently motivated to make an effort to agree on slowing down or halting the arms race, if only to be relieved of its enormous cost. Even if all goes well, a formal agreement cannot be expected before the latter part of 1970, if then.

Nuclear Issues in American-Soviet Arms Talks

The ABM debate in Congress is linked to prospects for success of SALT. The Nixon administration has taken the position that an anti-ballistic build-up, to serve primarily to protect the nation's missile sites, is necessary despite initiation of disarmament talks. Phase I of the Safeguard anti-ballistic missile program, calling for Safeguard installations at two missile sites,[28] began after Senate opponents failed, on a 50-50 tie vote, to block ABM deployment. The Defense Procurement Act for 1971, which passed the House on May 6, 1970, would authorize the Safeguard program to proceed to Phase II, providing ABM protection at 12 missile sites. Congressional opponents are prepared to fight again when the Phase II measure reaches the Senate floor, probably in July 1970. The Senate Armed Services Committee on June 17, 1970, approved the building of a third Safeguard site, to defend ICBM installations at Whiteman Air Force Base in Missouri, but rejected administration plans to begin developing four other anti-missile sites to provide a "thin" defense against a potential missile threat from China.

"Continued Chinese progress in nuclear weapons" was one of the reasons the administration asked Congress to fund "an orderly, phased Safeguard program for ballistic defense," Deputy Secretary of Defense David Packard told the Senate

---

[28] At Grand Forks, N.D., and Malmstrom, Mont., Air Force bases. See *CQ Almanac 1969*, pp. 257-259, and *CQ Weekly Report* of Jan. 23, 1970, pp. 206-208. The Defense Department disclosed on May 26 that Minuteman III deployment began in North Dakota on April 18.

Defense Appropriations Committee on April 8, 1970. "There is new evidence that [Communist China] continues to advance toward an ICBM capability." If it should achieve that capability by early 1973, which defense planners consider possible though not probable, this could mean China would have from 10 to 25 operational ICBMs on launchers by 1975.

Opposition to Safeguard is based primarily on the claim that, in the event of a full attack, it could not destroy enough of the incoming missiles to prevent severe damage to cities and population. It is argued that even without an ABM defense enough missiles would be left after an attack to inflict unacceptable retaliatory damage on the attacker; thus the nuclear deterrent is operative without the Safeguard. The extremely high cost of the ABM system makes it vulnerable to budget cutters. Department of Defense estimates of the cost of Phase I and Phase II now run to more than $15 billion.[29]

Beyond these complaints, critics hold that to begin deploying the system now is provocative and certain to lead to further escalation of the arms race at an increasingly burdensome cost and with no gain in security from nuclear attack. Much the same position is taken in regard to the administration's program for equipping missiles with multiple warheads. "Deployments of ABM or Mirv and especially of both together will disturb the comparative stability of the present nuclear peace maintained through mutual deterrence," G. B. Kistiakowsky, a former presidential science adviser (1957-63), told Congress. "Such deployments...induce an acceleration of the arms race rather than encouraging meaningful arms control agreements."[30] George F. Kennan, the author and former diplomat, is among those who have warned that "plunging ahead" with the new weapons imperiled the SALT talks.[31]

The Senate approved, by a vote of 72 to 6 on April 9, 1970, a resolution requesting the President to propose an immediate U.S.-Soviet suspension of testing and deployment of all offensive and defensive strategic nuclear weapons. Dr. John S. Foster Jr. testified on June 4 that to call off the ABM and Mirv deployments "is more likely to damage the U.S. negotiating position." Unofficial reports that the administration

---

[29] Testimony of Lt. Gen. Alfred D. Starbird, Safeguard System Manager, to House Appropriations Subcommittee for Department of Defense, April 8, 1970.

[30] Testimony before Subcommittee on Arms Control, International Law and Organization, a unit of the Senate Foreign Relations Committee, May 28, 1970.

[31] Testimony before Senate Foreign Relations Committee, Feb. 6, 1970.

intended to use the ABM and Mɪʀᴠ programs as bargaining points at the Sᴀʟᴛ talks gained credence from Foster's further statement that the deployments were not "irreversible" and that both Safeguard and Mɪʀᴠ could be "eliminated" if a mutual agreement to do so was negotiated at Vienna.[32]

While it calls for no celebration, the nuclear anniversary arouses at least a modicum of cautious optimism. "If a nuclear holocaust was to be avoided," a Washington reporter wrote in looking back over 25 years of the Cold War, "each side [at the Sᴀʟᴛ talks] was compelled by the stark facts of the nuclear age to talk with the other side; yet each was consumed with doubts about the other's intentions."[33] Despite the accumulated mistrust and mutual terror arising from the past 25 years, the United States and Russia appeared in the early summer of 1970 to be edging closer than ever before toward some sort of understanding on arms control.

---

[32] A few weeks earlier, on May 12, Secretary Laird told the Senate Armed Services Committee that if a Sᴀʟᴛ agreement required dismantling of ABMs, "we would have to regard Safeguard as money well spent, since it may have encouraged agreement at Sᴀʟᴛ."

[33] Chalmers M. Roberts, *The Nuclear Years: The Arms Race and Arms Control, 1945-70* (1970), p. 121.

COMMON MARKET VS. THE UNITED STATES

by

Yorick Blumenfeld

1971
Oct. 13

COMMON MARKET VS. THE UNITED STATES

BRITAIN'S APPROACHING DECISION on whether to join the European Economic Community ("Common Market") weighs heavily on this country's economic future. Economists on this side of the Atlantic are hopeful but apprehensive about an enlarged Common Market. They wonder whether it would become primarily a partner or competitor of the United States in world trade. American fears of the latter come at a time when economic troubles at home have brought on trade deficits and undermined the supremacy of the dollar in global commerce.[1] The Common Market countries and Britain have been at odds with the United States over a number of economic restrictions—including a 10 per cent surcharge on imports—President Nixon imposed Aug. 15; in at least one instance they have warned that retaliation might be forthcoming *(see page 90)*.

The present six-member Common Market of France, West Germany, Italy, Belgium, the Netherlands and Luxembourg is already the world's largest trading bloc. Its exports of $45 billion in 1970 were greater than America's and amounted to nearly one-fifth of those shipped from industrial countries. If Parliament approves British entry when it votes the question Oct. 28, and then Ireland, Norway, Denmark follow, the community will become a 10-nation economic power accounting for almost one-third of all world trade. It also embraces a bigger population and more industrial workers than the United States. The target date for admission of all four countries is Jan. 1, 1973.

Parliamentary approval has been treated in the British press during recent weeks as a foregone conclusion. Prime Minister Edward Heath and the ruling Conservative Party are committed to taking Britain "into Europe" after years of rebuffs. "Tories who were dismayed by the effects of the Suez invasion in 1956, with its proof that Britain was no longer a first-class military power, have joined hands with a

[1] See "World Money Crisis," *E.R.R.*, 1971 Vol. II, pp. 693-714.

smaller group on the Left, who despaired of our miserable odyssey from one crisis to another," the *New Statesman* commented editorially. They "see our membership of the EEC as a return ticket to power and prosperity."[2]

Britain's dealings with the Common Market have been long and tortuous, marked by periods of chill and warmth on both sides. Britain refused to take part in the 1956 meetings which led the following year to the Treaty of Rome and the formation of the Common Market. The country responded by organizing, in 1959, the European Free Trade Association, consisting of Austria, Britain, Denmark, Norway, Portugal, Sweden and Switzerland—the "outer seven" nations.[3] In 1961, the Conservative government changed its attitude toward full membership in the EEC, and Britain applied that year for entry.

After difficult and lengthy negotiations, accompanied by British concessions, President Charles de Gaulle of France pronounced the first of his vetoes at a now-famous press conference in Paris on Jan. 14, 1963. He said Britain was too "insular and maritime" to become integrated into Europe. The second attempt at gaining entry came early in 1967 after the Labor government of Harold Wilson reversed its previous opposition to admission. Again a Gaullist *non*, this time in November of that year, ended the second round of negotiations. However, the British did not formally withdraw their application; and in December 1969, with de Gaulle now out of office, the EEC invited Britain to reopen negotiations. These began in June 1970, the same month Labor lost control of Parliament in general elections[4] and was replaced by the Heath government. Heath continued to pursue the goal of Common Market membership while Wilson subsequently returned to his former stance, that of opposition— at least to the terms that have been negotiated.

Public Opinion and Terms of Britain's Admission

Popular support for "going into Europe," which was at its height when Britain made its first application in 1961, seems to have melted away. Today scarcely more than 20 per cent of the British people are prepared to supply pollsters with a

---

[2] "The Case for Entry Not Proven," *New Statesman*, Oct. 1, 1971, p. 421.

[3] Finland has since been accorded "associate" status in the association.

[4] See "British Election, 1970," *E.R.R.*, 1970 Vol. I, pp. 425-442. See also "Common Market: Start of a New Decade," *E.R.R.*, 1967 Vol. I, pp. 103-120, and "Britain, the United States and the Common Market," *E.R.R.*, 1961 Vol. II, pp. 521-538.

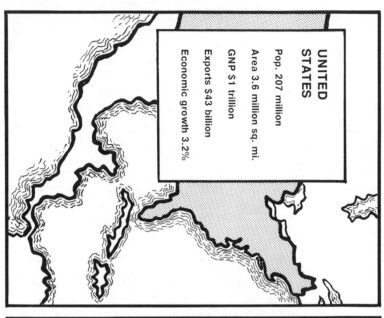

UNITED STATES

Pop. 207 million

Area 3.6 million sq. mi.

GNP $1 trillion

Exports $43 billion

Economic growth 3.2%

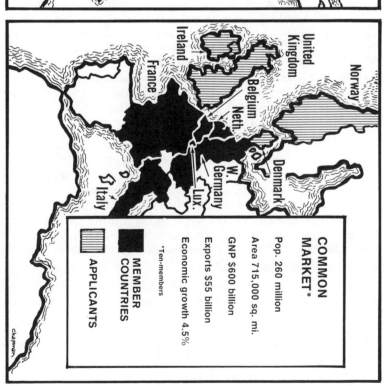

COMMON MARKET*

Pop. 260 million

Area 715,000 sq. mi.

GNP $600 billion

Exports $55 billion

Economic growth 4.5%

*Ten-members

MEMBER COUNTRIES

APPLICANTS

Norway

United Kingdom

Ireland

Belgium

Neth.

Denmark

France

W. Germany

Lux.

Italy

chapman

"yes" answer. "The reason usually given for this slump is simple attrition," John Mander wrote in *The New Leader* in the early summer. "The Gaullist vetoes of 1963 and 1967 have left their mark: Why expose oneself to such humiliation a third time?" Mander rejected this reasoning. "My own feeling...[is that] popular recognition that 'we' will not influence the decision anyway...accounts for the 'no' vote."[5]

The Economist was moved to complain, on Sept. 25, that the national debate on the issue was "subsiding in public indifference." "This is not so much because the public is indifferent to whether Britain should join Europe," the magazine added, "but rather because the electorate sees no point in getting worked up over what it regards as the foregone conclusion that Parliament will vote for Britain's entry anyway."

The opposition Labor Party was divided over the issue and unable to capitalize on the negative reaction of public opinion. When the party held its annual political conference at Brighton the week of Oct. 4-8, Common Market foes put Labor on record opposing entry on terms negotiated by the Heath government. Labor delegates also asked the government to hold new parliamentary general elections to let the electorate express itself on the question of joining or staying out. But the Labor delegates refused to approve a resolution placing the party in opposition to Britain's entry on any terms. Moreover, the deputy party leader, Roy Jenkins, remained an outspoken advocate of entry.

British and Common Market negotiators announced at EEC headquarters in Brussels on May 13, 1971, that all major issues regarding Britain's application for membership had been resolved. They agreed to a five-year transitional period, comprising six steps, for Britain's adoption of the Common Market's troublesome agricultural policy. In a major concession to the French, the British accepted the principle of giving full "community preference" to EEC products, beginning in 1973.

A government White Paper, presented to the House of Commons on July 7, added details of Britain's entry terms. These included the following:

● Britain would be represented in the European Investment Bank with the same voting weight as France and West Germany,

---

[5] John Mander, "Dragging Britain into Europe," *The New Leader*, June 28, 1971.

and it would pay a contribution (about $450 million) similar to theirs.

● EEC members would consider Britain's proposals for adjusting its rules on capital movements to Common Market nations.

● All British dependencies except Gibraltar and Hong Kong and all developing nations in the Commonwealth except those in Asia would be given the choice of entering into trade agreements or association with the community.

● Asian Commonwealth nations would "benefit from the enlarged community" [the White Paper added] and would be assured that the Common Market would "examine trade problems which might arise."

● Hong Kong would be included in a plan of trade preferences.

The White Paper's main theme was that the terms for admission were "fair and reasonable" and provided an opportunity that might never arise again. Emphasizing the disparity between Britain's slight economic gains over the past decade[6] and the far better progress of Common Market countries, the 20,000-word paper stated that there was no way except through membership to provide Britain with a sufficiently large market to stimulate economic expansion.

Question of Commonwealth and U.S. Farm Exports

British resistance to European economic integration goes beyond purely economic questions. But the arguments, pro and con, have a strong economic rationale. British international trade is bound at present by the Commonwealth preference system. Exports from Commonwealth nations receive preferential duty rates in the United Kingdom of England, Scotland, Wales and Northern Ireland, and British exports receive favored treatment in Commonwealth markets.

By accepting membership in the EEC, Britain would have to replace this system with one giving preferences to trade among member countries. While the relative weight of the Commonwealth in British trade has declined, several Commonwealth countries—New Zealand most of all[7]—would suffer from losses in the British market. In addition, the British would lose the benefit of cheap food imports from overseas and would be forced to accept the higher agricultural prices of the Common Market. These prices are set and supported by member governments, which buy up excess supplies at

---

[6] See "Britain in the 1960s: Descent from Power," *E.R.R.*, 1967 Vol. II, pp. 697-716.

[7] New Zealand exports 85 to 95 per cent of its butter, cheese and lamb to Britain.

guaranteed prices. Imports are charged a variable levy, calculated as the difference between the lowest world price and the guaranteed internal price. The price of food in Britain was recently estimated to be 18 to 26 per cent below Common Market levels.

Raymond Lubitz, an economist at Columbia University, contends that not only British consumers but American agricultural exporters might suffer from British membership in the Common Market.[8] No issue has caused more problems between the Common Market and the United States than American farm exports. U.S. exports of industrial goods to the EEC have increased in recent years, mainly as a result of successive reductions in tariffs, especially since the Kennedy Round of tariff negotiations was completed in 1967. But U.S. farm exports to the community declined 20 per cent from 1966 through 1969. They rose in 1970, edging close to the 1966 level. Subsidies that the Common Market pays its growers have increased the competition American food shippers face in other foreign markets.

Washington is concerned that British farmers might be encouraged by Common Market price supports to increase their production and consequently diminish their purchases of American feed grains. These purchases currently amount to about $100 million a year. The British-American tobacco trade, valued at about $150 million a year, is in an exposed position also. American tobacco experts calculate that this trade might be halved by greater British imports from Greece and Turkey under preferential trade agreements between those countries and the Common Market.

By American standards, farms in the Common Market countries are small and inefficient. And they are 13 times as numerous, in terms of total population, as in the United States. Foreign trade officials in Washington contend that these countries should reduce their price supports or take other steps to limit surplus production. But John Whitehorn, deputy director general of the Confederation of British Industries, argues that human and social, as well as economic, problems are involved. Writing in *Industry Week,* Aug. 9, 1971, he noted that in Italy 40 per cent of the work force is in farming. The average size of Italian farms is only 12 acres.

---

[8] Raymond Lubitz, "Round Three: Britain and the Common Market," *Columbia Journal of World Business,* July-August 1971, p. 77.

EEC officials in Brussels can point out in their defense that U.S. agricultural exports to their countries, valued at $1.9 billion in 1970, have doubled since 1958. The sale of soybeans alone has exceeded $500 million a year. N. William Hazen, projecting U.S. trade trends, foresees a decrease in grain, meat and fruit exports to Britain if it becomes part of the Common Market but an increase in soybean exports because the Common Market lets them in duty free.[9] As for industrial goods, he projects a slight increase because British tariffs would be aligned with lower Common Market tariffs on these goods.[10]

Membership Quest by Denmark, Ireland, Norway

Britain's admission to the Common Market would remove it as the pivotal country in the European Free Trade Association. Unlike the EEC, the association is devoid of supranational features and is aimed not at the establishment of a common market or common external tariffs but at the elimination of internal barriers to trade among the member nations. Moreover, its provisions apply only to non-agricultural goods. Two member countries of the "outer seven" besides Britain—Denmark and Norway—are candidates for membership in the Common Market. Britain's entry would presumably push the two countries closer to acceptance of terms now being negotiated for entry; it is also expected that Ireland, another candidate for entry, would be similarly influenced because of its close trade ties with England.

Negotiations between the Common Market and Denmark, Norway and Ireland on terms of entry have yet to reach final form, however. In all three countries, referendums are expected to be held in 1972 on the question of accepting or rejecting membership. The outcome of the voting will be legally binding only in Ireland, where changes in the national constitution are regarded as a requisite to membership. In Norway and Denmark, the balloting will offer the national parliaments an expression of voter sentiment when they formally consider the question.

A Gallup poll taken in Norway during July 1971 recorded that, for the first time, those who favored membership out-

---

[9] The EEC considered placing an indirect tax on vegetable oils, a soybean derivative. But this would have made margarine more expensive and would have discouraged the use of animal feeds based on oil seeds. Such feeds tend to increase the cow's milk production and butterfat content.

[10] N. William Hazen, "U.S. Foreign Trade in the Seventies," *Columbia Journal of World Business*, September-October 1971, pp. 54-55.

numbered those who did not, 36 to 30 per cent. But a vast number of Norwegians were still undecided. The Storting, the Norwegian parliament, voted the previous month, 113 to 37, to continue negotiations. The 37 negative votes were one short of the number that would bar the country's membership in the EEC when the ultimate decision is made by the Storting following the national referendum. A three-fourths majority will then be required for ratification.

In Denmark, only the far-left parties have expressed concerted opposition to the country's bid for admission into the European community but parliamentary elections held Sept. 21, 1971, left the picture clouded. A five-sixths majority is required for ratification in the Folketing, the Danish parliament. In all three countries—Denmark, Ireland and Norway—the ruling parties and many of the opposition parties support the principle of membership.

American Aims Involving European Unity

POLITICAL AND ECONOMIC unification of Europe has been among the goals of American foreign policy ever since the end of World War II. When Congress authorized the Marshall Plan for aid to European recovery, it declared that the "policy of the people of the United States [is] to encourage the unification of Europe." Paul G. Hoffman, first head of the European Cooperation Administration, repeatedly urged the countries receiving Marshall Plan aid to integrate their economies into a single, large market free of all internal trade barriers. As NATO commander, Gen. Dwight D. Eisenhower declared in London on July 3, 1951, that "Europe cannot obtain the towering material stature possible to its people's skills and spirit so long as it is divided by patchwork territorial fences." Later, as President, Eisenhower gave full backing to the Treaty of Rome.

President Kennedy likewise spoke of a strong united Europe. At an Independence Day address in Philadelphia in 1962, Kennedy said: "We do not regard a strong and united Europe as a rival but a partner...capable of playing a greater role in the common defense, or responding more generously to the needs of poorer nations, of joining with the United States and others in lowering trade barriers, resolving problems of commerce and commodities and currency and developing coordinated policies in all economic and diplomatic areas."

President Nixon, in his State of the World message on Feb. 25, 1971, affirmed that America's policy of supporting the expansion of the European Economic Community had not changed. "We welcome cohesion in Europe because it makes Europe a sturdier pillar of the structure of peace," he said. But fears began to grow in Washington that a unified Europe might become an inward-looking rival.

Some Americans now contend that the Common Market is reverting to economic nationalism. They say that it is erecting trade barriers against American products and is luring other nations into special arrangements which discriminate against American products. The *Economist* argues that the United States, officially, still urges the community to enlarge for two reasons: "First, Europe gives America a galloping continental market outside its own...to which its companies and business influence can export America's capitalist and innovative way of life. And second, the Common Market promises (in its better moments) to become a strong, united political Europe which might one day, by fending however cussedly for itself, reduce one of America's major defense burdens in the world.[11]

Europeans, on the other hand, tend to regard the United States as a superpower trying to dominate them economically. There has been great resentment, particularly in France, at the way gigantic U.S. corporations have used the dollar to gain control of European industries. At the same time, members of the European community contend, the United States has erected barriers to protect its own industries whenever foreign competition has appeared on its home markets.

The British see themselves as being able to bring better understanding between the United States and continental Europe on these matters. The London *Times* wrote editorially June 29, 1971, that the four applicant countries to the Common Market—Britain, Denmark, Ireland and Norway—are all much closer to the United States in terms of economic philosophy than are France or Belgium. "It is not unrealistic to hope," the *Times* added, "that they will oppose any

---

[11] "A Europe of Ten," *The Economist*, May 22, 1971, p. 50.

trend towards European economic autarchy and give the community a more outward looking internationalist character." W. O. Campbell Adamson, director general of the Confederation of British Industries, said in a speech to the National Foreign Trade Council in New York on Feb. 17, 1971, that "British participation in the EEC will help to realize more quickly the political gain which the United States looks for in the unification of Western Europe."

Threat to Anglo-American Special Relationship

In World War II the United States and Britain fell into the habit of close and continuous official consultation. The habit persisted, with notable exceptions, for years afterward. This "special relationship"—as the English called it—extended to nuclear endeavors and was so intimate that it moved President de Gaulle to cast the first of his two vetoes against British membership in the Common Market. He thought Britain should turn its gaze across the English Channel rather than the Atlantic Ocean. American support for the pound sterling in successive financial crises was viewed by the French as unreconcilable with the aims of monetary autonomy and stability within the community.

Walter Lippmann observed at the time of an attack on the pound in the world money markets in 1967: "No one who knows British opinion can doubt that these proud people are irked by their financial dependence on Washington and that they yearn for a more independent role." Nevertheless, there are numerous Britons who feel little attraction to the EEC and would much prefer that their country remain in an unequal relationship with a partner which shares so many institutions and traditions.

Prime Minister Heath emphasized in an address to the American Bar Association in London on July 19, 1971, that "our ultimate purpose must be a more balanced defense partnership with you." Heath said he believed this aim would best be realized with Britain in the Common Market. And for the Labor Party, Roy Jenkins said in Parliament on July 23 that he, too, wanted to see Atlantic ties maintained, but upon the basis of a far more equal partnership between America and its European allies than has been possible for the last 20 years. However much some Englishmen may desire to take a more independent stance, they are aware of economic realities. American companies currently control more than 10 per cent of British industry and their strength is greatest in the main growth industries. For example, these companies control more than half of the British motor-car industry.[12]

Comparison of U.S. and Common Market Strength

An enlarged EEC would approach the size and economic power of the United States. The 10-nation community would not only account for almost one-third of all world trade, as compared with 14 per cent for the United States; it would also hold most of the world's gold and foreign exchange reserves—more than $35 billion worth. That is three and one-half times more than the United States holds. The American market is nearly two and one-half times the size of the EEC in purchasing power, however, and this gives U.S. companies enormous resources. It is this strong home market that has enabled American companies to compete so effectively abroad. America is far less dependent on foreign trade than Europe or Japan, as is shown in the following table of exports expressed in proportion of gross national product:

Belgium	43%	Italy	14%
Netherlands	35	France	11
West Germany	19	Japan	10
Britain	16	United States	4

In terms of economic growth, the Common Market has far outstripped the United States. From its inception in 1957, the gross product of the six countries, after adjustment for inflation, increased by 95 per cent, compared with 61 per cent for the United States and 42 per cent for Britain. The community's dynamism was best illustrated by the rapid expansion of its trade with the rest of the world. From 1958 to 1968, EEC exports to non-member countries rose by 122 per cent, while Britain's exports rose by only 78 per cent. If Britain's foreign trade had expanded at the same rate as the community's, the volume would have passed the $40 billion mark—instead of the actual figure of $34.5 billion. Projections indicate that the gross product of the expanded community would approach $1 trillion by 1980.

However, not all experts attribute the rapid economic growth of the six countries to the formation of the EEC. The British research organization, the National Institute for Economic and Social Research, has shown that growth rates in the six countries were higher before the Common Market

---

[12] D. J. Ezra, "British Industry and the Common Market," National Westminster Bank *Quarterly*, August 1971, p. 10.

AMERICAN TRADE WITH COMMON MARKET

(in millions of dollars)

	EEC imports from the United States	EEC exports to the United States
1965	5,692	3,424
1970	9,038	6,633

SOURCE: EEC information office, Washington, D.C.

---

had started functioning (1954-57) than in years afterward (1958-69). Charles Kindleberger and Edward Denison have argued that the fast growth rate was due partly to the existence of a low-priced labor supply drawn to industry from agriculture and migration—migration primarily from southern Europe and North Africa.[13]

Low wage rates in European industry have until recently been matched by the low productivity of European labor. However, the consensus of American manufacturers in Europe is that the Common Market labor force is no less skilled than the U.S. labor force and that once the quality of the equipment, facilities and supervisory skills improves, productivity in Europe will rise to American levels. A heavy European investment in plant and equipment over the past decade has resulted in the virtual rebuilding of such industries as steel and chemicals.

While American business officials generally agree that the EEC is going to become an ever-stronger exporter, American specialties such as aircraft, space equipment, telecommunications, computers and most electronic parts will continue to have a great advantage over European products for some time to come. Moreover, with Britain joining the EEC, U.S. industry will have an even stronger foothold in the Common Market. American direct investments in Britain have a book value of more than $7 billion.

Although there is no question that some of the Common Market's preferential agreements put a number of American exporters at a comparative disadvantage, the EEC still buys more from the United States than it sells to this country *(see table)*. And despite American complaints about tariffs, the Common Market's non-agricultural imports from the United States have been growing at a rate of about 9 per

---

[13] Charles P. Kindleberger, *Europe's Post-War Growth: The Role of Labor Supply* (1967) and Edward F. Denison, *Why Growth Rates Differ* (publication of the Brookings Institution, 1967).

cent a year and now exceed $7 billion annually. Europeans also note that when American congressmen complain about the low prices of European-made products on the U.S. market, it is very likely that these products were made by companies owned or managed by Americans. Moreover, a large share of the profits from these American investments in Europe is returned to the United States.

An enlarged European community might, in time, seek common policies on military as well as economic questions. French President Georges Pompidou suggested at a news conference in Paris on Jan. 21, 1971, that a European confederation could cover the major fields of government, including political decisions. Francois Duchene, director of the Institute for Strategic Studies, London, has theorized that "the urge to launch the European community on a more political course might well move into the area of defense" in face of rising European anxieties over the prospect of a reduction of American military forces in the North Atlantic Treaty Organization.

"A more coordinated West European defense system could not replace the American nuclear guarantee, but it would reinforce it and make it more credible," Duchene wrote. "A European operation would also be attractive as the only way to bring the heirs of De Gaulle back into the Western fold without a formal tie to NATO."[14] France severed its military, but not political, ties with the organization in 1967. The five other Common Market nations are also members of NATO; of the four countries seeking membership in the Common Market, only Ireland is not affiliated with the organization.

Atlantic Trade Problems and Opportunities

THE UNITED STATES has encouraged and welcomed the economic growth of Japan and Western Europe, for political as well as economic reasons. But the conviction has been growing in Washington in recent years that both Japan and the Common Market must allow American products to compete more readily in their countries. Kenneth N. Davis Jr., then an Assistant Secretary of Commerce, voiced that thought in a speech in March 1970, saying: "It is time for

---

[14] Francois Duchene, "A New European Defense," *Foreign Affairs*, October 1971, pp. 76-77, 78.

Japan and Europe to respond more fairly than heretofore to 20 years of U.S. leadership in expansionist world trade policies."[15]

Europeans take a different view about which side is guilty of being protectionist. They point out that while the EEC has eliminated 11 quotas on imported goods since 1963, the United States has added 60 in that time. Quotas, unlike tariffs, limit the amount of goods that can come into a country. Except in special circumstances, they are contrary to the international trading rules established by the General Agreement on Tariffs and Trade.[16] It is also recalled in Europe that during GATT negotiations in 1960, the Common Market offered to reduce its tariffs by 20 per cent. These reductions were made despite the fact that the United States was unable to reciprocate.

Europe and the United States accuse each other of maintaining non-tariff barriers to trade. Europeans, among other foreign exporters, regard the "American Selling Price" as a symbol of this country's protectionist tendencies. The duty on certain goods is computed not on the value of the product but when it reaches American shores—the traditional way— but on the U.S. sales price of a comparable item made in the United States. During the celebrated Kennedy Round of GATT negotiations[17] in 1967, the Johnson administration agreed to seek congressional repeal of the American Selling Price system in return for tariff concessions by Western European nations. But the Johnson administration was unable, and the Nixon administration has been so far, to bring about repeal.

American trade officials look upon the Common Market's preferential trade agreements with other nations as a violation of the spirit, if not the letter, of GATT principles of free trade. Member countries of GATT are committed to the concept that all countries are to benefit from tariff reductions extended by one country to another. Sen. Hubert H. Humphrey (D Minn.), the Democratic presidential candidate in 1968, took up this issue in speaking July 30, 1971, at the

---

[15] See "Competition for World Markets," *E.R.R.*, 1970 Vol. II, p. 593.

[16] GATT, as the organization is known, embraces a set of principles and rules on tariff and non-tariff barriers that is subscribed to by 77 nations.

[17] These negotiations were named for President Kennedy, who upon assuming the presidency in 1961 made tariff cuts and an expansion of foreign trade part of his legislative program. The Kennedy Round negotiations began in Geneva in 1963 and were completed in 1967.

Trade Policy Research Center in London. He accused the EEC of "taking a series of steps which add up to a shift from multilateral trade...to regional and bilateral special arrangements and the formation of a preferential trading bloc."

Common Market's Response to Nixon's Surcharge

Ralf Dahrendorf, the EEC commissioner responsible for foreign trade matters, disagrees. He contends that the organization supports "the rules of free international trade out of conviction, not just necessity." Dahrendorf added: "We do not want a trade war, for we have other instruments to settle our differences."[18] Dahrendorf has been outspoken in his criticism of the 10 per cent surcharge on U.S. imports which President Nixon imposed Aug. 15 in his economic plan to stop inflation, speed recovery from the 1970 recession, reduce unemployment, bring American foreign trade back into balance, and force revaluation of several foreign currencies in relation to the dollar.

There was growing recognition in the world that the American economy was not performing well. The U.S. balance-of-payments deficit reached a record $5.53 billion in the first quarter of 1971—a record surpassed in the second quarter by a deficit of $5.77 billion. Far more worrisome was the growing likelihood that the United States would end the year with its first trade deficit since 1893. While American exports continued to grow, imports grew faster. The surcharge was intended to help reduce imports and, according to several experts, provide the Nixon administration a bargaining tool in trying to make foreign governments revalue their currencies.

The EEC was at first unable to agree on a unified response to the American "challenge." Finance ministers of the six Common Market nations and Britain, meeting in Brussels four days later, could not reconcile French and West German differences over what common monetary policy to adopt in response to the dollar crisis. They did announce after a second meeting on Sept. 13 that they had reached agreement. Their joint statement, accepting the U.S. contention that it was time to restructure the world monetary system, proposed the following as preconditions:

- An official devaluation of the dollar by raising the price of gold for intergovernmental transactions above the prevailing price of $35 an ounce.

---

[18] Ralf Dahrendorf, "The Common Market, the U.S., and Japan," *The Atlantic Community Quarterly*, Spring 1971, p. 62.

● A gradual end to reliance on "national currencies (the dollar)" as reserve units in world trade and monetary relations.

● Retention of gold as the principal common denominator of international monetary relations, with increased emphasis on Special Drawing Rights issued by the International Monetary Fund.

● Realignment of the world's major currencies, "including the dollar," to restore equilibrium to the system of international payments.

● Restoration of fixed parities among the major currencies, but with greater flexibility in exchange rates to inhibit future speculation.

● Revocation of the U.S. surcharge.

Secretary of the Treasury John B. Connally told delegates to the annual meeting of the International Monetary Fund in Washington, Sept 30, that the United States would remove the surcharge if other leading countries would let their currencies "float" freely upward in relation to the dollar and if some countries took "specific" measures in the coming weeks to reduce barriers to American exports. Testifying the following day before the Senate Finance Committee, Connally stuck by his basic position that the United States would not remove the surcharge "until we can be assured there will be a turnaround in our balance of payments." He added, "We are not going to have a trade war—we don't want it, nobody wants it." He said that "beyond question we have set the stage for negotiations" on the monetary issues.

Europe did not appear to be pacified, however. The Common Market countries formally protested to the United States Oct. 4—Britain had done so earlier—against other aspects of the Nixon economic plan. These involved requests to Congress for tax credits on new machinery and equipment produced in the United States and for a tax deferral on business earnings from export sales. The EEC warned that these measures, if passed, might lead to retaliation. The protest, delivered to the American ambassador to the Common Market, J. Robert Schaetzel,[19] characterized the measures as being in violation of GATT agreements.

Dollar Crisis as Spur to EEC Monetary Union

Although President Nixon's action failed to give the needed stimulus for the immediate creation of a European monetary union, it seemed certain to speed up plans to weld the trading bloc into a single currency area over the next decade. It was

---

[19] A new EEC ambassador to the United States, Aldo Maria Mazio, is expected to arrive in Washington late in October 1971 to assume his post.

agreed in Brussels in February 1971 that the central banks of the six nations would set up a special fund by mid-1972 for stabilizing exchange markets. This fund could eventually serve as the basis of a European version of the U.S. Federal Reserve System. Existing central banks would act as Reserve Banks do in the U.S. system, and a new executive group would formulate community-wide policy in much the same way the Federal Reserve Board does.

A separate start was made through the issuance in January 1971 of EMUs, or European Monetary Units, by the European Coal and Steel Community.[20] The EMU is defined in terms of gold at the value of the dollar at par. Robert Prinsky reported that the unit "could be an important first step toward the use of a common currency within the Common Market and could help unify the capital markets of the Six."[21] However, few experts believe that monetary union can come about in the next few years. Neither Britain nor France shows much desire to delegate its national authority over monetary matters to Brussels.

A goal of complete monetary union within the community by 1980 was set when the six heads of state met at The Hague in December 1969. A commission published a detailed plan[22] the following March outlining the steps to be taken to reach this goal. Under terms of this plan, each country is now required to state its economic goals and to harmonize its tax structure with the others. In the second phase, to be instituted in the mid-1970s, fiscal systems are to be completely harmonized and capital markets integrated. Complete monetary integration is the goal of the third phase at the end of the decade.

Benefits to U.S. Industry From Unified Market

One obstacle to the expansion of American trade with the EEC has been the divergence of industrial standards on the two sides of the Atlantic. The aim of the United States, as well as of an enlarged community, will be to remove technical barriers to trade and obtain uniformity in national standards

---

[20] The European Coal and Steel Community is the oldest (1954) of three "communities" embracing the same six countries. The other two are the EEC and the European Atomic Energy Community (EURATOM).

[21] Robert Prinsky, "A European Monetary Unit," *The Atlantic Community Quarterly,* Spring 1971, p. 85.

[22] Known as the Second Barre Plan, named for its author, Raymond Barre. Under the first plan, the member countries agreed to reduce the margin within which their currency exchange rates could vary from one another and to set up a $2 billion reserve fund to extend credit to any one of them that was running up temporary payments' deficits.

and methods of testing. Under Secretary of Commerce James T. Lynn said in Washington June 18, 1971, that it looked increasingly likely that within two or three years there would be a European patent office. Seventeen European nations are drafting an agreement for a European patent system. It is likely that European patents will then be available to American companies.

Jean-Jacques Servan-Schreiber, editor of the influential Paris newsweekly *L'Express,* has characterized the Common Market as "the new frontier for American industry, its promised land." Some of that promise has obviously been fulfilled. American business investments in Europe may total $60 billion in real—in contrast to book—values. In comparison, European investments in the United States are estimated at $25 billion. American dollars in private hands in Europe— "Eurodollars"—have increased almost fivefold since 1964, growing from $11 billion to $52 billion.

More of the promise remains to be fulfilled, especially in an enlarged Common Market. Over the past decade, some European nations have outdone each other to attract American companies. Belgium, Luxembourg, and the Netherlands have made conditions particularly favorable to American investors. In this regard, the Treaty of Rome is helpful to foreign companies inside the Common Market. Article 58 of the treaty provides that they will be assured the same treatment as local producers.

And yet, American dominance of world finance and trade is showing signs of fading. The U.S. balance-of-payments deficit, the weakening of the dollar as an international currency, and the growing economic muscle of Japan and Europe all point to America's diminished status. Japan and the Common Market have already become great centers of industry and trade in the non-Communist world. With the enlargement of the Common Market in prospect, its relative strength in this tripartite setting will increase. A single market embracing nearly all of the industrial countries in Western Europe may work to America's disadvantage in the short run, but not necessarily over the course of years. That is the judgment of many economists and political thinkers on both sides of the Atlantic.

RUSSIA'S RESTIVE CONSUMERS

by

Yorick Blumenfeld

1 9 7 1
Mar. 17

RUSSIA'S RESTIVE CONSUMERS

T HE POLITICAL INFIGHTING taking place as the Soviet Communist Party prepares to open its 24th Congress in Moscow on March 30 is thought by experts to center on the question of how much to concede to Russia's restive consumers. That the Party Congress has been delayed a full year[1] indicates Kremlin planners have had great difficulty in laying out the ninth Five Year Plan (1971-75) for the development of the Russian economy. Draft directives of the plan were announced in Moscow on Feb. 14 and are destined to be approved by the Congress. While the stamp of consent is usually automatic, the plan's emphasis on the need to raise living standards and augment the output of consumer goods is bound to put strains on the Soviet leadership—a leadership which often is portrayed as uncertain and divided.

Russia's economic problems, ranging from stagnation to inflation, have attracted far less notice than America's in the past year. This is due, in part, to Soviet reluctance to produce statistics. However, Western observers perceive that the Brezhnev-Kosygin regime has failed to make the economy function more smoothly, as it promised to do. And it has failed to meet many of the goals of the last Five Year Plan. These failures have affected the long-suffering Soviet consumer. He is frustrated by his frequent inability to find such everyday items as gloves, towels and razor blades or even food staples like meat, fish, and fresh fruits and vegetables. Robert Conquest, a Soviet-affairs analyst, speaks of "a great reservoir of discontent among the masses."[2]

Russians, however, have traditionally shown a far greater tolerance than Poles, Czechs, Hungarians or Yugoslavs[3] for

---

[1] The Congress, theoretically the supreme body in the Soviet Communist Party, ordinarily meets not less than once every four years. It was last convened—the 23rd Congress—March 29, 1966, when the last Five Year Plan (1966-70) was approved. The 1971 Congress is scheduled to convene for 10 days.

[2] Interview published in *U.S. News & World Report*, Dec. 28, 1970.

[3] See Anthony Sylvester, "Yugoslavia's Consumers Call the Shots," *East Europe*, January 1971, p. 23. See also "Poland in the Eastern Bloc," *E.R.R.*, 1967 Vol. II, p. 943.

the shortcomings of their leaders. While Russia's economic problems are serious, they are not regarded as acute enough to force an overhaul of the archaic distribution system or a change in the over-centralized and bureaucratic economic direction from Moscow. The Soviet consumer has remained quieter than his Eastern European neighbors despite queues and shortages. He has seen some progress over the past decade. Each year, more Russians move into slightly better quarters, enjoy greater amenities, and receive a slightly improved variety of consumer goods. While these improvements are not dramatic, over a period of years they are noticeable.

Fears That Polish Consumer Revolt Will Spread

Yet it is obvious that food riots in Poland during December 1970 left their mark on the Kremlin. These riots in the Baltic shipbuilding cities of Gdansk, Gdynia and Szczecin led to Wladyslaw Gomulka's removal from political control in Poland—he was First Secretary of the Polish Communist Party—and had the effect of warning those planners in Moscow who refused to adopt new methods in the Soviet Union. The fact is that Gomulka was seeking the very path which Russian leaders have considered a means of escaping economic stagnation. Gomulka's first step in trying to move from a state-controlled economy toward a market economy was to raise food prices to a realistic level. Ever since 1948 Polish workers have enjoyed subsidized food at the expense of Polish farmers.

It was the insensitivity of the Polish United Workers' [Communist] Party to the consumer which finally brought the country to the brink of a total breakdown. Bitterness had been mounting since the fall of 1970 because prices of coal and shoes were raised just as the weather was turning cold. But to raise the prices on flour, meat, jam and coffee at a time when people were buying extra food for the Christmas holidays was an invitation to disaster. Workers took to the streets, forcing the country's top leadership to resign. A politburo member from Silesia, Edward Gierek, replaced Gomulka. The Warsaw daily *Polityka* commented on Dec. 30 that "personnel changes will not bring money into the treasury, or goods into the economy, but they should introduce a new style of decision-making on basic problems."

Gierek made concessions to discontented Polish workers and housewives immediately upon taking office. His first act was to announce a two-year price freeze on all food items. Then he increased assistance to low-income and fixed-income families, at a cost of about 8 billion zlotys a year—more than $300 million at the official rate of exchange. This action was quickly followed by hints that a popular-priced car would be manufactured to satisfy the Polish demand for automobiles. *Trybuna Ludu.* the official party newspaper, called the decree of the Council of Ministers of Jan. 8, which officially sanctioned many of Gierek's reforms, "a charter protecting the consumer."[4]

As industrial strife continued in a number of Polish cities, Gierek promised on Jan. 19 that additional meat and processed poultry would become available. Much-sought-after goods such as soup concentrates, chicken broth, instant coffee, jellies, pies and preserved vegetables would be imported in greater quantities, he added. Moreover, the new Polish leadership abandoned the current Five Year Plan and replaced it with a plan for 1971 only, while a new program for 1972-75 is devised to put more foodstuffs on the market. But all these measures did not suffice. When thousands of Polish textile workers in Lodz went on strike in mid-February, the Gierek regime rescinded the price increases on food and meat which Gomulka had imposed in December.

Poland's new leaders realize that if they give in too quickly to popular pressure there is the risk the country will be paralyzed by rising demands and further strikes. On the other hand, if they do not respond quickly enough, new riots might break out and plunge the country into chaos. The London *Times* wrote editorially on Feb. 17 that "the problem of the Polish government is whether the appetite of the workers will grow with what it feeds upon—whether the workers, having felt their new power, will decide they must press their advantage as far as they can while the present climate lasts, or whether they will be satisfied for the moment and give the government a breathing space in which to work out its plans for the future."

Dan Morgan, Eastern European correspondent of *The Washington Post*, wrote on March 13, 1971: "The core of the problem is the combination of growing nationalism and the

---

[4] The "charter" specified that prices of industrial goods would be lowered as production increased and costs were driven down; that steps would be taken to supply the market with an increased number of inexpensive commodities; that price abuses would be corrected; that manufacturers, rather than central authorities in Warsaw, would set prices, subject to scrutiny by several national agencies; and finally that consumer research would be conducted on a large scale to coordinate supply and demand.

pressures of industrialization in the Communist bloc. Gierek's unusual strategy of defusing these tensions by negotiating with the workers and making concessions may not please the Soviet leaders. But in the case of Poland, Western analysts wonder seriously whether the Kremlin has any real alternative for the moment between supporting him and intervening militarily on a massive scale." "For the moment," Morgan added, "Moscow is adopting a very low profile. It seems to have no desire to awaken the latent, fanatical patriotism that always is just beneath the surface in Poland."

What is certain is that Moscow urgently wants to quell labor and consumer unrest in Poland before it spreads. Russia has come to the aid of the Polish leadership with a line of credit— of about $500 million, it was rumored in Warsaw. The credit was extended to Poland for the purchase, among other things, of more than two million tons of grain from Russia. The grain will be fed to livestock in the hope of putting more meat and poultry on Polish tables. This assistance represents a genuine sacrifice for the Russian people, who suffer from a chronic shortage of meat and poultry themselves and whose standard of living remains considerably lower than that of the Poles.[5]

Plan for Improving Russian Standard of Living

The most significant aspect of the Soviet Five Year Plan to be approved during the 24th Party Congress is that the output of consumer goods is scheduled to increase more (44 to 48 per cent) than goods for heavy industry (41 to 45 per cent). This would suggest that the primacy of consumer goods will be formally recognized. But such statistics may provide distortions. The London *Economist* suggested on Feb. 20, 1971, that "the ordinary Russian who tries to study the plan will not find in it great changes in his life." According to the new plan, the average wage will rise from 122 rubles a month in 1970 to 147 rubles in 1975—equivalent to $135 and $164 at the official rate of exchange. Soviet authorities value the ruble at $1.11 but it buys less than 25 cents' worth of imported goods.

Writing in Moscow's *Literaturnaya Gazeta* (Literary Gazette) of Feb. 17, 1971, a deputy chairman of the State Planning Committee, Nikolai N. Mirotvortsev, said $10 billion would be invested in light industrial production in the coming plan—

---

[5] The Poles may suffer in the end, however. According to news accounts from Warsaw, Poland must repay Russia in hard currency, not in Polish zlotys which are virtually worthless outside Poland. And Poland must build 34 ocean-going merchant ships for Russia at low prices.

twice as much as during the past five years. Mirotvortsev promised that by 1975 there would be 85 radios, 72 washing machines, 72 television sets and 64 refrigerators for every hundred families. In a report to the Supreme Soviet on Dec. 8, 1970, Nikolai Baibakov, chairman of the State Planning Committee, said production deadlines would be fixed for "full gratification" of consumer demands. Baibakov blamed unidentified ministries for not building up production capacity for consumer goods and for not doing market research to enable them to produce the right goods.

Buried in the stacks of favorable statistics in Baibakov's report to the Supreme Soviet was casual mention of many shortcomings in the planned economy. One of the most important items was that industry had failed to meet the production goal for mineral fertilizers by three million tons. It is still uncertain whether a 70 per cent rise in agricultural investment, announced in 1970, will show results when the 1971 Party Congress meets. Mikhail A. Suslov, a member of the ruling politburo and the leading ideologist, acknowledged in a speech in November 1970 that "the present level of farm production cannot be recognized as adequate." The nation's food requirements "were not being fully satisfied," he said. A significant omission in Baibakov's report was the figure for the 1970 grain harvest. Baibakov did reveal that total agricultural yields rose by only 6.5 per cent that year, against the planned 8.5 per cent, despite Suslov's claim of three weeks earlier that Russia had reaped "the biggest harvest in the history of agriculture."

Every visitor to the Soviet Union wonders how consumers, with their relatively low wages, can afford the expensive goods offered on sale at various shops. It is bewildering that a secretary, who earns 70 rubles a month, buys second-hand Italian knee boots which cost more than her monthly salary. Charlotte Saikowski, a correspondent for *The Christian Science Monitor,* walked through the "private" Moscow market and found that a dozen white eggs cost $3, pears cost $2 a pound, and a 15-pound turkey cost $25. As the average Soviet wage in 1970 was 122 rubles ($135) a month, it is hard to believe that buyers can be found. The fact is that a lot of money is chasing few goods in Russia.

Communist planners have been vexed in the past few years by inflationary pressures resulting from record-high personal savings. Because of inflation, rumors have circulated in Russia that the Kremlin plans either to reform the monetary system or increase prices to drain off these savings. As a result, Russian consumers have started buying more durable goods such as pianos, chandeliers and other available items, thereby causing shortages in state shops and driving up prices on the black market.

Private Sales and Illicit Trade Amid Shortages

K. S. Karol, a Russian-born writer, sought to explain in a British magazine the complex workings of the Soviet economy after a recent visit to his homeland. He contended three economies exist side by side.[6] At the official level, the one portrayed in the statistics, there are rigidly controlled prices set by the state. The second economy, "which functions according to its own laws and allows people to redistribute both money and consumer goods among themselves according to their needs," is obviously supplied by illicit means. The third economy is for the power elite—party and state officials, high-ranking officers in the army and the police, "trusted" writers, filmmakers, and university officials. At these *volchebnye magaziny,* run for the privileged, the buyer can find anything provided he pays in dollars and produces a certificate showing where he obtained the dollars. "What separates 99 per cent of the Soviet population from Communism," Karol quoted a Russian as saying, "is this damned certificate which prevents them from shopping in these luxury stores."

For the majority of Russians, if they can afford it at all, the "second economy" is their source of most delicacies. It is supplied by stolen goods, by items deliberately diverted from factories, and by private entrepreneurs. Georgians, for example, take advantage of cheap airline fares to carry fruits, vegetables, poultry and flowers to areas in short supply. A Georgian knows that he will earn more from three boxes of lemons than he will by smashing all production records at the local factory. Curiously, Soviet authorities do not crush this thriving market—an implied admission that it serves a need that the state economy cannot fulfill.

Even under the Czars, Russians were never renowned for their retailing skill. But under Communism, the problem of supply and demand has become chaotic. While stockrooms and warehouses bulge with unwanted knitted sportswear, refrigerators are in such demand that prospective purchasers must wait up to three years.. Consumers may look in vain for pillows and blankets, or pencils and table knives, until a small supply

---

[6] K. S. Karol, "Conversations in Russia," *New Statesman,* Jan. 1, 1971, pp. 8-10.

suddenly surfaces on the market. When the sought-after items appear, they often are sold out in an afternoon. Housewives rush to telephone their relatives, who quickly get in line to buy extra quantities for themselves and their friends. On one occasion in the summer of 1970, foreign correspondents in Moscow witnessed screaming mothers and slugging fathers being clubbed by police because their patience had run out along with the supply of baby carriages in the Children's World Store.

Trud, the newspaper of Soviet labor unions, stated in September 1970 that the department in the Soviet Ministry of Trade that examines the critical problem of supply and demand on behalf of the nation employed only six persons. Stores and suppliers do nothing to coordinate their efforts. *Trud* reported that there were a million unsold and unwanted small-screen TV sets in warehouses and consumer outlets in Russia, and that part of the surplus had existed for seven years. Nevertheless, it added, small sets continued to be produced because they were specified in a Five Year Plan.

A plant manager responding to questions from a Soviet newsman explained that he received a plan for the production of buckets, pans and tea kettles from the ministry. The manager decided to produce buckets and pans but only a few tea kettles. The tea kettle, with its handle, lid and pouring spout, required a complex manufacturing process which would reduce factory profits. The result of such practices is a mentality of scarcity; one week there is no soap powder, and the next week there are no razor blades. Shoppers tend to hoard whenever supplies are available.

Quality is the other big failing in the Soviet economy. Products tend to be full of flaws, inferior in styling and of shoddy materials. The Soviet Minister of Trade, Alexander I. Struyev, said that 20 per cent of all industrial products in 1969 proved to be defective and had to be returned to the manufacturers or marked down in price. Under the new Five Year Plan, profits from substandard articles will go entirely to the state—not to the producing factories, as they do for ordinary goods. Moreover, they will not be accepted as part of the factory's plan fulfillment. When quality and style are taken seriously, standards can be met. This is shown not only in science but in articles as prosaic as army boots. But when the shoe manufacturer knows he will dispose of every pair he makes, regardless of defects, it is the consumer who has to bear both the pain and the cost.

Past Struggles to Raise Production

SINCE THE REVOLUTION of 1917, Soviet publicists have never tired of pointing out that in 1913 Imperial Russia ranked behind England, Germany and France in the production of steel and pig iron. In coal output, Russia stood in fifth place; and in electric power, sixth. Today the Soviet Union is first in Europe in all of these categories. Moreover, it is first in world production of wool textiles, tractors and sugar, as well as coal and iron ore, and second only to the United States in many other categories.

It is impossible to obtain valid statistics in some areas of the Soviet economy. Plan-fulfillment reports typically point up achievements and camouflage disappointing results by lumping several items together, according to Paul Wohl, Soviet-affairs specialist of *The Christian Science Monitor*. The situation was so bad under Stalin that Soviet economists could not reliably estimate the production capacity, output and reserves of Russian industry. Economic reporting improved markedly under Nikita S. Khrushchev. But since his removal from power[7] in 1964, the old methods of cover up and dissimulation have returned. Statistical honesty has been sacrificed to political expediency. Such tactics restrict the study of Soviet economic development.

Sacrifices Under Stalin to Benefit Basic Industry

Immediately after the Bolsheviks assumed power in Russia they were faced with the breakdown of the entire economy. Three years of struggle in World War I (1914-17) were immediately followed by a lengthy and disruptive civil war. By 1921, with the inhabitants of the cities starving, Lenin decided that if the country was to survive a new economic policy would have to be instituted. Private trade was tolerated; business managers were permitted to operate privately under state license. These were only temporary concessions based on necessity. They did not move the country toward Communist goals. Millions of peasants still went barefoot and everything from fabrics to furniture remained in short supply.

---

[7] Khrushchev was First Secretary of the Central Committee of the Soviet Communist Party, the post now held by Leonid I. Brezhnev, who shares authority with the Chairman of the Council of Ministers (Premier) Alexei N. Kosygin.

After Lenin's death in 1924, Stalin emerged victorious in a struggle with Leon Trotsky. Assuming dictatorial powers, Stalin decreed in 1928 that there was to be a full-scale collectivization of agriculture and a total suppression of the kulaks, or private farmers. At the same time, he set the Soviet Union on a program of forced industrialization to overtake the West.[8] A frenetic drive toward a planned economy, known as the first Five Year Plan, was launched in that year. Tremendous sacrifices were demanded of the Russian people. Human needs were subordinated to the expansion of the state. Families were uprooted and moved to where their labor was needed. It was a time of hardships, shortages, and unending toil. Failure to meet work goals brought severe punishment. Managers and workers could be put to death for faulty production.

John Maynard, in his book *Russia in Flux*, stated that "one of the aims in the USSR is to give freedom of choice to the consumer."[9] It was evident, however, that Russian industry was far too busy trying to provide the necessities of life to give much attention to individual taste. The question of standardization of products arose as an issue of policy during the first Five Year Plan. A Russian writer of the period said: "It is necessary to decide...on what levels of quality or on what standards to maintain development? Here two roads are possible: the road of English industry of producing dear things of specially high quality, and the road of American industry, developed on the simplified production of goods of mass consumption."[10]

Failure of Forced Collectivization of Agriculture

If the lot of the worker was difficult under the first Five Year Plan, the lot of the peasants was much worse. Because agricultural workers, farming their own land, consumed 90 per cent of what they raised, Stalin decided that collectivization was the only answer. The kulaks were liquidated; by 1934 about five million of them had disappeared. The peasants who were herded off into the new state and collective farms resisted strongly. In protest, they slaughtered their livestock. The costs were so severe that Stalin confessed to Winston

---

[8] See Bernard Pares, *A History of Russia* (1965 edition), pp. 527-531, and David and Vera Mace, *The Soviet Family* (1963), p. 31.

[9] The book was originally published in England in 1939, titled *Russia in Flux: Before October*. An American edition, with the title shortened to *Russia in Flux*, was published in 1948, followed by a paperback reprint in 1962.

[10] M. Aronovitch, "Problem of Standardization in the Reconstruction of Industry," *Planovoe Khoziaistvo*, Nov. 5, 1929, pp. 122-23.

Churchill during a wartime conversation that had he to do it over again, he would never attempt collectivization.[11] However, Stalin fulfilled his three objectives: (1) he broke the political power of rural Russia, (2) he financed industrialization by robbing the peasants, (3) and he increased farm output by combining the individual plots into larger units.

Yet the inefficiency of Soviet agriculture continues to this day, posing the constant threat of a food crisis. During the past decade, the Russians were still struggling to regain the dietary levels of 1913 and 1928.[12] The Kremlin was forced to make large purchases of grain from Canada, Australia, and the United States. Although Russia cultivates almost twice as many acres as the United States, it produces one-third less grain.[13] Here again Soviet consumers have suffered because of Kremlin ideology. Private plots, normally about an acre per household, today supply the nation with 30 per cent of its total agricultural output and 12 per cent of its marketed produce but account for only 3 per cent of the cultivated land.

Regardless of how inefficient collectivization may be, Soviet leaders will not abandon it. However, they no longer make it the stepchild of industrial development. According to the latest planning, the incomes of collective farmers—in addition to what they derive from private plots—will rise considerably faster than those of other workers during the next five years. As for agricultural production, it is scheduled to rise more slowly in 1971 than it did the previous year.

First Secretary Leonid I. Brezhnev told the Communist Party's Central Committee July 2, 1970, that "as we all know, the demand of the population for livestock produce, especially meat, is not being satisfied by far." Over the past 10 years the old price structure had encouraged collective farmers to raise grain rather than cattle or poultry. Then, as the demand for meat rose, the farmers took to over-slaughtering. Soon the meat shortage became more acute. Although Brezhnev said that by 1975 Russia should produce 15.6 million tons of meat a year, compared with an average of 11.4 million tons over the past five years, even this modest increase will be difficult to attain. Soviet housewives will probably continue to

---

[11] Recounted by Harrison E. Salisbury, *Russia* (1967), p. 53.

[12] See "Soviet Communism After Fifty Years," *E.R.R.*, Vol. II 1967, p. 760.

[13] Zbigniew Brzezinski and Samuel P. Huntington, *Political Power: USA/USSR* (1964), p. 302.

complain about scrawny chickens that cost $2 a pound, about beef that is good only for stew, and about salami that is heavy with fat.

Attempt in Past Decade to Insert Profit Motive

While Stalin was alive no criticism of his view of economics was tolerated. Shortages or defects were ritualistically attributed to "enemies." The country's development progressed erratically with little relationship to the fulfillment of plans. Under Khrushchev, a long-suppressed debate broke out between those who wished to increase the production of consumer goods and those who wished to retain the emphasis on basic industry. As conditions improved and consumers began to discriminate between products, obstacles arose. Buyers favored table radios made in the Baltic states, for example. The heavy, ungainly models turned out by Moscow factories continued to pile up in stores and warehouses. The same thing happened to hundreds of other products ranging from lampshades to red velvet curtains. Production quotas were based on old items; to introduce a new product or change models meant risks which few factory managers were willing to take. Innovation might easily cost the manager his own bonus for "plan fulfillment."

An economist from Kharkov, Prof. Evsei Liberman, put forward a thesis in 1962 that what was beneficial to manufacturing enterprises would also benefit the country at large. Liberman proposed that factory managers fix prices and determine their output on a competitive, cost-price basis. Instead of each factory being assigned fixed requirements in rubles, feet, or tons, the managers would adjust production to supply and demand. Profitability would thus enter the economic system. Production bonuses, wages, salaries and raw-material prices would all reflect actual market conditions rather than the desires of economic planners sitting in Moscow.

Premier Alexei N. Kosygin announced in September 1965 a sweeping reorganization designed to introduce the profit motive. All industrial enterprises were to be working under the new system by the end of 1968. However, the central planners were soon frightened by the specter of local economic independence and initiative. Various groups, especially those geared to the old ways, began to obstruct the profit system. Obstacles also arose because capital goods continued to receive priority in raw materials. Matches, for example, remained scarce because the needs of paper and building industries come before those of the housewife. To make the system efficient required further decentralization—and at this the Kremlin planners balked.

Numerous economists and forward-looking managers began to complain that implementation of the reforms was only marginal. Christopher Johnson, managing editor of the London *Financial Times,* wrote Nov. 23, 1970: "The Soviet system still gives power to the ministries to decide who should produce what, how much of it, and at what price. Variations from the norms are often negotiated by agreement at the local level, but there is still too little scope for initiative by enterprising managers, too little wholesale trade of producer goods, and too little feedback from the market to indicate what consumers actually want."

The time for reforms seems to be running out. In a booklet on economic theory published in Moscow in February 1971, even Prof. Liberman appears to have changed his mind about profit being one of the most important criteria of success. Liberman is now advocating "democratic centralism" in planning. Under this Stalinist approach, the state and the planning boards plot out all the bases, elements and needs while the factories and other organizations just fill in any omission in the plan. If the 1971 Party Congress approves this course, it will amount to a throwback to the Thirties when all that mattered was the fulfillment of production targets—and the consumer be damned.

Modest Gain for Soviet Citizen in Recent Years

Despite the difficulties in the Soviet economy, it continues to grow. And living standards are slowly rising—a fact that is generally recognized by experts even after making allowances for exaggeration in Soviet claims. It used to be that there was only the one drum-type washing machine on the market, and now there are machines with twin tubs. Today three models of color television sets are being produced and more than 60 models of portable transistors. Every other family in the Soviet Union, authorities proclaim, have both a television set and a washing machine.

One only needs to travel through the outskirts of Moscow or Leningrad to observe the tremendous emphasis being given to new housing and construction. Russia claims to have built the equivalent of 10.3 million new apartments since 1966, rehousing more than 50 million people. And yet much remains to be done. The housing program for 1970 fell 10 per cent below the planning goal and therefore the target for 1971 will be only marginally larger. Materials for housing are sometimes diverted to secondary and even unauthorized projects like VIP dachas and party offices.

Speaking in Moscow on April 13, 1970, Brezhnev said that Russia has produced 100 million tons of steel a year and could produce more. But the essential question, he went on to explain, was not how much could be produced "but at what price and at what effort in labor." This relatively enlightened attitude reflects that the debate over economic priorities may gradually be shifting in favor of the Soviet consumer.

Direction of Efforts to Meet Demands

RUSSIANS YEARN for automobiles no less than people in other lands where they are scarce. At the beginning of 1970 there were reported to be 1.2 million cars in personal use throughout the Soviet Union, a small number for 242 million people. About 30,000 Muscovites have waited since 1968 to buy a Moskvich car for 4,800 rubles—over $5,000 at the official rate of exchange—and more would join the list if they were allowed to do so. "To register for a car now," a trade official told the youth newspaper *Komsomolskaya Pravda,* "is like queuing up for a piece of the moon." The pudgy old Volga, for those Russians lucky enough to get one, sells for 5,600 rubles. Even used cars command exorbitant prices. Editorial Research Reports found in July 1970 that a 1967 Chevrolet Impala was selling for 10,000 rubles in Moscow; year-old Volgas were going for about the same prices as new ones; and a small Zaporozhets had lost only 25 per cent of its sales value after four years of driving.

Pravda reported Sept. 9, 1970, that the first automobiles had rolled off the assembly line at the Volga River town of Togliatti where they were being built under terms of a 1967 agreement between Soviet authorities and the Fiat Company of Italy. The new car[14] was supposed to signal the coming of the motor age in the Soviet Union. But the huge plant has fallen behind schedule and it is unlikely that its production

---

[14] Named the Zhiguli and modeled on the Fiat 124. It is powered by a four-cylinder, 92-horsepower engine.

goal of 660,000 cars a year for 1972 will be reached by 1975. Western estimates of current production range from 150 to 400 cars a day.

Giovanni Agnelli, chairman of the Fiat Company, said soon after the plant's opening that highways, gasoline stations and spare-parts plants would later be needed in Russia. He indicated that to provide these facilities would entail a shift in Moscow from defense to consumer spending. In the past, whenever the central planners felt they were not meeting popular consumer demands, they tended to blame the "aggressiveness of imperialism" for forcing the Soviet Union to spend immense sums on military arms. It is true that even now the latest arms program, calling for naval expansion and strengthening of missile capability, means that many Russians will forgo many items they badly need.[15]

Perhaps because of the Kremlin's inability to meet consumer demands for private cars, an active lobby has risen against them. The objectors point out that even if new factories were producing cars at capacity, only about 5 per cent of the population would have use of a car. *Literaturnaya Gazeta,* taking up this argument, published a plan in 1970 to expand taxi services in large cities so that taxis could take individuals on medium-range trips of 40 to 50 miles. But then, in one of those contradictory moves which seem to plague Russian planning, Soviet authorities closed down the entire rent-a-car system. This "socialist answer" to private car ownership consistently lost money, caused repair problems, and filled the Soviet law courts with complex claims.

Izvestia noted that if a person who hired a car smashed a bumper, for example, he had to pay the daily rental fee for as many days as it took to repair the car. Spare parts being scarce and service facilities insufficient, Moscow correspondent Bernard Gwertzman reported in *The New York Times,* it was not unusual for a person who had hired a car for one day to pay hundreds of rubles in penalties while it took months to find a new bumper and put it on.

When a Russian is lucky enough to buy a car, his troubles just begin. There are only 14 repair stations for Moscow's

---

[15] The Institute of Strategic Studies in London has estimated that Russia's overt defense budget, which was not increased in 1971 and remained at 17.9 billion rubles, represents only one-third of actual military spending. About one-half of the Soviet science budget is believed to be used for military purposes.

80,000 private cars. Unless the car owner is prepared to offer the garageman a bribe, the usual answer to any request for repairs is "come back in three months." Moreover, paying a friend to make repairs is illegal under Soviet law, which protects the state monopoly on repairs. For lack of antifreeze and winter oil in the bitter Russian winter, most private owners are forced to store their automobiles under canvas at the first frost in October.

Some experts on Soviet policy—Victor Zorza is one—contend that the state could find no more effective and beneficial method to absorb the inflationary spending power of the Russian citizen than to step up automobile sales. The obstacles are political, not economic. Japan increased its car production from 165,000 in 1960 to three million in 1970. Russia, which turned out 140,000 cars in 1960, doubled that figure in 1970. It is thought that some Russian officials fear the automobile will increase not only the owner's mobility but his personal freedom.

Expediency of Using Imports to Placate Shoppers

During the New Year's holidays of 1971, shoppers in Moscow and Leningrad were able to buy Dutch chickens, Romanian pork, Australian mutton and Egyptian oranges. The Soviet government makes substantial purchases of food and consumer items abroad whenever it is politically expedient. But the Soviet Union is determined not to depend on imports, even though domestic production might be costlier.

Despite trade embargoes imposed by the United States,[16] the Soviet Union has imported an impressive quantity of industrial equipment from the West.[17] In recent years, with Russia's fund of Western currency in short supply, the Soviet Union has resorted to barter arrangements. Typically, a Western company agrees to build a large project in return for a share of the profits on its output. Aside from a project like the Togliatti automobile plant, these ventures make an impact upon the Russian consumer only in the long term. A railroad being constructed today might deliver fresh fruit to him a decade later but it does little to satisfy his immediate needs and wants.

---

[16] A significant shift in American trade policy toward Communist countries became evident in December 1969 when Congress passed the Export Control Act, lifting many restrictions on East-West trade. The basic change from a 1949 law, which the new legislation replaced, was to remove restrictions on the sale of certain products to most Communist countries, including Russia. However, the United States continued to maintain a total embargo on exports to China, Cuba, North Viet Nam and North Korea.

[17] These imports between 1955 and 1968 were valued at $4 billion.

A shortage of skilled labor is one reason for the relatively slow growth of many industrial sectors, including the manufacture of consumer goods. Russia has a huge labor force in agriculture which it cannot divert to manufacturing because of the perpetual threat of food shortages. Soviet authorities thus must recruit housewives, pensioners and invalids to join the 90 million Russians already employed in industry.

The labor shortage has been aggravated by the political objective of populating Siberia. Stretching from the Urals to the Bering Sea, this vast region is virtually a wilderness broken only by developments clustered along the trans-Siberian railway. It is a remarkably rich area in oil, gas, other minerals and timber, but the cost of exploiting them has been enormous. The Soviet government has committed itself to develop local industries in Siberia. But as of now, nearly all consumer goods are sent in from European Russia.

Living conditions in Siberia, while slowly improving, are below those of the western regions. The average Siberian has less floor space than the resident of Leningrad or Moscow. He pays more for heat, food and clothing. He also has fewer schools, doctors, consumer services and cultural amenities. Charlotte Saikowski reported that in the Irkutsk region heating costs 90 per cent more, clothing 18 per cent more, and food about 5 per cent more than in central Russia.[18] In the past decade Siberia lost 730,000 more persons than it gained. The population of the Soviet Union is shifting southward, not eastward as the economic planners intended.

Industrial Mergers as Way of Boosting Production

The ninth Five Year Plan (1971-75), with its exceptional emphasis on increasing the standard of living and the output of consumer goods, outlines a number of basic reforms in Soviet industry. Russia's weakest areas have been in the assimilation of new technology, automation and management techniques. Some Soviet planners believe that the best way to stop the duplication and waste of labor and materiel is through vast industrial mergers. All the steps from the extraction or production of raw material to the finished product would be under the control of a single gigantic enterprise in each field.

Thus far, the Russians have proceeded slowly with this idea. *The Christian Science Monitor* reported Sept. 4, 1970, that there

---

[18] Charlotte Saikowski, "Wanted: People for Siberia," *The Christian Science Monitor,* April 7, 1970.

have been about 600 amalgamations accounting for 8 per cent of the total industrial output. These conglomerates are developing along two main lines. The first is the amalgamation of small concerns that are supplying different items to the same factory—say, a plate-glass plant and an electric battery factory supplying Moscow's Likhachev automobile works. The second line involves the formation of immense industrial complexes on regional, republic, and even national bases. Such amalgamations are already proceeding in food, chemical and light-manufacturing industries. Although the merger process is relatively new, it appears to have heartened Communist planners by its performance. Productivity has risen.

However, the idea that size alone will help increase efficiency is an illusion which continues to plague Soviet economists. Russia is still trying to catch up with the United States by means of gigantic investment projects. The Bratsky power station, for example, is now the world's most powerful, and the Fiat car plant may one day produce a million cars a year. But such projects always take longer to build and cost more than was intended. Moreover, cost advantages of large-scale production taper off after a certain point.

"Gigantism" for its own sake can lead to a waste of investment resources. For example, in developing huge computer plants, the Soviets invested heavily in second-generation machines when the United States had already introduced third-generation computers. Having made a large initial investment, the Russians were reluctant to change.[19] This experience has been repeated again and again in other sectors of Soviet industry.

In trying to catch up with the United States over the last decade, the Soviet Union has made significant progress in many areas. It is now first in the production of coal, cement, bricks, machine tools, tractors, washing machines, cotton fabrics and footwear. In the manufacture of trucks, buses, cars, as well as the production of electric power, fertilizers, plastics and artificial fibers, it lags far behind. However, catching up to the United States is no longer the ultimate goal.

Khrushchev, in his purported memoirs, suggested the introduction of "as much freedom as material conditions would permit."[20] Evidently there are some leaders in the Kremlin who

---

[19] Gertrude E. Schroeder, "Soviet Technology: System vs. Progress," *Problems of Communism*, September 1970, p. 20.
[20] *Khrushchev Remembers* (1970).

believe that it would be unwise to improve material conditions too swiftly. Mikhail A. Suslov, the ideologist, said in a speech in Moscow in November 1970 that after the emphasis on materialistic rewards there must also be "moral incentives." But the Russian people have had their appetite whetted for material goods which for so many years were denied them. And the Soviet leadership shows signs that it realizes this appetite must be appeased even if it cannot readily be sated.

RECONCILIATION WITH CHINA

by

Helen B. Shaffer

1 9 7 1
June 16

U.S.-CHINA RECONCILIATION

NO RECENT NEWS was more evocative of the past—and more prescient of the future—than the accounts of the American Ping Pong team's recent (April 10-17) tour of mainland China. For this unexpected visit, undertaken at Peking's invitation, cracked the barrier of hostility that has existed since 1949 between that country and the United States. The visit obviously signaled a change in American relations with China, a change that could lead eventually to a new configuration of global power relationships. For many it raised hopes for a speedier end to the war in Viet Nam and a lowering of tensions that threaten new wars. Fear and distrust persisted, however.

At first it seemed that two decades of icy hostility had begun to melt down into a mutual willingness to let bygones be bygones. China's leaders spoke of renewing old friendships with Americans. President Nixon signaled his pleasure by lifting trade and travel bans and by expressing a personal wish to visit China. Memories of the past of what has been called America's long love affair with China began to flood the American consciousness.

Sober second thought made it clear that the spring thaw had barely begun and that new freezes may lie ahead. On both sides hard truths were reasserted about issues that bar reconciliation. One requiring immediate consideration is the future status of the other China—the Nationalist government of Chiang Kai-shek, known as the Republic of China, which governs only Taiwan and a few neighboring islands but claims all of China as its rightful domain. The United States must decide whether to revise its position on admission of the People's Republic of China to the United Nations before the U.N. General Assembly convenes in September.

The Senate Foreign Relations Committee scheduled four days of hearings between June 24 and 29 to assess America's position on the U.N. question and others in regard to China, including whether this country should establish diplomatic relations with the People's Republic. So far the renewal of contact between America and China has moved along the lines of a people-to-people relationship. Leaders of the two governments have said they will welcome travelers from the other country but they have not yet—openly at least—sought a formal relationship between their governments. The situation recalls the period before the resumption of formal relations between the United States and the Soviet Union in 1933, some 16 years after the Russian Revolution. Then, too, major issues blocked agreement. But sentiment for recognition grew and American fears of Bolshevist infiltration receded as the result of friendly contacts with Russian individuals.[1] Eventually the expectation of mutual benefit from reconciliation overrode differences on issues. The same expectations of an end to the U.S.-China impasse are rising today.

Since 1949 the only official contacts between the United States and China have been the "Warsaw talks." The talks between ambassadors of the two countries, 136 in all, began in Geneva in 1955 but have been held in Poland since 1958. They are secret by mutual consent. The talks were barely resumed early in 1970 after a two-year hiatus when China broke them off again—this time in protest of the U.S. invasion of Cambodia. No talks have been scheduled since then, although liaison officers of the two embassies in Warsaw continue to maintain contact.

Reopening of Contacts in 'Ping Pong Diplomacy'

"The ping heard round the world," as *Time* magazine put it,[2] was first sounded on April 6, during the international championship table tennis competition in Nagoya, Japan, when the team from China invited members of the American team to visit the mainland before returning to the United States. No group of Americans had been allowed into China since the Communists took control in 1949. "We have...extended the invitation for the sake of promoting friendship between the peoples of China and the United States," the spokesman for the Chinese team, Sung Chung, said.

The invitation was accepted and on April 10, the 15 Americans—nine players, four officials, and two wives—walked

---

[1] Secretary of State Cordell Hull (1933-1944) wrote of that period: "For some time we had informally exchanged views with Russians through...American citizens in contact with the Soviet government and the informal Soviet representatives in the United States. I frequently received some of these Americans, including engineers working on industrial projects in Russia, who strongly favored recognition." —*The Memoirs of Cordell Hull* (1948), Vol. I, pp. 296-297.

[2] *Time*, April 26, 1971, p. 25.

across a bridge from Hong Kong into Communist territory, where they were greeted by a delegation of smiling Chinese officials who escorted them to a train that took them to Canton. During the week of their visit, the Americans were kept on a full schedule of sightseeing, playing and entertainment.

They visited Peking, Shanghai, the Great Wall, a university and a rural commune. They participated in an exhibition Ping Pong match before a cheering audience of 18,000, attended a ballet staged by the wife of Party Chairman Mao Tsetung, and were guests at a party April 14 at which Premier Chou En-lai engaged the visitors at length in good-humored chitchat. Chou impressed the visitors as a surprisingly genial host. In his formal greetings to them, he said: "You have opened a new page in the relations of the Chinese and American people. I am confident that this beginning again of our friendship will certainly meet with the majority support of our two people."

117

Equally significant with the invitation of the players, Peking permitted five American newsmen to enter China to report the trip. Chou said at the April 14 party that more American journalists would be granted visas to come to China, although "they cannot all come at one time." Since then other newsmen have been allowed entry, and it was reported that American applications for visas were being received cordially at the newly opened Chinese embassy at Ottawa, Canada. Tillman Durdin, a veteran *New York Times* reporter in the Far East who was allowed a 30-day visit, reported on his return to Hong Kong in mid-May that China's leaders said they favored a regular flow of visitors from the United States. He said that a "trickle" had already begun.

Nixon's Lowering of Trade and Travel Barriers

Peking's "Ping Pong diplomacy" was recognized as a serious and planned step in the formulation of a new foreign policy rather than merely an impromptu gesture of good sportsmanship. A State Department spokesman, Charles W. Bray III, described Peking's invitation to the team as an "encouraging development...clearly consistent with the hopes expressed by the President and Secretary of State that there could be greater contact between the American and Chinese peoples." There were indications that the State Department had encouraged Graham B. Steenhoven, president of the U.S. Table Tennis Association, to reciprocate with an invitation to the Chinese players. Steenhoven announced on April 20, after his return to his home in Detroit, that he had extended such an invitation and that it had been accepted. White House Press Secretary Ronald L. Ziegler said that the U.S. government would welcome a visit by a Chinese team.

On the day that Chou talked with the American players, April 14, the White House announced that a 20-year embargo on trade with China would be relaxed. The announcement stated:

1. Visas for visitors from the People's Republic of China would be expedited.

2. U.S. currency controls would be relaxed so that China could use dollars to pay for exports.[3]

3. American oil companies would be allowed to provide fuel to ships or planes going to or from China ports (except on Chinese-

---

[3] The ban on dollar-trade with China, imposed in December 1950, was formally lifted on May 7 when Secretary of the Treasury John B. Connally Jr. announced that he had issued a "general license" allowing Americans to transact business with the government or citizens of China and to use dollars in these transactions.

owned or chartered craft going to or from North Viet Nam, North Korea, or Cuba).

4. U.S. vessels would be permitted to carry Chinese cargo between non-Chinese ports; U.S.-owned foreign flag carriers would be allowed to call at Chinese ports.

There followed on June 10 a further relaxation of trade restrictions when the White House announced a long list of goods that American businessmen could export to China. The items included farm, fish and forestry products; tobacco; many kinds of fertilizers and chemicals; coal; rubber and textiles; some metals; agricultural, industrial and office equipment; household appliances; some electrical appliances; automobiles; consumer goods; roadbuilding and construction equipment, and some relatively unsophisticated computers. The inclusion of construction equipment was regarded as significant because it was known that the Defense Department wanted to keep it off the list. The department's opposition to the sale of locomotives was also known, and they did not appear on the list.

Outlook for Presidential Visit to Mainland

President Nixon has raised the possibility of paying a visit to the long-forbidden land. At a meeting with the American Society of Newspaper Editors in Washington, April 16, Nixon expressed the hope that he could visit China some day. However, he was "not sure" it would happen while he was in office. He returned to this theme at a news conference, April 29, saying: "I hope and, as a matter of fact, I expect to visit mainland China sometime in some capacity. I don't know what capacity but that indicates what I hope for the long term." Edgar Snow, an American writer who has had access to Chinese leaders for years, said Chairman Mao told him in December 1970 that Nixon would be welcomed in China, whether as a tourist or as President of the United States.[4]

Snow said that during his six-month stay in China in the fall and winter of 1970-71, he learned that "foreign diplomats in Peking were aware...that messages were being delivered from Washington to the Chinese government by certain go-betweens" to assure Chinese leaders that Nixon had a "new outlook" on Asia and wanted to end the impasse in Sino-American relations. It was believed there, Snow said, that Nixon had offered to send personal representatives to Peking. During the

---

[4] Edgar Snow, "A Conversation with Mao Tse-tung," *Life*, April 30, 1971, pp. 46-47.

period of Ping Pong diplomacy, it was rumored in Washington that the President had chosen the Senate Majority and Minority leaders, Mike Mansfield (D Mont.) and Hugh Scott (R Pa.), to serve as his emissaries if the warmup of relations should make such a trip advisable.

Significance of Relatively Few Public Protests

Perhaps the most significant aspect of the thaw in relations was the weakness of the outcry against it. In view of the political blood that had been spilled in the United States in years past over the question of who was responsible for China's "going Communist," the equanimity with which most Americans accepted the prospect of a reconciliation was a sure sign that the times—and public opinion—had changed. Sen. Scott observed that less than a decade ago such overtures as the administration had made toward China would have sent "shock waves" over Congress.

Sen. Mansfield told the Senate that "the change is long overdue." Sen. Edward W. Brooke (R Mass.) professed to see the "first steps toward removing the fears and prejudices which have...distorted our visions of each other." The Assistant Senate Majority Leader, Robert C. Byrd (D W. Va.), said the United States "must accept" the fact that a Communist government rules all of mainland China. Sen. Robert Dole (R Kan.), chairman of the Republican National Committee, said that ping pong diplomacy could hasten the ending of the war and help re-elect Nixon.

There were some dissents from expected sources, but with little effect on the course of events. Leading figures in the so-called China Lobby that for years has supported Nationalist China's claims expressed displeasure. Former Rep. Walter Judd (R Minn.), chairman of the Committee of One Million Against the Admission of Communist China to the United Nations, charged on April 12 that "powerful forces" were bringing pressure "in the hope of forcing President Nixon to accept Mao on Mao's terms." Anna Chennault warned against the hazards of trade dealings with a poor and Communist China. Judd, a former medical missionary in China, has long been identified with a hard-line anti-Communist policy in the Far East. Mrs. Chennault is the Chinese-American widow of Maj. Gen. Claire L. Chennault, who headed the U.S. Air Force in China during World War II. Though Mrs. Chennault holds no official position, she is influential in Washington.

The most politically interesting dissent was attributed to Vice President Spiro T. Agnew. According to published accounts, he told reporters in remarks intended to be off the record that he disagreed with the administration on China;[5] that he had argued unsuccessfully at a meeting of the National Security Council against over-eagerness in bidding for contacts with China, and that he regarded the American team's visit as a propaganda victory for China.[6] The White House sought to play down the remarks. Press Secretary Ziegler said on April 20 that the Vice President had authorized him to say "there is absolutely no disagreement between [him]...and the President's decision regarding the initiatives taken in relation to the People's Republic of China."

Meanwhile, the new possibility of travel to China stirred interest among businessmen, scholars and inveterate tourists. As applications for visas from Americans began to rise, major U.S. airlines sought authority to fly to leading Chinese cities. The president of Trans World Airlines, Forwood C. Wiser, said on May 8 in Hong Kong that TWA would operate charter flights to China if the Peking government granted permission. United Air Lines also has applied for flight authority. Najeeb E. Halaby, president of Pan American World Airways, told shareholders in Miami on May 4 "we see a real possibility of resuming service" on the China route Pan Am served in 1947-49. He said Pan Am had been "quietly" seeking an approval from Peking for three years.

The president of Xerox Corporation, C. Peter McColough, told stockholders on May 20 that a London subsidiary had missions in Peking exploring market possibilities. In Washington, a Committee on Scholarly Communication with the People's Republic of China, an adjunct of the National Academy of Sciences, was trying to communicate with a counterpart science academy in Peking in order to arrange for the exchange of persons, journals and invitations to international meetings. Among members of the committee are leading China specialists A. Doak Barnett of the Brookings Institution, Jerome A. Cohen of Harvard and Alexander Eckstein of the

---

[5] His remarks were said to have been made in a three-hour session with nine newsmen at the Republican Governors Conference at Williamsburg, Va., April 19, 1971.

[6] Agnew was quoted as saying press coverage of the visit was too favorable to the Chinese. He was said to have objected particularly to the use of the adjective "exquisite" by Associated Press correspondent John Roderick in describing the tact of the Chinese in pitting a second-string team against the Americans in an exhibition match—thus protecting the guest team from the humiliation of a severe defeat. Chinese teams won the matches, but by narrow margins.

University of Michigan. The desire of Americans to go to China is nothing new. There are still many Americans who remember it well as it was in the old days and are curious to see what 22 years under communism have done.

America's Love-Hate Complex About China

AMERICANS HAVE long had strong sentimental ties with China. They were forged by generations of American traders, missionaries, businessmen and teachers, many of whom lived for years in China and raised their families there. The influence of these ties on U.S. foreign policy in Asia has been pervasive. It helped account for the great swell of sympathy for the Chinese during the Japanese invasion in the 1930s and it sharpened the bitterness when China went Communist.

Over the years the American feeling about China has been a composite of good and bad. Former Secretary of State Dean Acheson called it a "love-hate complex,"[7] but it had many shades in between. Affection for the Chinese was genuine, but it did not necessarily include an appreciation of Chinese sensibilities. American altruism and philanthropy were mixed with avarice and bigotry, and admiration was tinged with condescension. Doubtless the Chinese had similarly ambivalent feelings about Americans, who came to them as friends and benefactors, but also as exploiters. So today the building of a new relationship must deal with both a tradition of friendship and a large residue of distrust and ill will.

Sen. Mansfield has described the two American images of China: One is "the image of the China of wisdom, intelligence, industry, piety, stoicism, and strength,...of Marco Polo, Pearl Buck, Charlie Chan and heroic resistance to the Japanese during World War II"; the other is "the image of the China of cruelty, barbarism, violence, and faceless hordes...the China of drum-head trials, summary executions, Fu Manchu, and the Boxer Rebellion."[8] Felix Greene, another long-time China watcher, wrote: "From our earliest contacts, China has exerted a peculiar fascination for Americans, a fascination compounded both of highest admiration and the deepest suspicion."[9]

---

[7] Dean Acheson, *Present at the Creation* (1969), p. 8.
[8] Lecture at the University of Montana, March 29, 1968, reprinted in the *Congressional Record*, April 15, 1971, p. S-4890.
[9] Felix Greene, *A Curtain of Ignorance* (1964), p. 2.

America's first contact with China was in search of trade. Even before the first Yankee clipper set sail under the American flag for Canton in 1784, the China trade had figured in the life of the American colonies. The tea of the Boston tea party had come from China. In the early years of the nation, trade with China was highly profitable. "There was a kind of China craze in those years. Wealthy matrons bought Chinese porcelain from returning skippers....Today, in the elegant... reception rooms of the Department of State [in Washington] there are proud displays of Chinese export porcelain. These are regarded as pieces of Americana."[10]

China had traded with the West since ancient times, but the traders had always been received as inferior supplicants or vassals, subject to the pleasure of the emperor, and their contacts with the Chinese were narrowly confined to designated representatives of the ruler. Trade in goods was mostly one-way. Europe craved the silks and spices of the East but China had little use for Europe's goods and demanded pay—tribute —in gold or silver.

United States Role in China During 19th Century

This situation changed in the 19th century when the imperialist nations of Europe, pressing for trade concessions, broke down China's carefully guarded barriers against foreign penetration. In so doing, they irreparably damaged the power and prestige of the Manchu dynasty. The British took the lead, the others followed. The change began with the Opium War[11] of 1839-42, which was essentially a show of British naval power to force the dynasty to open up the country to foreign exploitation and to grant Britain trade concessions.

These concessions were extended after another unequal contest between China and the combined British and French forces in 1856-60. Coastal and river cities became "treaty ports" available to foreign ships. British settlements—enclaves subject only to English law—were established. The entire country was opened to travel, trade, missionary work, investment and settlement. Other nations—Belgium, France, Germany, Japan, Russia, the United States—gained similar privileges in the course of the century.

---

[10] Marvin Kalb and Elie Abel, *Roots of Involvement: The United States in Asia 1784-1971* (1971), p. 22.

[11] So-called because the war was touched off by China's effort to stop the illegal sale of opium, purchased in India, to the Chinese. The underlying issue, however, was Britain's drive for more trade as opposed to China's effort to resist foreign penetration.

"Throughout the process of the opening of China, the United States followed through portals cut by the British, avoiding the aggression and inheriting the advantages."[12] U.S. "extra-territorial rights," equal to those granted other foreign nations, were first established in a U.S.-China treaty signed in 1844. The United States could reap the rewards of an open China with an easy conscience, for it had taken no military action to gain them nor did it seek to win outright possession of Chinese territory for colonial purposes. American military power was nevertheless available to protect U.S. commercial interests.

These interests lay in the background of decisions that led to the Spanish-American War and the acquisition of the Philippines. "American businessmen feared that European aggression against China would rob them of their investment there," Marvin Kalb and Elie Abel said in tracing the evolution of U.S. policy in Asia. "They looked upon the Philippines as a fine fallback position." Albert Beveridge, a Republican senator from Ohio at that time, summed up the prevailing view. "Just beyond the Philippines," he said, "are China's illimitable markets. We will not retreat from either."[13]

By this time the United States had come to regard itself as protector of China against the threat of partition by the colonizing nations. China, for its part, was eager to modernize in the western manner. A bond of friendship grew up between the American and Chinese peoples. "It was a strangely symbiotic relationship. Its strength lay in the promise each people held out for the other. Its mortal weakness [was] that this friendship concealed ulterior motives on one side and repressed deeply felt humiliations and grievances on the other."[14]

Missionary Influence on America's China Policy

The opening of China came at a time when the proselytizing zeal of American churches was at a high level. China became an irresistible magnet for missionary work. "China's vastness excited the missionary impulse; it appeared as the land of the future whose masses, when converted, offered promise of Christian and even English-speaking dominion over the world."[15] The first American missionary arrived in China as early as 1811 but the main growth came later in the century. By 1925, there

---

[12] Barbara W. Tuchman, *Stilwell and the American Experience in China 1911-45* (1971), p. 29.
[13] Marvin Kalb and Elie Abel, *op. cit.*, pp. 31, 35.
[14] Greene, *op. cit.*, p. 11.
[15] Tuchman, *op. cit.*, p. 31.

were 8,000 missionaries in China, most of them American. Their influence far outweighed their number and the number of their conversions. By the eve of World War II there were no more than 2.25 million Christians in China (1.5 million Roman Catholic and 750,000 Protestant). But the missionaries and their converts held favored positions in the western-dominated parts of China and they provided major channels, through their schools, hospitals and other establishments, for the promulgation of western ideas.

Of particular importance was the influence of the missionaries on the minds of Americans back home and indirectly on foreign policy. "Hardly a town in our land was without its society to collect funds and clothing for Chinese missions...and to hear the missionaries' inspiring reports," Dean Acheson wrote. "Thus was nourished the love portion of the love-hate complex that was to infuse so much emotion into our later China policy." The author of another account said: "It would be hard to over-emphasize the extent of the influence of the missionaries in shaping and directing the Far Eastern policies of the United States....Beginning with President McKinley, they received...special recognition from the executive branch.... For many years missionaries, businessmen and government officials collaborated in the movement to implant American social and economic institutions in China; and of the three the missionaries were by far the most powerful."[16]

Their view of China became the American view. They sympathized with the privations of the people in an industrially backward, strife-torn country and took the view that America was obligated to help them.[17] "Congregations all over the United States listened to the returned missionary... tell of the deserving qualities of the Chinese people and of the great reservoir of future Christians. Along with the public impression that America had saved China's integrity by the doctrine of the Open Door, missionary propaganda helped to create the image of China as protege, an image which carried an accompanying sense of obligation toward the object of one's own beneficence."[18] Undetected by most Americans for many

---

[16] Richard Van Alstyne, *The Listener* (1961), quoted by Greene, *op. cit.*, p. 4.

[17] A China scholar has suggested that "to gain support for their efforts, they [the missionaries] probably exaggerated the poverty, the lack of popular culture, and the general absence of humanistic values among China's lower classes." —Ishwer C. Ojha, *Chinese Foreign Policy in an Age of Transition: The Diplomacy of Cultural Despair* (1969), p. 77.

[18] Tuchman, *op. cit.*, p. 32. The Open Door doctrine refers to U.S. policy, enunciated in 1899 and pressed on other nations, that called for equality of commercial rights in China among foreign interests. It was intended to forestall the threat of the partitioning of China by imperialist powers.

years was the undercurrent of resentment and sense of humiliation in China over its subservience to the foreign intruder.

American friends of China sincerely believed they could help China by leading it to adopt American ways. The revolution of 1911 that wiped out the Manchu dynasty and established a nominally republican government was accepted as a sign that China was on the way to becoming another western-style democracy, potentially strong and, of course, a true friend of the United States. This image of China contributed greatly to the shaping of America's policy on Asia as World War II drew to its close. Memoirists of Franklin D. Roosevelt's presidency (1933-45) recalled that his sympathy for China was profound, that he was fond of recounting anecdotes of his trader-ancestors in their dealings with the Chinese, that his mother had spent considerable time as a girl in China, and that his home contained many mementos of the family's China ties.

"Out of this background," Acheson wrote, "came...a notion of President Roosevelt's which seemed quixotic to Churchill and Stalin: that China, with our help and under our tutelage, would rise from its ashes to the position of a great power and play a beneficent role after the war in bringing stability to Asia." At the Yalta Conference in February 1945, Roosevelt bargained for China's future. "Through his efforts, [Nationalist] China was included as one of the five permanent members in the United Nations Security Council when such recognition could be justified only by a sentimental regard for her fight against the Japanese, and not in terms of any objective standards of power. Though fully aware of the many limitations of Chiang Kai-shek's government, Roosevelt was determined to assist in its revitalization."[19]

But China was divided. The forces of Chiang and Mao fought to a showdown, despite American efforts to reconcile them in the interest of a unified China. American support had long been committed to Chiang, a Christian convert. He and his Wellesley-educated wife were familiar figures and had come to symbolize the China that Americans knew and liked best.

Mao's triumph set the stage for one of the most vindictive periods in American political history. Its theme was: "Who lost China to the Communists?" Americans returning from

[19] Sidney Warren, *The President As World Leader* (McGraw-Hill paperback edition, 1967), p. 267.

China, who had witnessed the victory of Mao's People's Liberation Army, brought home stories of severe disillusionment. "The great shock...was that their beloved Chinese liberals, the Americanized university professors and their students, went over to the revolution...."[20]

McCarthy Era Acrimony Over 'Who Lost China'

Disillusionment over China helped to split the bipartisan support of foreign policy that had prevailed during the war. It gave the Republican Party an effective battle cry: the charge that the Democrats were "soft on Communism." The outbreak of war in Korea in June 1950 and the intervention of 200,000 Chinese "volunteers" in that war five months later magnified the import of the charge. President Truman, Secretary of State Dean Acheson, and Gen. George C. Marshall were among those charged with having given away America's Chinese birthright.

During the McCarthy era[21] the "soft on communism" attack often centered on the "loss" of China. For five years, 1950-54, Sen. Joseph McCarthy (R Wis.) carried on a highly effective vendetta against the State Department and other federal agencies that he said were riddled with Communists and their dupes. The "old China hands"—Foreign Service men and scholars with long experience in China—were major targets. The State Department was virtually drained of its China experts; some were drummed out of government service.

James C. Thomson Jr., an East Asian specialist in the State Department from 1961 to 1966, believes that American involvement in Viet Nam is a legacy of the McCarthy era. The department's Bureau of Far Eastern Affairs was "purged of its best China expertise, and of farsighted, dispassionate men, as a result of McCarthyism." Those who remained, Thomson feels, were committed to the containment and isolation of China. "Career officers in the department, and especially those in the field [in Viet Nam], had not forgotten the fate of their World War II colleagues who wrote in frankness from China and were later pilloried by Senate committees for critical comments on the Chinese Nationalists."[22]

---

[20] Tom Engelhardt, "Long Day's Journey: American Observers in China, 1948-50," in *China and Ourselves* (1965, edited by Bruce Douglas and Ross Terrill), p. 105.

[21] Beginning with McCarthy's speech in Wheeling, W. Va., on Feb. 11, 1950, in which he charged that 57 Communists were working in the State Department, ending on Dec. 2, 1954, when the Senate formally "condemned" him for conduct unbecoming a Senator.

[22] James C. Thomson Jr., "How Could Viet Nam Happen?" *Atlantic Monthly*, April 1968, pp. 47, 53.

"We interpreted the advent to power in China of Mao Tse-
tung's Communist regime...as the conquest of China by
Moscow," Louis J. Halle has written. "There were those among
us who knew the historical, geographical and strategic circumstances that, in the long run, made anything but conflict between Mao's China and Moscow virtually inconceivable, and
who knew as well the long record of conflict between Mao and
Moscow. They were, however, intimidated into silence, or if
they tried to speak out their careers and reputations were
ruined by accusations of treason."[23]

The policy toward mainland China, as cast in Cold War
terms, remained fixed during the Eisenhower years (1953-60).
Early in 1955 the United States and China stood on the verge
of a military showdown over the tiny islands of Quemoy and
Matsu lying in the Taiwan Strait a few miles off the China
mainland. At Eisenhower's request, Congress authorized the
use of American forces to defend the islands which, occupied
by Chiang Kai-shek's forces, had come under Communist
artillery attacks from the mainland. As it turned out, American
forces were not sent to the islands; by April of that year Chou
En-lai said "the Chinese people do not want to have war with
the U.S.A." and expressed a willingness to negotiate the
issue.[24]

In the midst of the Quemoy-Matsu crisis, the Senate ratified
a mutual defense treaty with Chiang's government in which the
United States pledged to defend Taiwan, the offshore islands
and "such other territories as may be determined by mutual
agreement" against attack from China. The United States regarded China as the aggressor trying to impose international
Communism on Asia. As recounted by Sen. Mansfield: "It was
assumed that if the endorsement of the free nations were with-
held, this regime...would wither and eventually collapse. On
this basis, recognition was not extended to Peking. The official
view was that the National Government...[on Taiwan] continued to speak for all of China."

Even as a more realistic view of the situation developed, few
politicians dared challenge the established position. President
Kennedy, according to Arthur Schlesinger Jr., "considered the

---

[23] Louis J. Halle, "After Viet Nam—Another Witchhunt?" *The New York Times Magazine,* June 6, 1971, pp. 42, 44. Halle is professor of foreign affairs at the Graduate Institute
of International Studies, Geneva.
[24] For details, see *China and U.S. Far East Policy 1945-66* (1967, publication of Congressional Quarterly Inc.), pp. 72-75.

state of our relations with Communist China as irrational" but thought "the international gains (if any) of admission [to the United Nations] would be far outweighed by the uproar it would cause at home." Eisenhower had warned Kennedy privately, Schlesinger added, that he would consider it necessary to return to public life if there was a threat of China's admission to the United Nations. Kennedy, with his slim majority, "felt that he could not take on the China problem"—not during his first term at least.[25]

Evolvement of Change in Peking and Washington

The atmosphere began to change during the Johnson years. The Senate Foreign Relations Committee held hearings in March 1966 to which a number of scholars were called to participate in a forum on "China and American attitudes toward China." The problem, as presented by A. Doak Barnett, then of Columbia University, was "how to reestablish a reasonable basis for contact and discourse between the United States and mainland China." In that year the United States eased restrictions on the travel of scholars to Communist countries, and President Johnson said in a televised speech that eventual reconciliation with China was necessary. He said the United States would seek to reduce tensions between the two countries. As a presidential candidate in 1960, Nixon strongly opposed admitting China to the United Nations. As a candidate in 1968, he said: "We simply cannot afford to leave China forever outside the family of nations."[26] As President, he took a series of steps to invite more contact. *(See box next page.)*

There is evidence to suggest that China began to reassess its position of hostility toward the United States near the end of the past decade. The reassessment came at a time when the Sino-Soviet dispute over Communist ideology had led to a bitter rivalry between Moscow and Peking which flared, in March 1969, into a series of armed skirmishes along the Manchurian-Siberian border. And it came after the turbulent Cultural Revolution of 1966-67 had subsided.[27] The upheavals wrought by five or six million Chinese students—the "Red Guards"—were aimed at purifying life in China. An unwanted

---

[25] Arthur M. Schlesinger Jr., *A Thousand Days* (1965), p. 443.

[26] CBS radio broadcast, Oct. 19, 1968. In the 1960 campaign Nixon said that to admit China to the United Nations would mock the interests of peace-loving countries, increase its power and "probably irreparably weaken" China's non-Communist neighbors.

[27] For background on the Sino-Soviet dispute, see "World Communist Summit," *E.R.R.*, 1969 Vol. I, p. 391, and on the Cultural Revolution, see "China Under Mao," *E.R.R.*, 1968 Vol. II, p. 565.

NIXON ADMINISTRATION INITIATIVES ON CHINA POLICY

1969 *July.* Eased restrictions on American travel to China and permitted tourists to buy Chinese goods up to $100 in value.
November. Announced suspension of an American naval patrol in Taiwan Strait.
December. Lifted the $100 limit on purchases of Chinese goods and permitted foreign subsidiaries of American companies to trade in non-strategic goods with China.

1970 *February.* Stated in the President's foreign policy report to Congress: "It is certainly to our interest... that we take what steps we can toward improved relations with Peking."
August. Removed restrictions that had prevented American oil companies from bunkering ships destined for China.

1971 *February.* Stated in the President's foreign policy report to Congress: "The United States is prepared to see the People's Republic of China play a constructive role in the family of nations."
March. Terminated all restrictions on the use of American passports for travel to China.
June. Announced a long list of goods eligible for export to China.

side effect was to make Peking's relations with other countries extremely abrasive. According to one count, by Oct. 1, 1966, the 17th anniversary of the People's Republic, China had picked quarrels with no fewer than 32 countries. Only five foreign governments[28] sent delegations to the Oct. 1 observances in 1967. President Johnson said in his State of the Union message to Congress, Jan. 17, 1968: "The radical extremism of their government has isolated the Chinese people beyond their borders."

However, a change may already have been in the making. Robert S. Elegant, who watches China from Hong Kong, had written the previous autumn: "Amid the turmoil of the last days of the Great Proletarian Cultural Revolution, there are signs that a profound change in the Chinese approach to the outside world is now in train. The Chinese pragmatists are being forced toward recognition that China is not so powerful—morally or materially—that she can impose her own order upon mankind."[29] The outer world did not receive confirma-

---

[28] Albania, the Congo Republic (Brazzaville), Pakistan, Tanzania, and North Viet Nam.
[29] Robert S. Elegant, "China's Next Phase," *Foreign Affairs*, October 1967, p. 140. See also "Hong Kong and Macao: Windows Into China," *E.R.R.*, 1967 Vol. I, p. 20.

tion of change—or even that a response would be elicited from Nixon's conciliatory gestures—until the American table tennis team received its invitation. "That a response from Peking finally came was not a surprise to President Nixon," Senate Assistant Minority Leader Robert P. Griffin (R Mich.) told the Economic Club of Detroit on May 17, 1971. "But I can tell you that no one was more surprised than he when Ping Pong became the vehicle for delivery."

Hurdles Marking Route to Reconciliation

THE CHIEF OBSTACLE to normal relations between the United States and the People's Republic of China is the existence of the other China—the Republic of China with its capital in Taipei on Taiwan. The United States has never wavered in its support for the latter's claim to represent China in the United Nations and for its hold on China's permanent seat in the U.N. Security Council. So far the United States has succeeded in defeating perennial efforts to supplant Taipei delegates with Peking delegates in the United Nations. But support for the American position has been shrinking. In 1970, for the first time, a majority voted in favor of the switch, but the vote was short of the two-thirds majority required for action on an "important question."[30]

The issue will come up again when the General Assembly convenes on Sept. 14, 1971. There is a good chance that this time—or by 1972 at the latest—Peking will make it. The General Assembly may vote again on whether this is an "important question" before taking up the issue itself. The question now is whether the United States will attempt to block what many observers believe is inevitable. Secretary General Thant suggested to a luncheon gathering of U.N. correspondents on June 3 that Peking's backers may have insufficient time to muster a two-thirds majority in 1971, if such a majority is again required.

Although there is no official confirmation, the United States

---

[30] The vote on a resolution to unseat the Taipei delegation and replace it with one from Peking, taken on Nov. 20, 1970, was 51 for, 49 against, with 25 abstentions, the resolution failing by 16 votes. The vote to declare the matter an "important question" requiring a two-thirds majority was 66-52 with seven abstentions. In 1965 the vote to admit Peking was 47-47.

appears to be moving toward a "two-China" position. A special presidential commission recommended on April 26, 1971, that the United States seek "as early as practicable" the admission of the People's Republic to the United Nations but without the expulsion of the Nationalist Republic of China. The 50-member bipartisan commission was headed by Henry Cabot Lodge, the Republican Party's leading elder statesman.

Earlier evidence of a change of tone was detected in the language of the American Deputy Permanent Representative to the United Nations, Christopher H. Phillips. He told the General Assembly on Nov. 12, 1970, the United States was interested in having the People's Republic "play a constructive role in the family of nations." America was "mindful of the industry, talents and achievements of the great people who live in that ancient cradle of civilization." But he insisted it was not right to expel one of the founding nations as a condition of admission.

The main trouble with the two-China policy is that neither of the two Chinas will have anything to do with it. Repeated statements of their leaders make it seem unlikely that either would ever agree to membership in an organization that included the other. It has been speculated that if Peking should be voted into the United Nations without a clause expelling Taipei, either the former would refuse to take the offered seat or the latter would walk out. If by some unlikely chance the two Chinas do end up in the United Nations, a decision will have to be made on which will hold the permanent seat on the Security Council.[31] This may raise the question of whether the seat—or any of the Big Five seats—should remain a permanent holding. Some fear too that a Peking delegate on the Security Council would exercise an obstructive veto similar to that exercised by the Soviet Union in earlier years.

The future of American relations with China will doubtless depend a great deal on how the two countries behave during the U.N. admission debate ahead and on its outcome. If the situation is resolved with a minimum of rancor on both sides, steps will probably be taken that will ultimately lead to U.S. recognition of the legitimacy of the Peking regime and to an exchange of diplomatic representatives.

---

[31] Originally composed of five permanent and six other members, the Security Council was expanded Jan. 1, 1966, to a membership of 15. Britain, China, France, Russia and the United States continue to constitute the permanent members—the Big Five.

Until that time contacts are likely to be limited to exchanges of scholars, scientists, journalists, Ping Pong players, and other special groups of people—and to links forged by trade. The most crucial of these contacts, in terms of the bearing on the future stability of international relations and hopes for peace, may well be in the area of trade.

Limiting of China Trade to Non-Strategic Goods

Segments of American business have shown keen interest in the potentiality of a new market of about 760 million[32] consumers, few of whom possess washing machines, electric refrigerators, automobiles, or other American necessities of life. But China is a poor country, consumer buying power is barely at subsistence[33] and the economy is tightly controlled. So a suddenly booming export market for American consumer goods can hardly be expected. But China has real needs for other goods that the United States could supply.

In a study prepared for the National Committee on U.S.-China Relations, Robert F. Dernberger, a University of Michigan economics professor, projected that under favorable conditions for growth and under the same terms that apply to U.S.-Soviet trade, China's purchases of American goods might reach $900 million by 1980, an amount equal to about 2 per cent of the current level of American exports. China's foreign trade, estimated at $4.3 billion a year and about equally divided between imports and exports, is small for a country of its size. It contrasts with America's 1970 total of $42.7 billion in exports and $39.9 billion in imports.

Under recent easing of trade restrictions, foreign-based subsidiaries of American companies have already sold to the People's Republic. General Motors dealers overseas, for example, recently sold China earth-moving equipment. China wants commercial aircraft, not necessarily new planes.[34] "They want plants to make fertilizers, chemicals and synthetics.... They lack spare parts (for communications and transport systems) that we could supply," Samuel Pisar, East-West trade expert, told an interviewer. "In return they have some

---

[32] Population estimate of the Population Reference Bureau, Washington, D.C., as of April 1970.

[33] Per capita income is estimated at $125 and Gross National Product at $80 billion, but these figures cannot be measured against the income and GNP of a fully developed, money-based economy.

[34] The president of Pan American Airways, Najeeb E. Halaby, said on April 13 that China was "one of the biggest untapped markets in the world for commercial aircraft" and that selling it used planes could "ease the surplus capacity" in the United States.

mercury, some silver, furs, silks, tapestries and even supplies for Chinese restaurants."[35]

If the United States is interested in tapping this market, it must compete with other developed nations—not only of the Communist bloc but America's friends and allies. Japan has now replaced the Soviet Union as China's main trading partner. Among the other leading China traders are West Germany, Britain, Australia, Canada and France. Canada, which established diplomatic relations with Peking in 1970, has sold vast quantities of wheat to China since early in the 1960s.[36] Competition from rival traders may be less a limiting factor for America's trade with China than self-imposed restraints due to fear of building up a hostile power.

Efforts to expand the China trade may well lead to a major debate on the benefits versus the hazards. Proponents of more trade complain that the Pentagon tends to slap the "strategic" label on almost any kind of export goods destined for a country outside the Western orbit, and this can delay or prevent the granting of export licenses for shipping particular items. China may well look upon American decisions on trade as a key to American sincerity in wishing to reduce tensions between the two countries.

Overcoming Old Fears About Peking's Intentions

A new image of China is unfolding in the American mind, replacing the image of the outlaw nation—sullen, unreasonable, unpredictable and bent on revolutionary conquest. The new image is hardly ideal in the American scheme of things, but it does describe a nation possessing at least some of the sturdier virtues, certainly a nation with which the United States may be able to deal in the normal way.

The most important change of American viewpoint, expressed by leading Asia scholars and "China hands" in the government, concerns the menace China presents to world peace. In simplest terms, the United States no longer believes China presents an immediate threat of military conquest in the name of world revolution. As expressed by Assistant Secretary of State Marshall Green before the Senate For-

---

[35] Quoted in *The Wall Street Journal,* April 28, 1971.
[36] See "Canada's Changing Foreign Policy," *E.R.R.,* 1970 Vol. I, pp. 85-86. Japan's exports to China in 1969 amounted to $380 million. In 1946, the first postwar year, American exports to China were $315 million; by 1949, the year of the Communist takeover, they had dropped to $83 million. See Laurence W. Levine, "The Prospects of U.S.-China Trade," *East Europe,* June 1971, pp. 2-6.

eign Relations Committee, Oct. 6, 1970: China "is not today considered to pose a 'juggernaut' type of threat to its neighbors and has been prudent in facing United States power in the area."

Altered circumstances accounted for the "evolution in our perception of the intentions of the People's Republic of China," Green said. In the early 1950s, what appeared to be close collusion between Russia and China implied a threat to enlarge Communist spheres of control "by force of arms if necessary." Today, he added, it is apparent that "world power...is polycentric and becoming more so." The deep schism between China and Russia, the rise of a strong Japan, and the declining appeal of China as a model for developing countries in the Far East alleviated earlier fears. Even the achievement of nuclear capability "will not necessarily make the Chinese more aggressive," Green said. "I believe they will continue to be deterred by overwhelming U.S. and Soviet power."

Some China-watchers believe that country will be too deeply concerned with internal matters for the foreseeable future to take on any outside military adventures. The recent news stories that have let the West glimpse the strange world of inland China tend to confirm the picture of a reasonably content, hard-working people with miles to go to catch up with the industrial West. They also depict a people ready to be friends despite two decades of propaganda portraying Americans as imperialist devils. A moratorium on the devil theme in international relations should be salutary for both sides.

EAST PAKISTAN'S CIVIL WAR

by

Richard C. Schroeder

CHAOS IN EAST AND WEST BENGAL
Massive Refugee Migration to Neighboring India
Causes of Rebellion in Culture, Economy, Politics
Charges of Genocide; Holy War Against Hindus
Threats of Famine and Epidemics From the War
U.S. Dilemma Over Arms Shipments to Pakistan

EAST PAKISTAN AND INDIAN HISTORY
Bengal as Seat of Ferment Since British Arrival
Ancient Background of Muslim and Hindu Hostility
Birth of a Divided Pakistan Carved From India
Growing Rift Between East and West Pakistan

PERILS OF STRIFE ON ASIAN SUBCONTINENT
Problems Created in India by Refugee Hordes
Possibility of War Between India and Pakistan
Interests of America, China and the Soviet Union
Challenge of Population Growth to Peace in Area

1 9 7 1
July 28

EAST PAKISTAN'S CIVIL WAR

O NE OF HISTORY'S greatest, and most sudden, migrations is taking place across the border that separates East Pakistan and India. Driven from their homes by violence, chaos and fear, as many as seven million Pakistanis have sought safety in the Indian states of West Bengal, Bihar, Assam, and Tripura. This mass movement has been compared to having the entire population of New Jersey abruptly flee to New York City and nearby counties. In one week, May 10-17, according to State Department figures, nearly one million East Pakistanis crossed the border into India.[1] The influx doubled the population of tiny Tripura in barely two months. As of late July, the migration continued at a rate of 75,000 to 100,000 a day, with no end in sight.

The refugees are escaping from a civil war in East Pakistan that has turned their riverine countryside into a lake of blood. Soldiers from West Pakistan are battling a ragtag but growing insurgent force intent on creating an autonomous, or even independent, Bengal state. Until 1947 when Pakistan was carved out of India, the area that is now East Pakistan was a part of India called East Bengal, and many of its people are still drawn by ancestral ties to the Indians of West Bengal rather than the West Pakistanis.

The struggle over "Bangla Desh," the Bengali homeland, is claiming a fearful toll of lives. By some Indian estimates, more than 700,000 Bengalis have been killed since fighting erupted in late March. A West Pakistani writer, Aijaz Ahmad, calculates the number of East Pakistani deaths at 500,000. Some other sources put the total so far at 200,000 The economy of East Pakistan lies in ruins and famine is threatened. Moreover, the refugee movement has placed terrible economic and social strains on India and raised fear of a cholera epidemic.

American concern is based not only on humanitarian considerations, but also on the possibility that the conflict could

---

[1] U.S.Department of State, Interagency Committee on Pakistani Refugee Relief. *Situation Report No. 5*, June 22, 1971.

ignite a war between India and Pakistan—and conceivably draw in China, Russia and the United States. The U.S. position is already uncomfortable because of the government's dual and perhaps conflicting relations with India and Pakistan. The United States has on its own and through international efforts sent refugee relief aid to India. But it has been an arms supplier of Pakistani military forces which are being portrayed in the world press as the aggressors in East Pakistan.

Causes of Rebellion in Culture, Economy, Politics

West Pakistan has made a determined effort to prevent news from East Pakistan from reaching the world. Western correspondents were removed from the country hours after war started with an outbreak of shooting in Dacca, the eastern capital, on March 25.[2] From available reports and from refugee accounts, there can be little doubt that massive bloodletting is taking place throughout East Pakistan, and that fear and terror prevail everywhere. The army holds a tenuous sway in most of the region. Guerrilla warfare rages between the regular troops from West Pakistan and the irregulars of the *Mukti Fauj,* the East Bengal "liberation army." Pakistani officials accuse India of supplying and sheltering the rebel troops along the border.

Although its causes go back many years, the crisis in East Pakistan came to a head on March 1 when Gen. Agha Mohammad Yahya Khan, in his role as President and Chief Martial Law Administrator, postponed the opening of a newly elected National Assembly. The task of the Assembly was to draft a new constitution, which would permit a return to civilian rule after 12 years under a military regime. In elections held in December 1970, the East Pakistan Awami League, a moderate body led by Sheikh Mujibur Rahman ("Mujib" to East Pakistanis), won 167 of the 169 Assembly seats allotted to the East, and an absolute majority of the 313 seats in the entire Assembly.

Since the Awami League had campaigned on a platform of autonomy for East Pakistan, it seemed certain that the new constitution would give the East a much larger measure of self-determination than it has enjoyed so far. East and West Pakistan are separated by 1,000 miles of Indian territory. Created out of the predominantly Muslim areas of India at

---

[2] A few newsmen were permitted to return, under heavy censorship restrictions, in late June. One of them, Sydney Schanberg of *The New York Times*, was expelled nine days after his return.

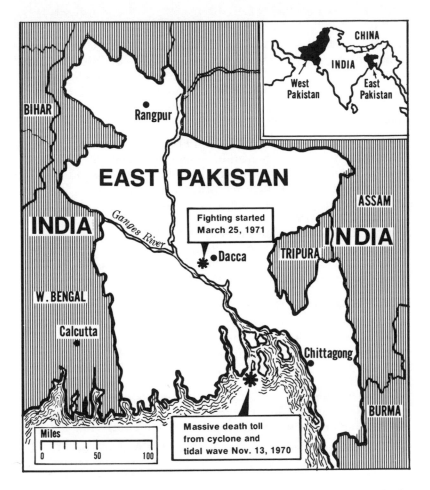

the time of independence, the divided nation has increasingly felt the strains produced by the disparate economies and cultural heritages of its two wings.

While the Awami League dominated elections in the East, the majority of the seats in West Pakistan were won by the People's Party under former Foreign Minister Zulfikar Ali Bhutto. The People's Party opposed any significant autonomy for East Pakistan as a threat to national unity. On Feb. 15, 1971, Bhutto announced that his party would boycott the Assembly unless the Awami League toned down its demands.

Without the participation of the majority party in the West, the National Assembly could not have drawn up a viable constitution. Gen. Yahya Khan quickly postponed the opening

141

of the Assembly, an action which enraged the East. Riots and strikes broke out in Dacca, the East Pakistan capital, and nearly 100 persons were killed in clashes with troops. When martial law was declared, Mujib launched a non-violent civil disobedience campaign which crippled the government and interrupted all business.

Gen. Yahya Khan flew to East Pakistan early in March for two weeks of talks with Mujib. When the discussions bogged down, the general ordered his troops—40,000 strong, and mostly West Pakistanis—to take command of the province. The Awami League was outlawed and Sheikh Mujib was arrested and reportedly flown to jail in West Pakistan to await trial.[3] Shortly thereafter, an additional 30,000 West Pakistani troops were airlifted in, leading to charges that Yahya Khan was merely "buying time" in his meetings with Mujib and that the takeover had been planned long in advance.[4]

Charges of Genocide; Holy War Against Hindus

With no advanced warning, tanks rolled through the streets of Dacca on the night of March 25. Machine guns and mortars were moved into place. At about 9 p.m., the troops opened fire, seemingly at random, shelling houses, firebombing crowded bazaars, shooting the homeless beggars who sleep on the pavement. Huge sections of shanty slums were gutted, and the inhabitants, including small children, were bayonetted by the soldiers in what seemed to be blind rage and hatred.

"The crackdown was brutal in the tradition of the Moguls and their bloody 15th and 16th century conquests," wrote Peggy Durdin in the *The New York Times Magazine* on May 2. It continued and even mounted in fury as time passed. Anthony Mascarenhas, a Goan who was correspondent for the English-language Karachi *Morning News,* a leading pro-government West Pakistan newspaper, fled to London to write about the horror he had witnessed in East Pakistan: "What I saw and heard with unbelieving eyes and ears during my 10 days in East Bengal during April made it clear that the killings are not the isolated acts of military commanders in the field. They are the result of deliberate...orders from the top."[5]

---

[3] President Yahya Khan said in an interview published in the London *Financial Times,* July 19, 1971, that Mujib would be put to trial "very soon." The trial would be by a military court and in secret on a charge, unspecified in the interview, which the president said would carry the death penalty.

[4] See Aijaz Ahmad, "The Bloody Surgery of Pakistan," *The Nation,* June 28, 1971, p. 817.

[5] Story in *The Sunday Times* of London, reprinted in *The Washington Post,* June 13, 1971.

The violence was soon being described in terms of genocide. *The Spectator,* the British weekly, commented on June 17: "There is no reason now to refrain from declaring, on evidence which is brave and strong, that the government and the army of Pakistan, which is to say the establishment of West Pakistan, is and has been for some weeks engaged upon the most extensive and barbarous exercise of genocide that the world has known about since the end of World War II."

At first, the slaughter seemed to be directed against all Bengalis; later it became more selective. More and more, Hindus were sought out and shot. The civil war took on the aspects of a *Jihad,* or Muslim holy war. The State Department noted in its reports on refugee movements that, at the start, the influx was evenly divided between Hindus and Muslims; later the ratio of Hindus to Muslims was two to one or even greater.[6]

It is worth noting that the West Pakistan troops apparently have had no monopoly on barbarism. "When the East Pakistan Rifles mutinied, their first reaction was to wipe out the non-Bengalis in their own ranks," a correspondent wrote. "A sadder story is that of the Biharis—Moslems from the state of Bihar....Being non-Bengali, they have been taken as supporters of the West Pakistan government and therefore spies. Many of them have been murdered by the Bengalis."[7]

Threat of Famine and Epidemics From the War

The specter of famine haunts the land, not only because the rice fields are untended, but because distribution systems have broken down. East Pakistan normally runs a deficit of two million tons of foodstuffs a year. By the most conservative estimates, the deficit will rise to three million tons this year. On July 13, Sen. Edward M. Kennedy (D Mass.) made public a survey indicating that widespread starvation would overtake East Pakistan by August unless emergency measures were put into effect immediately.[8] Ten days later he released confidential State Department cables in which U.S. consular officials in Dacca reported that famine there was a "real possibility"—in apparent contradiction to statements made by department officials in Washington.

---

[6] The Baltimore *Sun* reported July 13, 1971, that an unpublished study made by the Indian government showed that Hindus made up more than 90 per cent of the refugees.

[7] T.J.S. George, "The Cross of Bengal," *Far Eastern Economic Review,* April 24, 1971.

[8] The survey was made by Joseph A. Ryan of the Agriculture Department and Elliot J. Weiss of the Agency for International Development, who were in East Pakistan June 3-21. Their report was submitted June 28 to the Senate Judiciary Subcommittee on Refugees, which Kennedy heads.

The New York Times reported July 13 that a mission sent to East Pakistan by the International Bank for Reconstruction and Development—the World Bank—described the two most critical factors in East Pakistan as being a "general sense of fear and lack of confidence on the part of most of the population" and a complete dislocation of communications.[9]

India has been able to provide for only about half of the refugees—and those in makeshift camps where a bare minimum of food, shelter, sanitary facilities and medical supplies are available. The other half wander aimlessly about, sleeping on city streets and foraging off the land. The refugees are often drenched by the driving monsoon rains, wracked by hunger and felled by disease. Untold thousands have been struck down by cholera and there is threat that it will spread throughout eastern India despite international efforts to provide vaccine and medicine.

Two months after the outbreak of violence in East Pakistan, U.N. Secretary General U Thant appealed for a world pledge of $175 million to help India provide for the refugees during a six-month emergency period. Less than a month later, United Nations officials reported $150 million in pledges had been received but that India needed an additional $400 million. The Beatles, the British rock musicians, scheduled benefit performances in Madison Square Garden, New York, to aid the U.N. relief fund.

U.S. Dilemma Over Arms Shipments to Pakistan

Washington has attempted to tread a fine line, supplying some $90 million in aid to Indian refugee care, yet hesitating to cut off all aid to the government of Pakistan, a military and political ally.[10] The rationale has been that the United States wants to preserve its leverage on the Pakistani government, and that cutting off aid will do nothing to help the beleaguered people of East Pakistan. It is also believed that Pakistani cooperation in helping arrange the trip of presidential adviser Henry Kissinger to China was connected with aid-giving. Kissinger flew from Islamabad to Peking, it was reported, on aircraft supplied by Pakistan.[11]

---

[9] The mission's report, obtained by the newspaper, had been made available to World Bank officials only on a confidential basis—presumably because it recommended that further long-term international economic assistance to Pakistan be suspended "for at least the next year or so" while emergency relief measures receive top priority.

[10] Pakistan is a member of the Southeast Asia Treaty Organization and the Central Treaty Organization, both of which the United States was instrumental in forming as a barrier to communism in Asia.

[11] See Crosby Noyes, Washington *Star,* July 25, 1971.

The ambiguous attitude has led some critics to charge this country with closing its eyes to a situation in which "there have been a hundred My Lais and Lidices."[12] *The New Yorker* magazine commented: "Not only has the unspeakable man-made disaster of recent months gone unnoticed here, but until the middle of April America was shipping military supplies to Gen. Yahya Khan's troops..."

The arms issue has been particularly troublesome to the United States. From various quarters, U.S. military assistance to Pakistan has been assigned a large part of the blame for continuing bad relations between Pakistan and India. Aijaz Ahmad wrote that American arms aid "threw the entire political culture of Pakistan off balance." "Coupled with the fear of neighboring India...the availability of weapons led quickly to a thorough militarization of all facets of national life." Chester Bowles, writing in the July 1971 issue of *Foreign Affairs*, commented that "our lavish arming of Pakistan since 1954 will surely be considered by historians as one of our major follies." American military assistance to Pakistan to date is estimated at between $1.5 billion and $2.0 billion.

Arms shipments were put under embargo when India and Pakistan went to war briefly in 1965 over possession of Kashmir.[13] Sales of "non-lethal" equipment were resumed in 1967, and, according to State Department spokesmen, have averaged $10 million a year since then. The Nixon Administration offered in October 1970 to sell Pakistan a squadron of F104 Starfighters, a squadron of B57 Bombers, and some armored personnel carriers. However, those items have not been delivered, according to administration sources.

On April 15, 1971, the administration said it had reinstated the ban on arms sales to Pakistan, and that no shipments had been made since the outbreak of the civil war the previous month. However, Tad Szulc reported in *The New York Times* on June 22, 1971, that at least two freighters had been loaded in New York harbor with military equipment for Pakistan since the ban was announced. Subsequently, four or five more ships were reported scheduled to sail for Karachi with military equipment. The administration, obviously embarrassed by

---

[12] So characterized by *Newsweek,* June 28, 1971, p. 43. Lidice was a village in Czechoslovakia razed in World War II by German forces who then killed the village men and deported the women and children in retaliation for the assassination of Nazi official Reinhard Heydrich. For details on My Lai massacre, see "War Atrocities and the Law," *E.R.R.*, 1970 Vol. I, pp. 4-6.

[13] See "Kashmir Question," *E.R.R.*, 1965 Vol. II, pp. 801-817.

the news, explained that the arms sales had been licensed *before* March 25, and that no attempt to interfere with their shipment would be made.

After the World Bank report was leaked, Washington officials said that economic aid to Pakistan had been suspended. Shipments of military supplies were continuing, however. For the current fiscal year ending June 30, 1972, the administration asked Congress for $118.3 million in economic aid, $5.5 million in military assistance and $8 million in technical assistance for Pakistan. But administration officials have said the money would not be disbursed until the situation in East Pakistan returned to "normal." The House Foreign Affairs Committee voted July 14 to withhold all aid until East Pakistan refugees are returned to their homes and "reasonable security" is achieved. Under terms of the House proposal, aid would be resumed when President Nixon reported to Congress that those conditions had been met.

East Pakistan and Indian History

EVER SINCE the British began to establish their dominion over the Indian subcontinent in the late 17th and early 18th centuries, Bengal has been a focal point of strife, revolt and social distress. There are today more than 120 million Bengalis —a population equal to that of the United States east of the Mississippi River. The majority—75 million—are in East Pakistan. The Bengalis consider themselves a race apart— and better than their neighbors. There is a rich Bengali cultural and literary heritage, extending back several centuries and culminating in the great poet Rabindranath Tagore (1861-1941), who won the Nobel Prize for Literature in 1913.

Bengali nationalism has been a factor to reckon with throughout modern Indian history. For Britain, Bengal was the seat of imperial conquest. The British won their first major victory in India at Plassey, near present-day Calcutta, in 1757. Fort William—the nucleus of the future city—came under attack the previous year from the Nawab, or native Muslim ruler of Bengal. He imprisoned 146 British subjects in a cell 14 by 18 feet wide, the infamous "Black Hole of Calcutta" where all but 23 died overnight of suffocation. The angry British mounted an expedition from Madras under Robert Clive, who decisively defeated the Nawab at Plassey.[14] In subsequent battles, the British broke the power of their French rivals, and by 1765 had won control of all Bengal, from where they gradually extended their reign throughout India. Calcutta became the capital of British India.

In their long years of ruling India, the British never succeeded in reconciling the divergent religions and races that have arisen over the centuries on that vast, populous Asian subcontinent. The history of India has been one of successive invasions. The earliest Indians were black men related to the aborigines of Australia. A handful of descendants of these first inhabitants remain today, in the hills of central and eastern India, the so-called "scheduled tribes."

Ancient Background of Muslim and Hindu Hostility

The first great wave of invaders were the Dravidians, dark-skinned Caucasians, who today form a majority of the population in the south Indian states of Mysore, Andhra, Madras and Kerala. The Aryans, from whom evolved present-day Hindu religion and culture, appeared in northern India about 1500 B.C. and gradually pushed their Dravidian rivals southward. Muslims first came to India from the west, in the early 8th century. For several hundred years, Muslim incursions were limited to raids for plunder, but in 1206 a Muslim kingdom was established in New Delhi. The next 500 years, to a greater or lesser extent, is the record of the gradual subjugation of a huge Hindu majority by a Muslim minority.

The great period of Muslim, or Mogul, ascendancy began in the early 1500s with the appearance of a Turkish chieftain, Babur, a descendant of Tamerlane. Babur came out of what is now Afghanistan to conquer the Punjab, Sind and Kashmir in northwest India, and then set up his capital at Delhi. Babur's grandson, Akbar (1506-1605), was the most voracious conqueror among the Mogul emperors, extending his rule southward to the Deccan plateau. The empire reached its zenith during the reign of Akbar's grandson, Shah Jahan (1628-1657), builder of the Taj Mahal and of a multitude of other notable monuments. His son, Aurangzeb (1657-1707), launched an ambitious but unsuccessful attempt to extend Mogul domination throughout the remaining portions of south India. The empire crumbled rapidly after Aurangzeb's death, and the British quickly moved into the vacuum that was left.

---

[14]. Clive earned the title Baron Clive of Plassey. But in the end, Bengal conquered Clive. An opium addict—a habit he picked up in his years in Bengal—Clive committed suicide in 1774. See Percival Spear, *A History of India*, Vol. II (1970).

Mogul emperors were fierce proselytizers for Islam. "They destroyed Hindu temples. They imposed a special tax on any Hindu who would not adopt Islam. They sometimes ordered that the Hindu gods should not be worshipped in public. They even skinned alive certain Hindu priests who disobeyed these orders."[15] The years of Mogul rule left scars which have never disappeared from the Indian body politic. "Hindus, of course, fully understand why they fear Islam, despite their huge numerical preponderance on the subcontinent....For about 550 years, from the thirteenth to the eighteenth centuries, Muslim conquerors exercised from Delhi almost uninterrupted, impious sway over large parts of Bharat Mata, of Holy Mother India, of the revered land, the very earth itself which forms an essential part of the Hindu religion....The shame of it has caused deep wounds in the Hindu mind..."[16]

Muslim resentment over the loss of the empire, and the rising British control, was nearly as deep as Hindu resentment that the empire had ever existed. Increasingly, Muslims withdrew from Indian public life, building a wall between themselves and the country's Hindu majority. After the Sepoy Rebellion[17] of 1857, the British tended to view Muslims with increasing distrust, and began to rely more and more heavily upon Hindus to staff the civil service and other public institutions.[18]

The Hindu-Muslim division is a religious one and not, in any sense, racial. The Mogul conquerors were not Arabs, but central Asian converts to Islam—Persians, Afghans, and Turks. The Muslim community of the Indian subcontinent is largely a converted one. One estimate is that 89 per cent of India's Muslims are of Hindu origin.[19] A noted Indian writer remarked: "Most Muslims of today...belonged to families that were Hindu not so long ago. Two generations back, the forebears of Sir Muhammad Iqbal, the poet, were Saprus—Kashmiri Brahmins— and (Mohammed Ali) Jinnah's ancestors, not so far removed either, were also Hindus."[20]

A Muslim reawakening began to take place in the last third of the 19th century. A movement toward reconciliation

[15] Beatrice Pitney Lamb, *India* (1965), p. 40.
[16] Ian Stephens, *Pakistan* (1967), p. 14.
[17] Sepoys were Bengali troops, both Muslim and Hindu, who objected to the use of animal grease to lubricate cartridges. In the wake of the rebellion, the Bengali regiments were dismantled and the rule in India was transferred from the East India Company to the British Crown.
[18] See Richard S. Wheeler, *The Politics of Pakistan* (1970), and Donald M. Wilber, *Pakistan, Yesterday and Today* (1964).
[19] See "Freedom for India *E.R.R.*, 1946 Vol. I, p. 178.
[20] Durga Das, *India from Curzon to Nehru and After* (1970).

with the British and, to some extent, with Hindu India was led by the statesman and educator Sir Syed Ahmad Khan, founder of Aligarh Muslim University, the most important Muslim institution of higher learning in India. As a result of Muslim political activism, the first partition of Bengal took place in 1905—it lasted until 1912—producing a Muslim state in East Bengal and Assam. In the same year, the All-India Muslim League was formed as a counterbalance to the Hindu-dominated Indian National Congress, created in 1885 to work for greater self-government in British India.

Birth of a Divided Pakistan Carved From India

In the beginning, the Indian National Congress and the Muslim League were able to work together for the evolving goal of eventual independence. Following World War I, however, hostility between Hindus and Muslims split the two. From 1924 until the partition of India in 1947, the Indian political scene was dominated by two forces: the Muslim League under Mohammed Ali Jinnah and the Indian National Congress under Mohandas K. Gandhi. By 1940, Jinnah and the League, despairing of ever reaching an accord with the Congress, finally embraced a ten-year-old plan for the creation of two nations out of India, one Muslim and the other Hindu. The name Pakistan was given to the Muslim portion.[21]

A British proposal on the future status of India, put forth by Sir Stafford Cripps in 1942, seemed to reflect a willingness on the part of Britain to accept the two-nation plan. The Congress and the League were unable to agree, and the pressure of the war soon ended Britain's willingness to discuss concrete steps toward independence. The post-war period was marked by impressive electoral victories by the League, and by a tragic rise in communal violence between Hindus and Muslims. By late 1946, a semi-repressed civil war was raging in the eastern Ganges plain, in Bengal, Bihar and the United Provinces. By early 1947, it had spread westward to the Punjab and the Northwest Frontier. As the chaos and savagery mounted it became apparent to all that India was destined to become two separate nations.

India and Pakistan both proclaimed their independence Aug. 15, 1947. Partition was followed by a wave of bloodletting

---

[21] There are various explanations of the name. By one account, it is taken from the Urdu word *pak*, pure, and from the Persian *stan*, land. Another theory is that the word is an anagram for the peoples of West Pakistan: Punjabi, Afghan (or Pathan), Kashmiri, and Baluchistan. Another explanation is that the acronym embraces a pan-Islamic federation, including Iran.

far greater than anything that had come before. The savagery of Muslims, on the one hand, and Hindus and Sikhs on the other, is matched, perhaps, only by the current strife in East Pakistan. The death toll exceeded 500,000, it is estimated, and refugees numbered 10-12 million. Hindus fled Pakistan and Muslims left India.

The horror of those days continues to poison Indian-Pakistani relations today. "The capacity of India and Pakistan to direct their mutual relations has been limited. Much of the time the leaders and the people of the two countries were buffeted almost helplessly by forces of deep-seated religious animosity, the bitterness of ancient as well as recent memories, the compulsion of circumstances and the pressure of world powers. India was partitioned on the basis of communal hatred, not of mutual understanding."[22] The current strife in East Pakistan threatens to exacerbate that hatred.

Growing Rift Between East and West Pakistan

The dream of a strong and unified Muslim state was frustrated almost from the beginning by substantial and growing inequities between the east and west wings of the new nation. The relation between the two has been described by many experts as a classic colonial pattern,[23] with East Pakistan the exploited and West Pakistan the exploiter. East Pakistan has been, throughout the period of independence, a supplier of raw materials and financial resources to West Pakistan. It has also provided a captive market for West Pakistan's manufactured goods. At the time of partition, East Pakistan produced 80 per cent of the world's jute. In the first decade of independence, East Pakistan accounted for from 50 per cent to 70 per cent of the nation's exports, but received only 25 to 30 per cent of its imports.

The disparity shows up in human statistics as well. Average per capita income in the West was 32 per cent higher than in the East in 1959-60 whereas 10 years later it was 61 per cent higher. Despite their edge in population, East Pakistanis make up only 16 per cent of the national civil service and 10 per cent of the army. Few East Pakistanis hold high military rank. Educationally, the East Pakistanis suffer the same fate. Between 1947 and 1967, East Pakistan's share of primary school enrollment declined from 80 to 61 per cent of the national total; secondary school enrollment from 53 to 40 per cent;

---

[22] Krishan Bhatia, *The Ordeal of Nationhood, A Social Study of India Since Independence, 1947-1970* (1971), p. 280.
[23] See Aijaz Ahmad, *op. cit.*, p. 815, and T. J. S. George, *op. cit.*, p. 57.

and university enrollment from 70 to 45 per cent. In agriculture, Richard Critchfield noted, "there has been a steady regression in agricultural methods over the past thirty or forty years....Bengal has witnessed a steady retreat from oxenpulled plows to the primitive hand hoes, a sort of green revolution in reverse."[24]

In the first decade of independence, East Pakistan seemed willing to accept its situation, in the belief that as the nation got on its feet, the injustice would be repaired. The political system was still evolving; there was a will to believe in the power of the democratic process. A steady rise in the power of the Pakistani military establishment stifled that hope; a military government took over in 1958, and the generals still hold sway today.

Perils of Strife on Asian Subcontinent

IN THE FIRST DAYS of fighting it seemed unlikely that the disorganized East Pakistanis could offer much resistance to the 70,000 West Pakistanis in their midst. But as the bloodshed mounted, the will of the Bengalis to fight back seemed to stiffen. "The prospect is for a long and sullen war," Sydney Schanberg wrote soon after the outbreak of fighting. "Most diplomats and foreign observers believe that the Bengalis, by hanging on, will eventually make life untenable for the West Pakistanis. But...it could be years before the Bengalis finally win their freedom."

He wrote later that East Pakistani resistance fighters had organized themselves into effective guerrilla units and were conducting hit-and-run attacks on army outposts and police stations, cutting roads and railways, blowing up bridges and assassinating collaborators. "As in most insurgencies, only a small percentage of the people are active participants or combatants, but the overwhelming majority of the 75 million East Pakistanis seem to be at least passive resisters."[25]

So far, Gen. Yahya Khan has shown no sign of willingness to compromise with the East. In a broadcast to the nation on

[24] Richard Critchfield of the Washington *Star*, in the *Alicia Patterson Fund* newsletter, May 2, 1971.
[25] Dispatch printed in *The New York Times*, July 16, 1971.

June 28, he closed the door to any accommodation with the Awami League, announcing that a handpicked group of "experts" rather than the National Assembly would draw up a new constitution, following guidelines laid down by the general himself.

There were reports that two army divisions recently formed in West Pakistan were ready for transfer to the East. Civil servants from Islamabad, the western capital, were being sent in increasing numbers to man the posts abandoned by Bengalis. The 1971-72 national budget showed a significant rise in military spending, although over-all spending was down. West Pakistan's economy began to show the strain of civil war. The war was costing more than $2 million a day and its disruption of economic life had cut in half the country's capacity to earn foreign exchange. Currency reserves fell below $200 million and the Pakistani government stopped making payments on the $5 billion national debt.

Problems Created In India by Refugee Hordes

At an estimated cost of 40 cents a day for each refugee, the over-all cost to India could exceed $1 billion a year. International aid is the only recourse. The United States has committed $90 million and Congress is considering $100 million more. Aside from costs, many Indians fear the social ramifications of the presence of so many refugees. Under the best of circumstances, the refugee camps are wretched, over-crowded quagmires, where thousands spend most of their day waiting in line for a plateful of rice. The potential for chaos is very near to the surface. There have already been clashes between refugees spilling out of the camps, and Indians seeking to contain them within. The Indian villagers not only fear the threat of disease, but they also feel the pressure on jobs and prices. Border areas already report rising food costs, and the desperate refugees are offering to work at any job for far less than the going wage. In Calcutta, a city on the border of breakdown even in normal times,[26] the mayor has tried to put the city off-limits to the refugees in the hope of preventing the spread of disease and strife. Hundreds of thousands have slipped in nonetheless.

A plan to resettle large numbers of the refugees in Indian states away from the border areas has apparently fizzled. The numbers of refugees overwhelmed the few planes avail-

---

[26] See "Urbanization of the Earth," *E.R.R.*, 1970 Vol. I, pp. 370-371.

able to transport them. Not even the beleaguered Indian railway system appears to be capable of moving the millions involved in less than half a year. In the interior states, officials balked at the huge rehabilitation task they were being asked to undertake. And, on reflection, the government of India decided that resettlement might make the task of eventual repatriation of the refugees doubly difficult.

The camps serve as active recruitment centers for *Mukti Fauj* agents who enlist any able-bodied man in the fight to win East Bengal. Indian officials fear that the camps may also provide thousands of new volunteers for Naxalites, pro-Peking terrorists who have operated in Calcutta and the surrounding West Bengal countryside for nearly four years.[27] Naxalite elements are believed to be involved in, although not in control of, the East Pakistan rebel movement.

New Delhi is pinning its hopes on the eventual return of most of the refugees to East Pakistan. "We must get rid of them," Prime Minister Indira Gandhi has said. "Some way has to be found. We cannot resettle such an enormous number."[28] But hopes of repatriation depend on a number of questionable possibilities. It is doubtful that even when the bloodshed ceases, the refugees can be persuaded to return to homes that have been destroyed, fields that have been trampled and an economy that has been shattered. There is a chance that many of the East Pakistan Muslims who have fled the wrath of the army and the Biharis might return if the guerrilla forces win. That, in turn, would likely trigger still another exodus, that of the 1.5 million Biharis in East Bengal. And under no circumstances is it probable that the millions of Hindus who have fled the bitter Muslim persecution will ever go back.

Possibility of War Between India and Pakistan

The violence has shattered, perhaps forever, the fragile unity of East and West Pakistan. Most observers now feel that the Bangla Desh movement is irreversible. It has also ended, for many years to come, any chance of meaningful political and economic cooperation between India and Pakistan. Joint development of the great river systems of the subcontinent, for example, long a dream of development experts, now seems out of the question. Likewise, the deepening ani-

---

[27] See "India 1971: Strained Democracy," *E.R.R.*, 1971 Vol. I, pp. 128-129.
[28] Quoted by Philip Potter in a dispatch from New Delhi published in the Baltimore *Sun*, May 26, 1971.

mosity appears to rule out any political initiatives designed to reduce Indian-Pakistani tensions over the long haul.[29]

Indeed, the greatest fear now is that the continuing civil war and the mounting refugee problem may provoke a fresh outbreak of hostilities between India and Pakistan. Some Indian army officers are known to be advocates of a "cleansing war." The present circumstances offer any number of pretexts for starting a fight. The continuing inundation of refugees offers India provocation enough to launch a war to stop the flow. Any of the numerous border incidents, which include shelling of Indian villages by West Pakistan troops and flights over Pakistan territory by Indian planes, could trigger hostilities.

Gen. Yahya Khan, the Pakistani leader, was quoted as saying that if India stepped up border activities, such as helping establish a guerrilla base in East Pakistan, he would consider it an attack. In that event, "I shall declare a general war—and let the world take note of it."[30] He said further, according to the same account, that he was not ready to accept a proposal to let United Nations observers into East Pakistan to supervise the return of refugees to their homes.

Perhaps the most serious danger of all lies in the growing possibility that the Awami League moderates may lose control of the Bangla Desh movement and that pro-Peking leftists may take over. "This would raise the possibility— perhaps specter is the better word—of the two Bengals uniting in a new, independent, extremely leftist and probably ungovernable republic," Richard Critchfield wrote. It is doubtful that the Indian army could maintain its current restraint in the face of such a threat from East Bengal. The Naxalite element in West Bengal could probably be counted on to move into open rebellion and guerrilla warfare in such circumstances.

Interests of America, China and the Soviet Union

The present strife, and the possibility of a war between India and Pakistan, provide a major challenge to the interests of the big powers in the Indian subcontinent. China is closely allied with Pakistan, and alone of the major powers

---

[29] See, for example, a proposal for a confederation of India and Pakistan, in which both Kashmir and East Pakistan would enjoy autonomy, in Selig S. Harrison "Nehru's Plan for Peace," *The New Republic*, June 19, 1971, pp. 17-22.

[30] Interview published in the London *Financial Times*, July 19, 1971.

PAKISTAN AT A GLANCE

	West Pakistan	East Pakistan
Area	365,529 square miles	55,126 square miles
Population	65 million (1971 est.)	75 million (1971 est.)
Religion	Islam	Islam, Hindu minority
Major languages	Urdu, English	Bengali, English
Capitals	Islamabad (national administrative capital) Lahore (capital of West Pakistan)	Dacca (national legislative capital and capital of East Pakistan)

has ·pledged renewed aid—including arms—since the outbreak of civil war in East Pakistan. Chinese troops are stationed along the mountainous frontier with India, only a few hundred miles from East Pakistan. In the event of war, the Chinese forces might not move to help Pakistan, but their presence is reason for concern in New Delhi. There is the memory of the 1962 China-India border war in the same mountainous area. A long-range objective of Chinese foreign policy continues to be the establishment of a solid Chinese presence in the Arabian Sea and the Bay of Bengal as a deterrent to American and Soviet naval forces in the Indian Ocean.[31] Intervention in East Pakistan could provide the chance to build such a presence.

Russia, like the United States, faces a dilemma in the present crisis. The Soviets have supplied aid to both Pakistan and India, and they see the Indian subcontinent as a fulcrum in the present struggle to contain China. However, they have been openly critical of West Pakistan's actions in East Pakistan and have called for an end to the bloodshed. A good part of the Soviet stand may be attributed to its close relations with India.

For the United States, the East Pakistan tragedy presents a situation in which this country stands to lose whichever way it turns. Outright condemnation of Pakistan, and support or encouragement for Indian intervention in East Pakistan, would lead to a rupture in relations between Washington and Islamabad. This would certainly mean the loss of important military bases, including the big installation at Peshawar[32] and various radar sites.

---

[31] See "Indian Ocean Policy," *E.R.R.*, 1971 Vol. I, pp. 189-206.
[32] From where Francis Gary Powers took off on his ill-fated U-2 flight in May 1960.

Even without the current crisis, both India and Pakistan face almost insurmountable challenges. The Indian sub-continent has, by any measure, the world's worst problems of overcrowding and population growth. All efforts, public and private, to bring the population explosion under control there have foundered badly. Pakistan's situation is by far the worse, bordering on the desperate.

Demographers projected that East Pakistan's population would double in about 20 years and by the end of the century approach the size of the current U.S. population—207 million as of 1970. The departure of seven million refugees relieves the pressure somewhat, but puts tremendous additional pressure on the neighboring states in India. East Pakistan's overcrowding was displayed to the world when a cyclone roared in from the Bay of Bengal, Nov. 13, 1970, pushing be-fore it a huge tidal wave which inundated hundreds of square miles of the low-lying Ganges delta. Perhaps as many as half a million people perished from drowning and from the disease and famine that followed. Demographically, the loss of half a million people made little difference to East Pakistan. They were replaced by live births in little more than a month.[33]

Such growth renders economic development nearly im-possible under the best of conditions. The maddening pres-sure of too many human beings may help explain the sav-agery of the East Pakistan civil war. It may be, as some gloomy demographers have predicted, that genocide, famine and pestilence are the natural alternatives to population control. If so, East Pakistan provides a horrifying glimpse into man-kind's future.

---

[33] Population Reference Bureau press release. Death estimates varied widely. The bureau used the figure of 500,000. The vice chairman of the League of Red Cross Societies, Kai Warras, told a news conference in Washington, Dec. 7, 1970, that the death toll was about 200,000.

Expatriate Americans

by

Helen B. Shaffer

NEW TRENDS IN AMERICAN EXPATRIATION
Reverse Migration: The Rising Outward Flow
Draft Evaders and Others in Canada, Australia
Return of Jews to Israel and Blacks to Africa
Lure of Life Abroad for Students and Retirees

AMERICAN EMIGRATION: PAST AND PRESENT
Flight of Loyalists During American Revolution
Post-Civil War Exodus Across the Rio Grande
Influence of European Experience on Americans
Attraction of Paris to 'Lost Generation' of 1920s
Little Americas Abroad: Military and Business

PROFITS AND PROBLEMS OF LIVING ABROAD
Executives' Good Life; Culture Shock Problems
Identity Conflict of Jews and Negroes Overseas
Difficulties of Refugees From Military Service
Tax Breaks and Citizenship Rights of Expatriates

1 9 7 0
<u>Nov. 18</u>

EXPATRIATE AMERICANS

OF ALL THE INDICATIONS of unwelcome change in the American way of life, none is quite so blemishing to the nation's self-image as recent reports of citizens quitting their native land to seek a better life elsewhere. Few Americans can be comfortable with the thought that the United States, pre-eminently the land to which other people seek to emigrate, should now be a supplier of people for settlement in other countries.

It's not that many Americans haven't gone abroad to live in the past. Expatriation has, in fact, always been an aspect of the American experience. But for the most part, expatriates have been special people—diplomats, foreign correspondents, artists and writers, employees of American firms with overseas interests. Today there is another special group of emigres—young men evading the draft law and deserters who refuse to serve in Viet Nam.

No one knows precisely how many are in this category: possibly there are 50,000 in Canada, the chief refuge of U.S. military evaders; 500 or so in Sweden; perhaps fewer than 100 in England; and a sprinkling in other parts of the world. They differ from most expatriates in that living abroad for them is involuntary. Sympathizers may call them political refugees, viewing their flight from military service as resistance to political oppression.

Certain other fugitives now living overseas have a similar view of themselves as victims, hounded from their own country. Among the best known are Eldridge Cleaver, the Black Panther leader, and Timothy Leary, high priest of the drug culture. Both face arrest if they return. Cleaver, now living in Algiers, left the United States in November 1968 when his parole was lifted for involvement in an alleged shoot-out with the Oakland, Calif., police. Leary, a former Harvard psychologist, escaped on Sept. 13, 1970, from a California prison where he was serving one to 10 years for possession of marijuana. As last reported, he was seeking a refuge in the Middle East.

For the majority, whose expatriation is voluntary, the stay abroad is often extended but rarely permanent. Many expatriates might be described as cosmopolites, who flit back and forth across oceans and continents: men with international business interests, movie stars, well-known writers, the so-called "jet-setters." Mrs. Aristotle Onassis, the widow of American President John F. Kennedy, is perhaps the most famous American who lives both in the United States and abroad. But even those who lived abroad for most of their adult years, as Gertrude Stein did in an earlier era, rarely lost their sense of being Americans. Few ever relinquished their citizenship.

Reverse Migration: The Rising Outward Flow

What is new and troubling about the latest chapter in the story of American expatriation is evidence that growing numbers of middle-class Americans are pulling up stakes, not for a fling at glamorous living abroad, not to find a refuge from jail or military service, but simply because they have decided that life would be preferable for them if they established a new home in another country. No one is certain how many Americans feel this way but, according to informed opinion, as many as 40,000 are leaving this year to settle down in other English-speaking countries.[1] Consular offices of countries favored by American emigres report a distinct rise in the number of inquiries about permanent settlement.

When S. J. Perelman, the humorist, announced that he, at age 66, was leaving the United States to spend the rest of his days in England, he did not seem to be so much of an odd case as an exemplar of a trend.[2] His reasons for leaving constituted a now-familiar bill of particulars against living in the United States, especially in the big cities. He mentioned pollution, confusion, traffic, violence, crime, bad manners, and the political climate. Like Henry James a century earlier, Perelman found life in the United Kingdom to be more civilized than at home. In England, he will be among 74,000 other Americans now living in that country.[3]

Many writers, past and present, have found it convenient, cheaper and more pleasant to do their writing abroad. The

---

[1] However, immigration continues to exceed emigration significantly. Immigration authorities report 359,000 were admitted to the United States on a permanent basis in fiscal year 1969.

[2] Perelman sailed from New York on Oct. 21, 1970, after selling his 91-acre farm and household possessions in Bucks County, Pa.

[3] U.S. Department of State, *Reports and Statistics,* Dec. 31, 1969.

EMIGRATION FROM U.S. TO CANADA

1946-55 annual average	9,090	1967	19,038
1956-66 annual average	13,433	1968	20,422
		1969	22,785

SOURCE: Canadian Embassy in Washington.

---

newer development in expatriation, however, is typified by an Indiana family whose departure for Vancouver was the subject of a picture story in *Life,* July 17, 1970. This middle-aged couple and their 10 children were described as a "prosperous, well-established family, with old roots in Indiana." Among reasons the 46-year-old head of the family gave for leaving was that he felt "society closing in," while life in British Columbia was happily like "stepping back a generation or so" into the life style of the American past. There has always been a certain drift of American citizens into Canada. Of all foreign nations, it has the largest complement of U.S. nationals. Official Canadian statistics show that more than 250,-000 Americans crossed the border as immigrants in 1946-69.

Draft Evaders and Others in Canada, Australia

American youths seeking to evade the draft account for part of the increase but not as much as is popularly assumed. Of the 22,785 Americans listed as having migrated to Canada during 1969, only 2,175 were males in the prime draft years of 20 to 24. Of course, many draft evaders did not enter Canada as immigrants. It is not known how many went in as visitors and then overstayed the terms of their visit. Estimates of the actual number of young Americans living in Canada because they don't want to serve in the U.S. armed forces range from 5,000 to 50,000.[4]

Of the 22,785 Americans who went to Canada during 1969 as immigrants, more than one-half (11,609) were women; 1,142 were in retirement years (65 and older), 6,472 were dependent children. Because of the careful screening by Canadian immigration authorities, family breadwinners (10,220 of the total) constituted an unusually well-educated and skilled group. The largest number of Americans in Canada settle in Ontario, but others scatter over all the provinces.[5]

---

[4] On his return from meetings with draft-age Americans in Canada early in 1970, Rep. Edward I. Koch (D N.Y.), an advocate of amnesty for those who evade the draft as an act of conscience, put the figure at 50,000.—House speech, Jan. 21, 1970.

[5] Destinations of U.S. immigrants to Canada during 1969: 9,400 Ontario; 5,675 British Columbia; 2,649 Quebec; 2,359 Alberta; 739 Nova Scotia; 654 Manitoba; 470 Saskatchewan; 463 New Brunswick; 222 Newfoundland; 101 Prince Edward Island; and 56 Northwest Territories and Yukon.

Australia has attracted American settlers ever since large numbers of American troops were stationed there during World War II. Australia welcomes immigrants, especially those from English-speaking countries and those with the kind of skills American emigres are likely to possess. Some 20,000 Americans are reported, unofficially, to have settled permanently in Australia over the past decade. The Australian government recently disclosed that its offices in the United States were handling 1,200 inquiries a day on migration to that country, 14 per cent more than a year earlier.

Approximately 3,400 Americans left to settle in Australia during the year that ended June 30, 1969, and the number is believed to have risen since then. The Australian Minister for Immigration has predicted an annual intake from the United States of at least 10,000 within a few years. Australia does not advertise for American immigrants, but it is warmly responsive to inquiries and provides financial assistance to approved immigrants to help pay their travel expenses.

A Melbourne editor who asked a group of American immigrants why they had come received both negative and positive responses. They had come to rescue their children from the danger of street crime, to get away from "the rat race" and from jammed freeways and crowded beaches, or else they had come because the people in Australia were friendlier, the pace was slower, land for farming and ranching was cheaper, and the air cleaner.[6] A survey by the Australian Department of Immigration in 1969 summarized the results as follows: 33 per cent had come because they wanted adventure, 16 per cent to escape the fast pace and tensions at home, 13 per cent because of good business and employment opportunities, 10 per cent because of marriage to an Australian, and 8 per cent because they had been impressed with the country during a previous visit. These reports do not show the number of Americans who changed their minds after a spell of expatriation and returned home.

Return of Jews to Israel and Blacks to Africa

American Jews in Israel constitute another special migration group that has grown in recent years. Until the Six Day War in 1967, Americans had contributed scarcely more than one per cent of the total immigration flow to that country. Israeli records show that 600 to 1,200 Americans a year set-

---

[6] Harry Gordon (editor of the *Melbourne Sun*), "Americans Are Emigrating to Australia," *The New York Times Magazine*, May 17, 1970, p. 75.

tled in Israel between the founding of the nation in 1948 and 1967. But in the latter year the number doubled to 2,100, rose to 4,600 in 1968, exceeded 6,000 in 1969, and is still rising. Israeli official records for the first nine months of 1970 show that 6,129 American settlers arrived, accounting for 20 per cent of the country's immigration for that period. According to estimates made by the Jewish Agency in October 1970, only 5 to 6 per cent of the Americans who came to settle since the 1967 war had returned—far fewer than before the war.[7]

A change in the background of the American Jewish migrants has been observed. Those who went to Israel and stayed in earlier years were either foreign-born or otherwise close to old world traditions. Premier Golda Meir of Israel is of that group. Born in Russia, she came as a child to the United States in 1906 and then migrated to Israel as a young wife in 1921. The newer crop includes many American Jews who are two to four generations removed from their immigrant forbears. The majority today are in the middle thirties and possess a high level of skills.

They are drawn by varying degrees of commitment to the Israeli cause. Some say they want to raise their children in a totally Jewish community, safe from encounters with anti-Semitism. Revulsion against the trials of life in urban America, especially black-Jewish tensions in the inner city, apparently has played some part in the exodus. New arrivals include professors sick of campus unrest and technicians who lost their jobs in the U.S. space program and expect to work in Israel's budding aircraft production industry.

A small but significant number of American Negroes have become expatriates—significant because the expatriate experience of the few has been absorbed, through the work of black writers, into the consciousness of the mass of American Negroes. Long before the present era of black awakening in America, frustration and despair over race prejudice drove many blacks to seek a better life abroad. Europe, especially Paris, has always been a favored destination. Some 1,500 Afro-Americans were said to be living in Paris in the late 1960s.[8] Since the founding of independent nations in Africa, the migration has been extended to those countries.

---

[7] Figures cited in a dispatch from Tel Aviv printed in *The New York Times,* Oct. 18, 1970. Harold Robert Isaacs reported in his book *American Jews in Israel* (1966) that of every six Americans who went to Israel in the years after independence, five returned to the United States.

[8] Ishbel Ross, *The Expatriates* (1970), p. 292.

Students form a special group of expatriates. The latest annual count by the Institute of International Education showed that 25,000 American were studying abroad in 1969, three times as many as 15 years earlier. In addition, more than 5,000 American scholars and college faculty members were pursuing their work overseas—a quadrupling of the earlier year's total. However, the count on students was "appreciably less than complete," so the actual total is higher than 25,000.[9] In addition, there are American students abroad who are not enrolled in foreign schools. Many of these students take a break from their studies to wander over Europe, and often into Asia and Africa. Some acquire a taste for the roving life and remain overseas for an extended period.

Retired Americans account for a growing number of expatriates. While not everyone who expresses a wish to retire in some out-of-the-way foreign place acts on that desire, there are many signs of Americans buying property abroad for vacation-retirement home sites. Social Security figures give some indication of the extent of Americans living abroad in retirement. As of March 1970, 220,205 recipients of benefits under the Social Security system were living abroad. Of these, 109,960 were retired workers, 4,431 disabled workers, and 105,814 dependents or survivors of the insured. Not all were American citizens, for benefits are based on the insured person's work history regardless of nationality. Some were immigrants to the United States who never became citizens; some are foreign wives and widows of American workers. Checks from the Social Security Administration go out to beneficiaries living in 60 or more countries. Most of them go to Canada, Italy and Greece, but Mexico is coming increasingly to the fore.[10]

Major components of the expatriate population are officials and employees of the U.S. government and international agencies, and American businessmen with foreign interests. Some 46,000 Americans work for the government abroad, chiefly for the Departments of State, Defense, Commerce, and Agriculture. Their dependents, combined with those of American military personnel stationed abroad, raise the total by nearly 420,000. Yet, 855,000 Americans who live abroad have no employment connections with the U.S.

---

[9] Institute of International Education, *Open Doors 1970: Report on International Education* (September 1970), pp. 5, 16-17. The largest numbers of American students overseas were in Canada, Mexico, United Kingdom, West Germany, and France, in that order.

[10] *Social Security Bulletin*, September 1970, p. 68, and February 1969, pp. 29-40.

U.S. CITIZENS IN RESIDENCE ABROAD

	U.S. government employees	Dependents of U.S. employees*	Other residents	Total
Total in 133 Countries	46,118	418,759	854,875	1,319,752
West Germany	6,826	162,550	50,676	220,052
Canada	412	5,691	172,134	178,237
Mexico	325	740	86,867	87,932
Britain	952	34,270	38,620	73,842
Japan	4,005	45,638	17,271	66,914
Italy	743	14,249	51,850	66,842
Philippines	1,734	31,222	26,771	59,727
Spain	616	14,543	20,093	35,252
Greece	272	4,543	20,835	25,650
Bahamas	23	190	24,000	24,213
France	488	956	20,333	21,777
Brazil	952	1,386	17,629	19,967
Switzerland	131	199	19,400	19,730
Australia	104	507	17,625	18,236
Israel	59	148	15,700	15,907
Venezuela	488	478	13,490	14,456
Belgium	462	2,987	10,500	13,949
Turkey	686	10,463	2,509	13,658
Colombia	875	897	10,106	11,878
Netherlands	216	2,818	7,753	10,787
Peru	144	406	10,100	10,650
Thailand	1,608	5,749	3,204	10,561
Bermuda	272	2,347	7,500	10,119

*Includes military dependents but not servicemen.
SOURCE: Department of State.

government. Continuing expansion of American business operations is encouraging this form of expatriation.[11]

Members of the armed services make up the largest single group of Americans abroad—1,032,620 as of June 30, 1970. It may not be strictly correct to call military personnel expatriates. But there is little question that military duty overseas has encouraged the growth of expatriation. Travelers everywhere have run into ex-GIs who have found some corner of the world to their liking and have settled down there, sometimes with a foreign wife.

A group of expatriates whose tradition goes far back in American history are the missionaries. According to the 1970 *Yearbook of American Churches,* 33,270 Protestant and 9,655 Catholic Americans were serving in overseas missions —an increase since 1968 of 22 per cent for the Protestants and 40 per cent for the Catholics.

[11] See "Where and How U.S. Companies Are Moving and Expanding in Overseas Markets," *Business Abroad,* May 1970, p. 14.

American Emigration: Past and Present

MOST AMERICAN EXPATRIATES have lived abroad by choice. Many, however, would have stayed home if it had not been for their fear of the consequences. In the course of American history there have been three waves of involuntary expatriation in this sense. Each was prompted by a war: the American Revolution, the Civil War, and the present war in Viet Nam.

It is estimated that 100,000 Americans loyal to the British Crown were exiled by the Revolution.[12] The population of the 13 colonies, including slaves, was about 2.5 million at that time. Some 40,000 Loyalists—Tories to their enemies—ended up in Canada, chiefly in the sparsely settled Maritime Provinces. Others became the first English-speaking population in what became the Province of Ontario.

Many Loyalists in the South fled with their slaves to the Floridas, when in British hands, only to find it wise to flee again when the territory passed back to Spain in 1781. Some eventually returned to the United States, but thousands moved on to the Bahama Islands and Jamaica, while lesser numbers joined other emigres in Nova Scotia and England. The mother country was naturally a favored destination. By the end of the Revolutionary War there were some 5,000 to 6,000 American refugees in England. Many left later for other parts of the British Empire, or to return to the states.

The exodus was not a single mass movement but a series of departures affected by the course of events. It began during the disorders preceding the Revolution, which some of the solid citizens viewed as a portent of anarchy. John Singleton Copley, the painter, took his family to England after witnessing a Boston mob in action in 1774; he was then 36 and he never returned.[13] Thousands left when the British evacuated Georgia and South Carolina. After the Battle of Yorktown, approximately 80,000 left the country with the British garrisons "to which they had flocked for protection."[14]

---

[12] Wallace Brown, *The Good Americans* (1969), p. 227.

[13] Copley would probably have gone to England, as other artists had, to polish up his skills in any event, but the mob action apparently clinched his decision to move at that time.

[14] Samuel Eliot Morison, *The Oxford History of the American People* (1965), p. 286.

Contemporary records—letters, diaries, claims reports, petitions—reveal many cases of extreme hardship among Loyalist refugees. Those in England found conditions unexpectedly difficult. Prices were higher, class distinctions sharper, poverty more prevalent, and job opportunities scarcer. "The general result of exile in Britain was much despondency and grief... and some insanity and suicide."[15] Many who went to Canada were unfit for the wilderness conditions they found there. The British government gave aid—land for settlers in undeveloped territories, subsistence payments to the needy, pensions to former royalist officers, and compensation for properties lost due to loyalty to the Crown. But this help was often insufficient to assuage refugee bitterness at what they considered ingratitude for their sacrifice.

Loyalist departures from the 13 colonies were of great importance to the development of Canada. "The loss to the United States was the British Empire's gain," American historian Samuel Eliot Morison has written. "Most of the exiles settled in New Brunswick, Nova Scotia, or Ontario, where they became leaders in their communities and helped to keep them loyal to England." The majority of the Loyalists, however, did not leave their homes. And unless they were active supporters of the Crown, they suffered little for their views. All 13 of the new states adopted punitive legislation against active Loyalists and much Loyalist property was confiscated or looted during the owners' absence. But most of these measures were withdrawn after the war. While some exiles who returned were mistreated, often at the hands of vigilantes, most were not and some went on to successful careers. Among returning Loyalists was a future mayor of New York, Cadwalader Colder.

Post-Civil War Exodus Across Rio Grande

The Civil War gave rise to another exodus. "Thousands deserted a prostrate South to go to Mexico, to journey up the Orinoco, to live on the Venezuela llanos, to cut hardwood in Brazil....Former governors, generals, colonels, congressmen, judges and mayors of small and large towns all over the South joined carpenters, blacksmiths, coopers, farmers and peddlers determined to live outside the damnable Yankee dominion."[16] Some left because they could not bear defeat or else feared retribution from the victors. Many Confederate soldiers, refusing to surrender, retreated into Mexico and then scattered

---

[15] Wallace Brown, *The Good Americans* (1969), p. 156.
[16] Andrew F. Rolle, *The Lost Cause: The Confederate Exodus to Mexico* (1965), pp. ix, 9-10.

—to Canada, Brazil, Cuba, Honduras, Jamaica, Venezuela, Egypt, and Japan.[17]

Many Southerners, finding postwar conditions abominable, hearkened to naive schemes for transplanting the Old Confederacy to new sites in Latin America. Within three to four years of the close of the Civil War, some 8,000 to 10,000 Southerners had left to seek new homes in Mexico and South America.[18] The going was rough and many returned to the United States or drifted to other parts of the world. A number of Charleston Huguenots, after generations in America, returned to France "to grope their way back to the heart of the old French culture."[19]

Of all Civil War emigres, the most successful was probably Judah P. Benjamin, a member of Jefferson Davis's Cabinet. Benjamin made his way to Cuba, then England, where he became a renowned barrister and Queen's counsel. Several southern generals found a warm welcome for their military skills in Egypt, among them Maj. Gen. William W. Loring who commanded an Egyptian army division, headed an expedition to Abyssinia, and received a title of Pasha.

Less fortunate were those who subscribed to the dream of Matthew Fontaine Maury, the famous hydrographer, of founding a New Virginia in Mexico. Emperor Maximilian's offer of free land was attractive, but the would-be settlers ran into ownership disputes, bad weather, dysentery, and bandit raids. Maury himself left Mexico in 1866, never to return. The victory of the rebel leader Juarez and the execution of Maximilian in 1867 put an end to the project. Hardly more successful were those who took up the land offers for sugar planters in Brazil and cotton growers in Venezuela in the 1865-70 period.[20] Approximately 4,000 Southerners settled in Brazil but few stayed long.

A much different, and in many ways more significant, form of American expatriation was the voluntary exile of artists, writers, scholars and others drawn to the great cultural centers

---

[17] Confederate General Jo Shelby never surrendered. He led remnants of his cavalry unit, the Iron Brigade, into Mexico where he offered to establish a foreign legion of ex-Confederate soldiers. Emperor Maximilian turned down his offer.

[18] Lawrence F. Hill, *The Confederate Exodus to Latin America* (1936), p. 5.

[19] Van Wyck Brooks, *New England: Indian Summer* (1940), p. 140.

[20] Promoters of the Venezuela project sought to establish "a distinctive state government...purely southern in all its characteristics," but the undertaking was doomed by insufficient capital and inadequate technical knowledge. Virtually all of the several hundred emigres returned, disappointed.—Alfred Jackson Hanna and Kathryn Abbey Hanna, *Confederate Exiles in Venezuela* (1960)

of Europe. Few knew or cared much about the tribulations of war refugees. But the European experience of a relatively few members of the nation's elite seeped into the consciousness of millions of American stay-at-homes. Of central importance, they sustained the new nation's connection with its cultural roots in Europe during the early years of independence. They became the medium through which European modes continued to influence American taste in art, literature, education, music, dress, decor, and manners.

Influence of European Experience on Americans

Americans abroad also did much to boost the confidence of the young nation in the worth of its own culture, for they were living proof to cultivated Europeans that all Americans were not barbarians and that the new world could produce worthy practitioners in arts and letters. The expatriates generated debates on the relative merits of the two civilizations—of the old world and the new—that compelled Americans to justify the home product for its freshness and vitality as opposed to the refined but decadent charms of Europe. At the same time they quickened a passion for European travel among prospering Americans that contributed an element of cosmopolitanism to their homeland.

The expatriation movement also proved that gifted Americans could live abroad for extended periods of time without losing their American identity—that, contrary to the current slogan, they *could* leave America and still love it. There are many examples of this, from Benjamin Franklin to expatriates of today. Benjamin West, the Pennsylvania-born painter who arrived in England in 1763 at the age of 25 and remained until his death in 1820, never lost his sentiment for his native land.

He loyally turned down a knighthood and he taught many of the best of America's younger painters in the belief that leadership in the arts would pass to America. Among the American painters who studied with him were Copley, Gilbert Stuart, Thomas Sully, Matthew Pratt, John Trumbull, Charles Wilson Peale, and Samuel F. B. Morse. Peale founded the first art school in the United States and Morse became the new nation's first professor of art, at New York University.

Some of the most American of writers in the early years of nationhood knew and enjoyed the expatriate experience. Washington Irving lived or traveled in Europe for 17 years before coming home in 1832. He returned 10 years later for a four-year stint as Minister to Spain. Irving frequently reassured friends and family that, though fascinated by Europe, he had not lost his love of America. It was at his insistence that he was relieved of his foreign post in 1846 and he contentedly spent the remaining 13 years of his life at his home near Tarrytown, N.Y. James Fenimore Cooper remained an ardent patriot throughout the years (1822-26) he lived abroad with his family, though he was accused of having been unduly influenced by the prejudices of Europe's aristocracy.

The pull of Europe on the sons of the American gentry was inevitable, for there were no schools in the United States of the caliber of Oxford in England and Gottingen in Germany. A number of 19th century Americans who studied in Europe later contributed importantly to the shaping of American education and scholarship. Their European stay included not only years of formal study, but extensive travel and association with foreign intellectual leaders. Many were received at the great salons.

These men included George Ticknor (1791-1871), Edward Everett (1794-1865), Joseph Cogswell (1786-1871), George Bancroft (1800-1891), and Charles Eliot Norton (1827-1908). Everett, a Greek scholar and teacher of Emerson at Harvard, served five terms in Congress. Ticknor, a long-time Harvard scholar, originated the departmental system in higher education. Cogswell, an intimate of Goethe, was a major builder of the Harvard and the New York City libraries. Norton became one of Harvard's great teachers and educational innovators. Bancroft wrote the first comprehensive and scholarly history of the United States.

Expatriation greatly increased and took several new turns in the latter part of the 19th century. This was the Gilded Age when new fortunes were made almost overnight, creating a new leisured class that, along with its less affluent imitators, felt a craving for "the finer things of life." A spell of living abroad became fashionable, for Europe was the home not only of great art and music, but of an elegant society that had no counterpart in the United States.

Many Americans who had no claim to esthetic or intellectual leadership flocked to Europe to do the rounds of artistic and historical monuments and, they hoped, to become part of a glamorous social circle. Some of the wealthiest Americans became collectors, draining the art treasure of Europe and ultimately enriching the public museums of the United States. Some became patrons of living artists. Others sought titled husbands for their daughters.

American expatriates of this period were models for the novels of Henry James, who is described by one literary critic as the expatriate writer who "converted the trans-Atlantic relation into a subject of major fiction."[21] James was one of a number of well-born and sensitive young men of his day who were repelled by the new prominence of raw commercialism and political opportunism. He was irresistibly drawn to the shelter of upper-class English society.

Mrs. Edith Wharton, another highly successful American novelist who spent most of her life abroad yet never cut herself off from America, wrote of James, a close friend: "The truth is that he belonged irrevocably to the old America out of which I also came and of which—almost—it might paradoxically be said that to follow up its traces one has to come to Europe.[22] By the early 20th century, an international community of writers, artists, patrons and their associates had come into being, in which American expatriates figured as prominently as Europeans. Among them were poets Ezra Pound and T.S. Eliot, writer and art-patron Gertrude Stein, dancer Isadora Duncan, and painters Mary Cassatt, John Singer Sargent and James Whistler.

Attraction of Paris to 'Lost Generation' of 1920s

The expatriate movement of the 1920s stands apart from all the others. For the first time those who chose to live abroad were not only the favored few of America's wealthy, social or intellectual elite, but thousands from the mass of middle America. Those who set the tone of the movement were the young writers and artists, usually impecunious, and their friends, some not so impecunious, who lived in Bohemian style on the Left Bank in Paris. These were the expatriates who gloried in the myth of the "lost generation," romanticizing their alienation from their American past. Among them were F. Scott Fitzgerald,[23] Ernest Hemingway, E. E. Cummings, Kay Boyle, Hart Crane, Louis Bromfield, Ford Madox Ford, Dashiell Hammett, Julian Green, Matthew Josephson, Alfred Kreymborg, Sidney Howard, Glenwood Westcott, and many others. Young painters, composers, dancers, and musicians were also part of the unprecedented concentration of American talent in Paris.

---

[21] Philip Rahv, *Discovery of Europe: The Story of the American Experience in the Old World* (1947), p. 269. See also Ernest Earnest, *Expatriates and Patriots: American Artists, Scholars, and Writers in Europe* (1968).
[22] Quoted by Ishbel Ross in *The Expatriates* (1970), p. 204.
[23] Fitzgerald was one of the few who came to Paris *after* making a lot of money from his writing—in this case publication of his first and sensationally successful novel, *This Side of Paradise* (1920).

These gifted Americans went to Europe not so much for pilgrimages to a romantic past as to breathe the freer air of the Paris boulevards—and take advantage of the favorable currency exchange. Though highly individualistic, they created a kind of community of free spirits, given to madcap adventures and unfettered artistic expression. In their gaiety, their cynicism, and their irresponsibility about practical matters, they acted out their scorn of what they saw as the provincialism, the puritanism, and the commercialism of post-World War I America.

"Paris was a great machine for stimulating the nerves and sharpening the senses," Malcolm Cowley wrote in a nostalgic remembrance of those years. Yet they were a restless bunch. "In those days, young American writers were drifting everywhere in western and middle Europe; they waved to each other from the windows of passing trains."[24] But Paris was the hub to which they always returned. Avant garde movements flourished in this atmosphere and many little magazines, some of them collectors' items today, were put together for small sums to publish and reproduce the new-style work.

Not all expatriates were artists and writers, but they were the ones who gave the movement glamor and conveyed its essence to a fascinated population back home. In the Prohibition Era, Europe became the playground of prospering middle-class Americans. Many American entertainers won success in the night spots of Europe. Black Americans in particular found not only social acceptance but professional opportunities that were closed to them at home. Josephine Baker, who became the darling of Paris as star of the *Folies Bergere,* never returned to the United States to live.

The stock market crash of 1929 put an end to the fun and games in Paris and most of the expatriate crowd came home. The glamorous expatriate of the 1930s was not the poet or the painter but the foreign correspondent—the John Gunthers, Vincent Sheeans, Dorothy Thompsons—covering the unfolding of new dictatorships and approaching war. After World War II, a new flow of Americans to foreign lands took place, but it was of a different character, reflecting the new global concerns of the United States. Foreign aid specialists, employees of international agencies, exchange students and scholars, technicians, businessmen and the

---

[24] Malcolm Cowley, *Exile's Return* (1963 edition), p. 135.

vast number of workers needed to man the facilities for American bases—from school teachers to commissary clerks —made up a new expatriate mix.

> As families were able to join army men stationed abroad and thousands of government officials...took off for Europe, small American communities grew up whose "Stateside" standards of living cut them off almost completely from the country in which they were situated....These unwilling residents transferred suburbia across the Atlantic—its schools, churches, supermarkets, moving pictures, theaters, and country clubs.[25]

Artists and writers still go abroad to pursue their craft, but the little Bohemias where expatriates can subsist on a song are fast disappearing. The popular image of the expatriate writer today is not the destitute Bohemian of the 1920s but the established writer, whose living style is comparable to that of any other successful American resident abroad.

Profits and Problems of Living Abroad

THOUGH LIVING ABROAD appeals to many Americans, the actuality often proves much less glowing than the dream. By and large the happiest expatriates are those with an interesting job or independent means and the knowledge that they can pack up and go home whenever they want to. Corporation executives abroad appear to be a relatively satisfied lot, especially when stationed in one of the great cities of western Europe. But like the GI's wife on an overseas base, they live in a world not too different from the one they left behind.

"Life for the American executive transferred abroad rarely is as completely foreign as the advice and literature on such a transfer leads him to believe it will be," *Dun's* reported. "...The American is good at transplanting his home-grown life style."[26] A study of Americans abroad, made a decade ago but still a basic reference, observed that "the American businessman is usually not lonely for other Americans when he lives abroad." Most business executives had little social contact with either foreign nationals or with other groups of expatriate Americans. They tend "to cluster into groups con-

---

[25] Foster Rhea Dulles, "A Historical View of Americans Abroad," *The Annals of the American Academy of Political and Social Science,* November 1966, p. 18.

[26] "An Executive Abroad," *Dun's,* August 1970, p. 48.

U.S. CITIZENS IN RESIDENCE ABROAD

1900	91,219	1940	118,933
1910	55,608	1950	481,545
1920	117,238	1960	1,374,421
1930	89,453	1970	2,400,000

*Figures include military personnel.

---

sisting of Americans of similar income, language, background, social interests and drinking habits."[27]

Living in London is so agreeable to most of the 5,000 American executives there, *Business Week* reported May 30, 1970, that it is no wonder many of them become Anglophiles. The taxis are roomier, good restaurants and golf club memberships are less expensive, and good college preparatory schools are available for their children. Even in places less like home than London, the corporation executive will usually find much that is familiar and comfortable. There are American chambers of commerce in 31 countries on five continents.

Technical and management personnel assigned by government or business firms to underdeveloped or remote areas have a harder time. They may suffer not only culture shock but "role shock," which is defined as "the frustrations and stresses associated with such discrepancies as between what a technical assistant views as the ideal role for himself and what he...finds the actual role to be abroad."[28] On the other hand, many foreign aid technicians like their overseas assignments because they can gain greater responsibility and more prestige than in the same work at home.

Wives of overseas personnel usually have a harder time adjusting to life abroad and this has proved as true for the wife of a corporation executive in London as for the wife of a foreign aid official in a backwater land. For it is the wife who has to handle the day-by-day problems of establishing and running a household and maintaining family hygienic standards. She deals with a far greater variety of individuals than her husband, who tends to associate only with those nationals who are involved in his work. While the prospect of having a household staff may appeal to the servant-less

---

[27] Harlan Cleveland, Gerard J. Mangone, John Clarke Adams, *The Overseas Americans* (1960), p. 117.

[28] Francis C. Byrnes, "Role Shock: An Occupational Hazard of American Technical Assistants Abroad," *The Annals of the American Academy of Political and Social Science*, November 1966, p. 96.

American housewife, many women who have had the overseas experience gladly go back to the conveniences of electrical appliances and supermarkets, and to privacy and independence in their household.

Many Americans think they can live abroad more cheaply than at home. This may be true, but only if they "go native"—that is, truly live in the manner of the local population. State Department studies of retail prices in 153 cities around the world show a relatively high cost of living in most places if the American attempts "to transplant, to the extent permitted by local conditions, an American pattern of living to the foreign city."[29]

Identity Conflict of Jews and Blacks Overseas

Even when conditions are most favorable to ready adaptation, as among Jews in Israel, there are problems. For one thing, living in Israel means a much more Spartan existence: housing is in short supply, beef is scarce, taxes are high, and wages are lower than in the United States. And there is, of course, an almost constant state of war or near-war. But the problem goes deeper than that. No matter how much they are committed to the Israeli cause, relatively few of the migrants from the United States give up their American citizenship. The door to their return therefore remains open, an important psychological consideration and one which sets them apart from immigrants who fled persecution and have no choice but to stay in Israel.

Interviews with 50 American settlers or would-be settlers in Israel several years before the 1967 war showed that many were "caught in a complicated set of push-and-pull pressures which had prevented them—in some cases for many years— from resolving their problem of national identity." "They were pulled strongly enough by Israel to cause them to migrate....But most of them clung strongly enough to America to find it impossible to become Israelis in the full sense of an unqualified acceptance of Israeli nationality."[30] Whether the more recent emigres will feel as much push-pull remains to be seen.

---

[29] On the basis of these studies, which exclude the costs of shelter and education, the Department has developed "Indexes of Living Costs" for each city, using Washington, D.C., as a base of 100. In 97 of the 153 cities, the index exceeded 100. Among them were Paris, 145; Vienna, 113; Rome, 122; Tel Aviv, 110; Stockholm, 130; London, 108; and Geneva, 116.

[30] Harold Robert Isaacs, *American Jews in Israel* (1966), p. 6.

A somewhat similar experience has been reported among black Americans living abroad, including those who have gone to Africa. Many of the latter found to their surprise that the Africans looked on them primarily as Americans, hence alien. A young American Negro woman who was sent to Tanzania as a school teacher and married there told an interviewer: "I realized very early in the game that...I'd never be anything but 'that American Negro who married so-and-so.' I'd never want to be anything else."

The black writer, James Baldwin, who spends much of his time abroad, may have struck a common note when he told the same interviewer, in Istanbul: "I am not now, and never will become...by my own desire—an expatriate. For better or for worse, my ties with my country are too deep, and my concern is too great. But I am an American artist, and I know exactly what Nathaniel Hawthorne meant when he wrote, from England, around 1861, that 'the United States may be fit for many excellent purposes, but they are not fit to live in.' Nearly all American artists have felt this...but we have all—usually anyway—gone home."[31]

Eldridge Cleaver, the Black Panther fugitive, told another interviewer recently at his headquarters in Algiers: "Of course, it's frustrating to live in exile. I'd much prefer to be there [in the United States]....All I do is toward the idea of going back, but not to surrender myself." An immediate project, he said, is to recruit black servicemen who have deserted and are in Europe into a revolutionary force.[32] The Black Panthers are one of a dozen so-called "liberation movements" which are recognized and given assistance by the Algerian government.

Difficulties of Refugees From Military Service

Among all expatriates, beyond doubt draft evaders and deserters have the hardest time of all. Recent reports indicate that the hospitality of the two countries which have been most receptive to the runaways—Canada and Sweden—is beginning to wear thin. So far, Sweden has granted them "humanitarian asylum" and provided food, housing allowances and medical care under the nation's welfare system. Nevertheless, the language barrier, the difficulty of finding

---

[31] Quoted by Ernest Dunbar in *The Black Expatriates: A Study of American Negroes in Exile* (1968).

[32] Sanche de Gramont, "Our Other Man in Algiers," *The New York Times Magazine,* Nov. 1, 1970, pp. 31, 112.

a job, the immaturity of many of the refugees, even the climate with its long winter nights, have made the experience anything but pleasant. About a dozen of these Americans were reported recently to be in prison for selling drugs. For most of them, the main problem is loneliness and a feeling of being cut off from home. According to American news dispatches from Stockholm, several have suffered nervous breakdowns and some have attempted to commit suicide. Approximately 50 have returned to the United States to face prison sentences.

The few deserters and draft evaders in England and the many in Canada face similar problems. Rising unemployment has made it difficult for the Americans to find work, especially if they arrive, as many do, with few skills. American companies will not hire them and employment by British or Canadian firms is strictly hemmed in by government restrictions. Aliens have two hurdles to overcome before they can begin to consider working for a living in most developed countries. First they must be admitted with the status of resident or immigrant and then they must successfully apply for a work permit. Canada is more hospitable to immigration than England, but both countries take steps to keep out individuals who are likely to become an economic burden.

Many of these young men are afraid to apply for any form of official status lest they lose their precarious haven. They, therefore, live in a kind of limbo, a waiting-out of the time until they can return home. Some have gotten into trouble. A spokesman for the Toronto Anti-Draft Program testified recently that the group had frequently been called on to put up bail for exiles charged with vagrancy, drug possession, and shoplifting. Columnist Stewart Alsop recently described his investigation of the situation of draft evaders and deserters in Canada as a "shattering and saddening...experience."[33]

Tax Breaks and Citizenship Rights of Expatriates

Despite the problems, many Americans still hanker for at least a taste of living abroad. For the top layer of business executives, for successful writers, for movie stars and the leisured class with independent income, living abroad can be a personal delight and a financial boon. Unless they draw their pay from the U.S. government, American expatriates may be forgiven taxation on a large part of their income.

---

[33] *Newsweek*, July 20, 1970, p. 88, and July 27, 1970, p. 80.

The Internal Revenue Service recognizes two categories of American expatriates for tax purposes: bona fide residents and those with a "physical presence in a foreign country." Bona fide residents may exclude from tax income up to $20,000 of earned income for a full tax year, or $25,000 a year if they have been a bona fide resident for an uninterrupted period of three years. Those merely "physically present" are allowed an exemption up to $20,000 a year if they have been in a foreign country for at least 510 days during any period of 18 consecutive months.

In both cases the exempt income must have been earned for services performed while abroad. This rule would cover an author who writes a book while living abroad or an actor who makes a movie overseas. The test of bona fide residence is not too precise and many claims are decided on a case basis by the Internal Revenue Service. In general, the bona fide resident is one who has set up permanent quarters for himself and family and settles down in the community, even if he ultimately intends to return to the United States. The key determinant is whether there is "an air of stability" about the stay abroad.[34]

There are virtually no official U.S. barriers to expatriation. The citizenship of an American living abroad is secure so long as he does not formally renounce it or take an oath of allegiance to another country. Enactments of Congress providing for withdrawal of citizenship for various acts while living abroad, such as voting in foreign elections, have been nullified by the court determinations in recent years. The courts have removed any distinctions between naturalized and native-born citizens in regard to the security of their citizenship during expatriation. By and large, the citizen who commits no act that would cause the government to refuse to renew his passport can live abroad indefinitely with no fear of losing his citizenship rights.

The odds are that more and more Americans will choose to live abroad, whether voluntarily or involuntarily. And as the world shrinks and differences between the living habits of nations diminish, the expatriate will become less of an odd figure in his host country and at home.

---

[34] U.S. Internal Revenue Service, *Tax Guide For U.S. Citizens Abroad* (Revised edition, October 1969).

GLOBAL POLLUTION

by

Richard C. Schroeder

1971
Dec. 1

GLOBAL POLLUTION

THE WORLD IS AWAKENING to a sense of crisis about the state of the environment. Dozens of countries, including the United States, have taken steps to control pollution. Scores of national and international meetings have examined in detail the deterioration of the environment. International agencies, ranging from the North Atlantic Treaty Organization to the United Nations Economic Commission for Asia and the Far East, from the Organization of American States to the World Bank, have instituted environmental programs. "The environment," remarks Barry Commoner, one of America's leading ecologists, "has just been rediscovered by the people who live in it."[1]

The rediscovery will culminate next year in "one of the boldest adventures in international cooperation ever attempted"[2]—the United Nations Conference on the Human Environment. In Stockholm, Sweden, for 12 days from June 5 to 16, representatives of some 131 countries and dozens of international organizations will gather to map a worldwide assault on the problems of pollution and depletion of the Earth's resources.

It will be an unprecedented and, in many ways, a very difficult conference. Developing nations are suspicious that concern about pollution may hinder efforts to promote economic growth. And noticeably missing from the agenda is any discussion of the mounting burden of world population growth. From the conference may come some mechanism to monitor what is happening to the Earth's environment, and some means to coordinate anti-pollution efforts both within and outside the U.N. To many officials, the conference represents a first step in the direction of rescuing the world from pollution. It is, at any rate, solid evidence that the environmental movement is not—as was once predicted—a passing fad.[3]

---

[1] Barry Commoner, *The Closing Circle* (1971), p. 5.
[2] Richard N. Gardner, "U.N. as Policeman," *Saturday Review*, Aug. 7, 1971.
[3] See "Protection of the Environment," *E.R.R.*, 1968 Vol. I, pp. 445-463.

The big question for the U.N. conference, and for all subsequent attempts to stop worldwide pollution, is whether the concern about the environment has come too late to do much good. Has man, in fact, gone too far to turn back? Can the nations make the hard political decisions that are necessary to establish worldwide cooperation in the face of the present crisis? Anything less than a full-scale international effort seems futile. The world's ecosystem is one; it is such that no nation alone can clean up its environment. The atmosphere carries industrial pollutants and pesticides all over the earth. Virtually every international waterway is polluted, and becoming worse year by year.

Growing Severity of Pollution on All Continents

Lake Erie is "dead,"[4] and so is the Lake of Zurich. The Baltic and Mediterranean Seas are dying. Lake Baikal in Soviet Siberia, the world's largest fresh-water lake, is being poisoned by effluent from pulp mills and industries. In the heart of Africa, the Zambesi River is polluted by raw sewage as it flows over Victoria Falls. Coastal waters of the South Seas are fouled by human and chemical wastes, and coral reefs are dying as a result. The once-lovely Rhine River is Europe's drainpipe to the sea, carrying the filth of cities and factories in such quantity that Germans say it ought to be called the Rinne, their word for sewer. By the time Rhine waters reach Amsterdam, they are so polluted that a Dutch newspaper reports it is able to develop photographic film in them.

Nearly every big city has severe smog problems. London has made improvements since the "killer smog" of 1952 contributed to the death of 4,000 persons. But conditions have worsened in many other places. Some of the worst smog problems today are found in Mexico City, Tokyo and Santiago, Chile. In the United States, for the first time, the federal government on Nov. 18, 1971, ordered 23 industrial plants and steel mills shut down temporarily at Birmingham, Ala., to relieve a smog crisis there. Pollution alerts were issued at half a dozen other cities in the eastern United States. But air pollution is not confined to individual metropolitan areas or nations. In Sweden, the nation's pine forests are withering under rainfall that bears sulphur compounds blown from Germany's Ruhr Valley. Pesticides from Africa have been found in the West Indies, 3,600 miles away.

---

[4] A condition caused by pollution-induced plant growth which shuts off sunlight and allows algae to decompose below the surface, exhausting the oxygen in the water. See "Coastal Conservation," *E.R.R.*, 1970 Vol. I, pp. 149-150.

The worldwide ecological movement is relatively new. The word ecology[5] entered the English language about a century ago. But the modern ecological movement is scarcely a decade old. In the United States, it is sometimes dated from 1962, the year Rachel Carson's book *Silent Spring* appeared, bringing the environmental crisis to public attention. Underlying the world environmental concern is the growing awareness that the capacity of the Earth to support human life is finite. There are definite limits to the Earth's resources, whether man abuses them or not. And there is suspicion that man may be approaching the limits of those resources in several areas,[6] including food and water.[7] Even those who have written glowingly of the so-called Green Revolution, which has doubled and tripled agricultural yields in certain regions, freely admit that improved agricultural technology may only have bought a few years of time for man to solve the problems of rapid population growth.[8]

Abuse and Fast Depletion of Earth's Resources

Per capita consumption of the Earth's resources is many times greater in the developed than in the developing countries. Efforts to close the economic gap between the world's rich and poor nations will inevitably increase the strain on resources. One scientist, Preston Cloud, has estimated that to bring the rest of the world up to the current U.S. level of consumption would require a yearly world output of 60 billion tons of iron, a billion tons of lead, 700 million tons of zinc and more than 50 million tons of tin—between 200 and 400 times the present world production levels. Dr. Philip Hauser, a sociologist, estimates that the world's resources could support a population of only half a billion people if they all consumed at the U.S. level.[9] Loren Eiseley, the anthropologist, has called man a "flame" that will eventually consume the world.

Depletion of the earth's resources is one side of the ecological dilemma; pollution is the other. Man the consumer is also man the poisoner. Pollutants that enter the earth's ecosystem at any point may be expected to spread across the globe. Air pollution and water pollution are generally treated as dis-

---

[5] Derived from the Greek word *oikos*, for household, it is a branch of science concerned with the inter-relationship of organisms and their environment.

[6] See Paul and Anne Erlich, *Population, Resources, Environment* (1970), pp. 51-112.

[7] See Robert Rienow and Leona Train Rienow, *Moment in the Sun* (1969); William and Paul Paddock, *Famine, 1975* (1967); and Rene Dumont and Bernard Rosier, *The Hungry Future* (1969).

[8] See "Green Revolution," *E.R.R.*, 1970 Vol. I, pp. 219-240.

[9] The present estimated world population is 3.7 billion.

tinct problems by environmentalists. However, French ocean-ographer Jacques Cousteau recently declared that "there is only one pollution because every single thing, every chemical whether in the air or on land will end up in the ocean."[10]

Cousteau fears that the damage being done to the oceans and world's great rivers by industrial wastes, oil spills, pesticides and other chemicals may be irreversible. "Twenty-five per cent of all the DDT compounds so far produced are already in the sea. They will all end up in the sea finally. But already 25 per cent has reached the sea—cadmium, mercury, all these problems." Another great oceanographer and marine scientist, Dr. Jacques Piccard, warned just a few weeks earlier that at the current rate of pollution, there would be no life in the oceans in 25 years. He said that the shallow Baltic Sea would be the first to die, and that the Adriatic and the Mediterranean would be next.

International Nature of Oceanic and Air Pollution

A United Nations report on marine pollution explains how an ocean can be "killed": "The ecological balance of the oceans can be upset in many ways. Some pollutants simply poison the animals and plants with which they come into contact. Other pollutants make such a demand on the oxygen dissolved in sea water—oxygen which is essential to the life of marine animals—that the living competitors suffocate. Some pollutants encourage the growth of a single species which either consumes or poisons other species. Still other pollutants accumulate in marine food chains and webs because they are not readily metabolized. Pollutants concentrated by food chains can reach levels which upset physiological functions."[11]

The U.N. document emphasizes the hazards of oil pollution, from accidental spills from tankers and the rupture of off-shore wells. "A recent estimate puts oil pollution from oil transport activities alone at one million metric tons per year and the total from all human activities at no less than 10 times this amount." Thor Heyerdahl, the Norwegian anthro-pologist-explorer, noted after his successful crossing of the Atlantic Ocean in the summer of 1970 that his papyrus raft, the Ra, encountered great blobs of tar-like material on the ocean surface on many of the 57 days it was at sea.

---

[10] Jacques Cousteau, "Our Oceans are Dying," *The New York Times,* Nov. 14, 1971.

[11] Oscar Schachter and Daniel Serwer, "Marine Pollution—Potential for Catastrophe (United Nations document OPI/444-06208), April 1971.

Experts are also concerned by the rising concentrations of the so-called "chlorinated hydrocarbons" in the sea. These consist mainly of the pesticides DDT, dieldrin and endrin. Another class of chemicals, the polychlorinated biphenyls, are also found in increasing amounts. Both classes of compounds are responsible for massive kills of marine life. "Levels of DDT contamination in marine fish may, in fact, be approaching levels associated with the collapse of fisheries for freshwater areas," the U.N. report states.

If possible, atmospheric pollution is even more ubiquitous than oceanic pollution. It comes from various sources—from industry, the heating of buildings, trash burning, jet airplanes. The principal culprit is the internal combustion engine. The U.S. Public Health Service has estimated that in the United States alone, the nation's motor vehicles spew into the atmosphere each year some 66 million tons of carbon monoxide, one million tons of sulphur oxides, six million tons of nitrogen oxides, 12 million tons of hydrocarbons, one million tons of particulate matter and assorted other dangerous substances, such as tetraethyl lead. Under certain conditions of wind and temperature, the combination of these gases can produce "killer" smogs. One estimate is that the average resident of New York City, simply by breathing the air of his city, "smokes" the equivalent of 38 cigarettes a day.

The steadily rising combustion of fossil fuels—coal, gasoline, fuel oil—presents still another global problem, which is only dimly understood. The Air Conservation Committee of the American Academy for the Advancement of Science has found that the amount of carbon dioxide released into the air has tripled since the beginning of the century, from three billion to nine billion tons. By the end of the century, industry and transport vehicles may be producing as much as 50 billion tons of carbon dioxide a year.

Technology Versus Ecology Since World War II

The committee observed that combustion could raise the concentration of carbon dioxide in the atmosphere by as much as 17 times. No one is sure what the result of such high concentration would be. Some scientists believe it would act as a "heat trap," raising the temperature of the Earth. One possible consequence could be the melting of the Greenland and Antarctic ice caps, raising the level of the oceans by as much as 250 feet and drowning every port city in the world.

Most pollution problems made their first appearance, or became very much worse, in the years following World War

II. Especially in the developed nations of the world, the principal factor was the technological revolution that transformed the nature of agricultural and industrial production. As a result of the new technology, and of vastly altered consumption patterns, the output of certain items which contribute heavily to pollution problems zoomed upward. According to Barry Commoner, production of non-returnable soda bottles increased 53,000 per cent in the quarter-century after the war; synthetic fiber output rose by 5,980 per cent; mercury used in chlorine production, by 3,930 per cent, and mercury used in mildew resistant paint by 3,120 per cent. DDT, detergents and synthetic plastics made their appearance on the market. Authorities estimate that human beings are now exposed to over half a million chemical pollutants, and that the number is increasing by 400 to 500 a year.

The new technologies have transformed the face of agriculture, as well as industry, in the developed countries. The steadily rising use of pesticides and fertilizers is one part of the story. Another is the evolution of "agribusiness"—the assembly-line approach to the raising of crops and animals. Cattle, for example, are not turned out to graze but are kept in feed lots; with little exercise, they gain weight much faster. But the concentration of their wastes in one small area constitutes another strain on the environment. In the United States, the volume of animal waste that finds its way untreated into rivers and streams is estimated to be ten times as great as the volume of human wastes.

A special problem of the technological age is radiation pollution. One source of exposure to radiation is isotype therapy and X-ray diagnosis and therapy, which has increased significantly in recent years. Until the leading powers agreed in 1963 to discontinue above-ground testing, the radioactive fallout from atmospheric explosions of nuclear devices represented a growing threat to human health. Scientists found alarmingly high levels of cancer-causing strontium-90 in humans all over the earth. Atmospheric winds carried radioactive ash from Hiroshima around the world in barely two weeks.

The newest threat of radioactive contamination stems from the proliferation of nuclear power plants to generate electricity.[12] Reactors constantly "leak" tiny amounts of radiation. While this leakage constitutes only a small fraction of the

[12] As of November 1971, 23 commercial nuclear power plants were in operation in the United States, 54 were under construction and 48 were being designed. See "Nuclear Power Options," *E.R.R.*, 1971 Vol. II, pp. 587-606.

"background" radiation received from the environment, there is a bitter scientific controversy about how dangerous these small doses are. A related argument concerns the disposal of radioactive byproducts of the power-generating process. The Atomic Energy Commission pins its hopes on storing the by-products in underground salt mines. Given the long radioactive life of such substances, many scientists fear that such storage may merely postpone the day of reckoning.

Lord Ritchie-Calder, the British author-environmentalist, has pointed out that in some atomic wastes the radioactivity can persist for hundreds of thousands of years. "With the multiplication of power reactors, the wastes will increase," he wrote. "It is calculated that by the year 2000, the number of six-ton nuclear 'hearses' [trucks] in transit to 'burial grounds' at any given time on the highways of the United States will be well over 3,000 and the amount of radioactive products will be about a billion curies, which is a mighty lot of curies to be roaming around a populated country."[13]

Still another pollutant of the modern age has only recently come to the attention of researchers: noise. In the crowded cities of the world, noise—from aircraft, construction, vehicles and amplified sound systems—is reaching levels beyond the capacity of humans to absorb without injury. Scientists have found that excessive noise can raise blood pressure, increase the cholesterol count, affect the heart and glands, harm unborn children and cause stress and irritability.[14]

Special Problems of Poor Countries

A HIGH RATE of population increase puts a heavy strain on resources and severely handicaps efforts to develop the economies of the poorer nations. Not only is the population of the poor nations rising fast, it is shifting to the cities at an even more rapid rate.[15] The urban growth has produced wretched ghettos and shanty. towns in the developing world, more squalid than any slum in the industrial countries. City govern-

---

[13] Lord Ritchie-Calder, "Mortgaging the Old Homestead," *Foreign Affairs*, January 1970, p. 211.

[14] "New Pollutant, Noise, Causing Deafness and Illness," in *Man's Control of the Environment* (publication of Congressional Quarterly), August 1970.

[15] Annual population growth is currently estimated at 2.9 per cent for Latin America, 2.7 per cent for Africa and 2.3 per cent for Asia, well above the 2.0 world average and Western European (0.6) and U.S. (2.0) marks. See "Urbanization of the Earth," *E.R.R.*, 1970 Vol. I, pp. 363-382.

ments are virtually powerless to cope with the swelling tide of humanity, and sanitary and social services are almost non-existent. As living conditions in the ghettos deteriorate, environmental problems rise.

Environmental decay, endemic disease and social disorder are bred in the overcrowding and misery of the slums. But air and water pollution, which are also increasing, come from the industries and technological advances. Industrialization, increased use of fossil fuels, and a sharp rise in the number of cars on the road are responsible. Mexico City has been singled out as having the highest carbon monoxide level in the entire world, exceeding even that of Los Angeles. Mexico City is ringed by 5,000 factories, which, experts say, account for 20 per cent of the pollution. Another 20 per cent comes from open burning of garbage. But the bulk of the city's smog—60 per cent of it—comes from the million cars, trucks and buses that jam the streets.[16]

Quest for Economic Viability at Expense of Ecology

The coming U.N. conference on the environment may prove to be a turning point for environmental protection efforts in the developing world. Early indications are that the developing countries will be willing and interested participants in the Stockholm discussions, and in any environmental arrangements which result from them. "Up to now, poor nations usually turned deaf when rich nations discussed ecological dangers. In developing countries there has been little demand for a cleaner environment," Irwin Goodwin wrote in *The Washington Post*, Aug. 8, 1971. A study by the Organization of American States noted that, "given the amply justified emphasis of policy upon raising living standards in Latin America, environmental protection tends to be viewed largely as irrelevant, and even as a hindrance to development."

Such a view has been quite commonly held throughout the developing world. An Indian government official was quoted as saying: "The wealthy worry about car fumes. We worry about starvation." Ceylon's Ambassador to the U.N., Hamilton Shirley Amerasinghe, has stated that "developing countries have of late been warned of the price that has to be paid in the form of environmental pollution for industrial development."

All developing countries are aware of the risks [he continued] but...their economists, and planners must not and will not allow

[16] "Saving Latin Environment: An International Task," *The Latin American Service,* July 28, 1971.

themselves to be distracted from the imperatives of economic development and growth by the illusory dream of an atmosphere free of smoke or a landscape innocent of chimney stacks.[17]

In Africa, an official of the Senegalese government, speaking of water pollution, has said, "The problem is indeed a serious one...we are reaching the point where even drinking water supplies are threatened." The official, Babacar Diop, then observed: "Solving this problem requires international measures. But that is not at all the same as to say that such measures can be considered a sort of compensation or a justification for transferring a part of the aid now given third-world countries to the fight against pollution.... I believe that it is absolutely necessary to fight pollution, but at the same time, pollution may bring with it certain 'advantages.' "[18]

Curiously, rich countries may also face economy-ecology dilemmas. In the United States, Democratic Party Chairman Lawrence F. O'Brien asked in a recent speech:

> What priority does air pollution have to a mother in the core city whose baby has been bitten by a rat? What priority does a polluted lake have to a family whose main recreation area is a littered alley?
>
> If we cannot solve the problems of poverty and squalor and racial bigotry that have created our slums, it will do us no good to solve the problems of water and air pollution and contamination that are despoiling our countryside.

The clear challenge ahead will be to reconcile the urgent need to raise living standards among the two-thirds of the world's people who are desperately poor and to prevent the environmental degradation that will eventually impoverish the entire Earth.

Pesticide Popularity in Third World Despite Harm

The reconciliation is likely to prove difficult, not only because of the demand in the underdeveloped world for more industry, but also because the application of modern technology to agriculture carries with it the threat of environmental damage. A fierce argument is now raging over the use of DDT and other pesticides. DDT (dichloro-diphenyl-trichloroethane) is one of a family of chlorinated hydrocarbons which, along with the newer polychlorinated biphenyls, are used extensively to destroy crop-killing and disease-carrying insects.

---

[17] Quoted by M. Taghi Farvar, *et. al.*, "The Pollution of Asia," *Environment* (magazine of the Scientists' Institute for Public Information, St. Louis), October 1971, p. 10.

[18] Quoted in *Topic* magazine, Issue No. 57, a publication of the U.S. Information Service. Interview reprinted from *CERES*, magazine of the U.N. Food and Agriculture Organization.

Extensive studies have shown that DDT is harmful to a broad spectrum of animal life, killing some species and damaging the liver, central nervous system and reproductive capacity of others. It has been blamed for massive fish kills, and for the inability of some fish-eating birds to develop shells sufficiently strong to protect their eggs—and offspring. Some medical research has indicated that the compound has harmful effects on humans.[19] Rats fed a steady diet of DDT have developed cancer, suggesting—but not proving—that humans might be susceptible also.

DDT is an extraordinarily stable compound which tends to become more and more concentrated the farther along the food chain it moves. DDT has been found in the fat of Antarctic seals and penguins, in the ice of Alaskan glaciers, and in the milk of nursing mothers all over the world. A Swedish toxicologist, Dr. Goran Lofroth of Stockholm University, has reported that nursing infants in Sweden consume twice the daily "safe" limit of DDT set by the World Health Organization.

As an insecticide, DDT has been found wanting by many ecologists. Insects tend to develop immunity to it, making necessary the application of ever-larger amounts and the continual development of newer and stronger pesticides. At the same time, DDT and the other pesticides may harm the natural enemies of the insect pests—birds, for example. For all these reasons, several developed countries, including the United States, have placed controls on the marketing and use of several pesticides and seem to be moving toward an outright ban on them.

The federal government has restricted domestic uses of DDT since November 1969 and the Environmental Protection Agency is expected to complete court-ordered hearings by January 1972 on whether to ban all uses in the United States. The agency estimated that 35 per cent of the former uses of the pesticide are now forbidden. The uses that are still permitted are mainly agricultural. No restrictions have been placed on exports of American-manufactured DDT. According to agency officials, Montrose Chemical, the principal U.S. maker, produced 123 million pounds of the pesticide in 1970 and exported 82 million pounds of it.

---

[19] Erlich, *op. cit.*, pp. 129-134. See also Samuel Mines, *The Last Days of Mankind* (1971), pp. 215-240, and Steven H. Wodka, "Pesticides Since Silent Spring," in *The Environmental Handbook* (1970), pp. 76-91.

Pesticides, especially DDT, have strong defenders in the developing world. Dr. Norman Borlaug, father of the Green Revolution, and developer of the "miracle wheat" strains now in use in many parts of the developing world, recently attacked "irresponsible environmentalists" for their opposition to the use of DDT and other chemical pesticides and fertilizers. "No chemical," Borlaug said, "has ever done as much as DDT to improve the health, economic and social benefits of the people of the developing nations."[20]

Borlaug's view is backed by the U.N. Food and Agriculture Organization, the single largest user of DDT in the world. The FAO opposes any ban on DDT because it has found no acceptable substitute for controlling the spread of malaria, yellow fever, elephantiasis, sleeping sickness and cholera. The organization also emphasizes the use of pesticides in protecting crops against the ravages of insect plagues, such as locusts, cotton worms and corn borers. *CERES*, the FAO magazine, has argued that "indiscriminate attacks on pesticides should be resisted by developing nations."

Modern technology has introduced into agriculture a host of other substances which, like the pesticides, can cause ecological damage. Among these are mercury compounds (used as fungicides), lead (used in automotive fuel), and phosphates and nitrates (used in fertilizers). Recently the Food and Drug Administration issued warnings against diethylstilbesterol (DES), a synthetic estrogen used to fatten cattle, which, it has been shown, may cause cancer in humans and animals.

Aswan Dam Example; 'Export' of Pollution Abroad

Developing countries typically need roads, power grids, oil pipelines for a viable economy. But all of them exact some price in environmental damage, and there is inevitably a trade-off between the economic benefits and the ecological disadvantages. Perhaps the cruelest choice comes in deciding to build dams. They control floods and provide irrigation water to raise farm yields. And they generate electric power. Unhappily, as a recent United Nations Development Programme-Food and Agriculture Organization report showed, "dams can raise more problems than they solve."

The classic case is the new high dam at Aswan, Egypt. Throughout history the lower Nile Valley has been periodically inundated by floods. The high dam now prevents flood-

---

[20] Quoted in *The New York Times*, Nov. 9, 1971.

ing. As a result, the rich river silt no longer fertilizes the delta lands, and commercial fertilizer must be used. Flood-borne nutrients no longer reach the sea, and the fish catch in the eastern Mediterranean is declining drastically. Paradoxically, the silt is now building up behind the high dam, and will eventually render it useless. Controlled irrigation from the new dam is salinating the soil bit by bit, making periodic flushing—an expensive process—necessary. Additionally, parasite-carrying snails are multiplying in the irrigation channels, and schistosomiasis, or biharzia, a debilitating tropical disease, is spreading rapidly.[21]

In a number of ways, the developed countries are a source of the ecological difficulties of the underdeveloped world. The United States, Japan and Western Europe supply the world with its automotive vehicles, its mills, factories and chemical plants. They drill the oil wells, build the refineries and supply the technology available to the developing nations. In the United States, new air pollution laws are so strict that copper smelting operations are being sharply reduced. *Vision*, a Spanish-language magazine which circulates throughout Latin America, notes that "in almost the entire nation it is virtually impossible to build a copper smelter." As a result, smelting operations are being moved to other countries; thus the United States, a big user of copper, is transferring a pollution problem abroad.

Gunnar Myrdal, the Swedish economist, has predicted a "people's movement in developed countries to end pollution and all the harmful effects of technology on the environment." But, Myrdal observes, "for Americans to be concerned enough to do something about the detrimental changing of local ecology by development projects in poorer countries, that will take time."

Perhaps the most important factor of all is the subtle export of attitudes from the developed countries to the less-developed world. The poorer countries have a strong desire and an unquestioned right to seek to raise their standard of living. To a certain extent, they try to do so by utilizing the technology that is made available to them; some environmental damage is accepted as a fair price for the effort. In the process, many political leaders and technologists appear to have adopted the traditional western view that a constantly rising level of consumption is necessary to economic health.

---

[21] See *Our World in Peril* (1971), edited by Sheldon Novick and Dorothy Cottrell, pp. 26-27.

Many ecologists believe, however, that development in the poorer countries cannot and will not follow the pattern of the industrial nations. The constraints are physical; the capacity of the earth is limited. "Just think," someone has suggested, "what would happen to the atmosphere if 700 million Chinese started driving big automobiles!"

Ironically, many leaders in the developing world have become afflicted with what is termed "growthmania" at a time when even the developed countries are becoming aware that fundamental changes in their own consumption patterns are inevitable. Paul W. McCracken, President Nixon's chief economic adviser, has stated: "simply producing more...if it means putting more smoke in the atmosphere...is not an adequate goal."[22] A leading economist, Kenneth Boulding, has begun to develop a non-growth-oriented economic theory under the title "The Economics of Spaceship Earth." Boulding argues that within the confines of the globe, there are no unlimited reservoirs for extraction or pollution, and that consumption and reproduction must therefore be minimized.

One problem that all industrial countries—and many less-developed countries as well—face in common is the skyrocketing demand for electric power. Electric power needs in the United States are doubling every decade. Every step up in generating capacity—whether through steam generator plants, nuclear power stations, or hydroelectric dams brings on some environmental disruption. And should the developed countries increasingly turn—as is expected—to nuclear power, the problem of waste disposal will become an international worry.

Movement For International Action

ENVIRONMENTAL PROBLEMS are as real in Communist as in capitalist countries. The pollution of Lake Baikal in Soviet Siberia has been amply documented.[23] In a recent issue, the *Proceedings* of the Association of American Geographers identified some 30 other examples of serious industrial and agricultural fouling of Soviet inland waters.[24] Earlier in

---

[22] Quoted by Hobart Rowen in *The Washington Post*, April 23, 1970. Herbert Stein succeeds McCracken as chief economic adviser, Jan. 1, 1972.

[23] For example, see Marshal Goldman, "The Pollution of Lake Baikal," *The New Yorker*, June 19, 1971.

[24] Article by Philip R. Pryde, reprinted in *Environment*, November 1970, pp. 30-39.

the year, the Soviet government reported a break in one of the country's biggest oil pipelines, located near the Ural River, which empties into the Caspian Sea. Smog and sewage disposal problems plague Soviet cities. In the Eastern European satellite countries, similar environmental problems abound: forests are dying, and industrial soot covers the cities. It is reported that Budapest, Hungary, is capable of treating only one-half of its sewage. The rest contaminates the Danube River.

Ray Vickers of *The Wall Street Journal* reported from Rome, Nov. 26, 1971, the Italian Communist Party had adopted the theme that capitalism causes pollution whereas only communism can provide the political framework for a clean environment. "This seems to be the official environmental party line emanating from Moscow today," Vickers added. "It's being worked into Red propaganda in Britain, France and elsewhere so consistently that there is a Soviet smell to the whole claim." When an Eastern European Communist country points its finger at capitalist polluters, "it indeed is a case of the pot calling the kettle black...."

> Pollution, however, is finally becoming an issue within the USSR [he continued]...as it is in the capitalist world. More and more newspapers carry feature stories about ecological damage, and conservationists are raising their voices against indiscriminate production without regard for the land, sea and air.
>
> At the ministry of health headquarters in Moscow, a half dozen officials met not long ago with a reporter to outline some of the steps now being taken to combat ecological damage and to protect the environment.

The situation of Japan, Asia's only thoroughly industrial state, is not very different from that of the developed western nations. Since the end of World War II, Japan has come charging pell-mell into the front ranks of the world's industrial powers, and has paid a fearful price in environmental degradation. To some visitors, Tokyo is the most crowded and most polluted city on earth. An observer has written:

> In Japan, pollution—whether you pronounce it with two l's or two r's—is a very dirty word. Because, for man and beast alike, there simply is no escape from it. It is in the air you breathe. It is in the rice and fish you eat. It fouls the beaches where you try to swim. It fosters some of the most baffling diseases in medical history. It pounds at people's eardrums around the clock, accelerating the flow of adrenalin and infringing on their territoriality.[25]

---

[25] Darrell Houston, "Remember When You Could See Mount Fuji?," *Alicia Patterson Fund Newsletter*, Jan. 13, 1971. See also "Emergent Japan," *E.R.R.*, 1970 Vol. I, pp. 171-172.

A persistent blanket of smog shrouds Japan's sacred mountain, Fuji. Within the city limits of Tokyo, factories discharge 1.7 million tons of waste gases a year; two million motor vehicles spew out 700,000 tons of carbon monoxide. Fifty-five per cent of the city's sewage is dumped untreated into the sea.[26] Significantly, the so-called minamata disease—now identified as mercury poisoning from tainted shellfish—was first detected in Japan. Another exotic affliction, Itai-Itai—a word that is translated as "ouch-ouch," since the victim aches all over—was traced to rice contaminated by cadmium from the exhaust gases and waste waters of zinc refineries.

The catalog of problems is as endless as it is repetitious. In Italy, seven out of every ten miles of the nation's waterways are polluted, and most of the larger lakes are dead. In Latin America, the big industrial centers such as Sao Paulo in Brazil and Buenos Aires in Argentina have turned their rivers into black and fetid industrial sewers. Even China, the sleeping giant, is awakening to environmental problems. Western newsmen who have been admitted to China in recent months reported seeing or being told of anti-pollution activities.

Economic Barriers to Control of Global Pollution

A number of other countries have begun to control pollution. Britain has established a cabinet-level post of Minister of the Environment, and given its holder, 37-year-old Peter Walker, formidable powers to intervene in the planning of transportation, housing, land-use and regulation of rivers and coastal waters. One result of rising British interest in a better environment is a 70 per cent reduction in air pollution in London, and the return of trout and pike to the lower reaches of the once heavily contaminated Thames River.[27]

For the past half a decade, Paris has been trying to cleanse its air. As an experiment, the city government has set up two 16-foot-high towers around a railway station, Gare de Lyon, with air filtering devices to remove dust and pollutants. In Santiago, Chile, the new Institute of Occupational Health and Air Pollution Research has been set up to gather basic information on the city's mounting pollution. The institute's work is supported by the World Health Organization and the U.N. Development Programme. Japan has hesitantly started its first anti-pollution efforts with the creation of an environmental agency whose task is mainly educational. The Japanese

---

[26] "Tokyo: the Problem City after the Shock," *Business Week*, Oct. 9, 1971.

[27] For background on Britain's environmental efforts, see "Protection of the Countryside," *E.R.R.*, 1971 Vol. II, pp. 557-563.

have sought anti-pollution advice from such diverse persons as Russell Train, chairman of President Nixon's Council on Environmental Quality, and Ralph Nader, the consumer advocate.

Considerable technology for limiting the contamination of air, water and soil has been available for many years. It is just beginning to be applied on any significant scale. And so far, the application of technology is strictly at the local, state or national level; no advances have been made on the international level. In the United States, clear-air and clean-water legislation are prompting industry to make major investment in clean-up techniques. Many states have instituted tax incentives to encourage industrial-pollution abatement.[28] The Atomic Energy Commission, under its new chairman, James R. Schlesinger, has emphasized environmental matters—an area in which the commission had long been accused of showing gross insensitivity. In recent months, the federal government has begun to seek indictments against officers of companies that are consistent polluters.

The chief obstacles to the widespread adoption of anti-pollution technology are economic. Barry Commoner has estimated the cost of halting pollution in the United States and repairing essential parts of the ecosystem at about $40 billion a year for the next 25 years—a total of one trillion dollars. Even such an enormous outlay would not bring the environment all the way back to where it was before the great technological leap after World War II.

Worldwide, the costs would be astronomical. The Organization for Economic Cooperation and Development has estimated that it would take an annual outlay equal to 2 per cent of the gross national product of the industrial countries just to ensure that environmental deterioration is gradual rather than rapid. In the United States alone that would amount to $20 billion. Holding the line against pollution, they say, would cost about 4 per cent, and repairing past damage while preventing future problems could cost three to four times that much.[29] At present, no nation is likely to make a commitment on so grand a scale. Even if a nation had the resources to do so, it "must bear in mind...the consequences of putting its industries and its economy at a competitive disadvantage, should other nations not follow suit."[30]

[28] See "Pollution Technology," *E.R.R.*, 1971 Vol. I, pp. 20-21.

[29] Figures cited in *The Washington Post*, Feb. 2, 1970.

[30] Michael Harwood, "We Are Killing the Sea Around Us," *The New York Times Magazine*, Oct. 24, 1971, p. 91.

Ecologists thus stress the need for an international approach. They cite the decline in levels of radioactive fallout in recent years as evidence that international agreements do have value. They point to the possibilities inherent in space technology for creating a worldwide environmental protection system. Under the earth resources satellite program, the National Aeronautics and Space Administration will soon launch Erts-A, an orbiting satellite with infra-red remote sensing devices capable of detecting pollutants from a height of 492 miles. Several such satellites, linked to computers on the ground, could form the basis for a global environmental monitoring system.[31]

Environmental programs have already been initiated by a number of regional and international organizations. The World Bank in 1970 appointed an environmental adviser to review all Bank projects for their ecological implications. The Organization of Economic Cooperation and Development, embracing the United States, Canada, Japan and 19 western European nations, has agreed to draft common pollution standards and to work toward a system of enforcement. Eight nations of the East and West—the United States, the Soviet Union, East Germany, West Germany, Britain, France, Italy and Poland—agreed in October 1971 to set up an international research center to investigate common problems arising from the spread of modern technology. The center, to be known as the International Institute of Applied Systems Analysis, would study such critical factors as population growth, food production, raw material depletion and all kinds of pollution.

Plan of Action Expected From Stockholm Meeting

Various U.N. councils and agencies have undertaken specific programs in such areas as natural resources, population, control of radiation emissions and health problems. The 1972 Conference on the Human Environment represents a giant step in international cooperation. The Conference, in the planning stages for the past two and a half years, is billed as an "action" meeting. Its mandate is to consider proposals in six major areas:

Planning and management of the environmental quality of human settlements everywhere.

Environmental aspects of natural resource management (including animal, botanical and mineral resources).

Identification and control of environmental pollutants and nuisances of broad significance.

---

[31] See Paul A. Dickson, "Sensitive, Remote Eyes Show Changes on Mother Earth," *Smithsonian* magazine, January 1971, pp. 14-20.

Educational, information, social and cultural aspects of environmental issues.

Economic development and environment.

Implications for international organizations of action proposals.

According to U.N. documents, possible courses of action include the signing of new international agreements; creation of a system for collection of data and monitoring of pollution levels; systematic exchanges of information among countries; promotion of scientific research into environment-saving alternatives for dangerous chemicals and pesticides; setting of international limits for chemical, physical and biological contaminants; and the formulation of national environmental policies.

A massive "Report on the State of the Global Environment" will be prepared and circulated before the meeting. It will contain country-by-country reports, and is expected to give the first comprehensive look at the enormously complex issues facing the participants. The delegates, representing the 131 U.N. member states, including the newly seated mainland China delegation, will be asked to approve a "Declaration on the Human Environment," drawn up in preliminary meetings by a 27-man steering committee. The declaration, containing "universally recognized fundamental principals," will serve as the charter of the world environmental movement in years to come.

It is apparent that the U.N. will not be transformed—not yet at least—into a world policeman to apprehend polluting nations. National sovereignty is not at issue in Stockholm. Given the short time the conference will meet—12 days in all—it is likely that the thousands of participants will be able to agree only on a few very broad policy issues. U.N. officials are putting special emphasis on the mass impact the meeting can have on public attitudes around the world. Environmental education and information programs are due to receive a boost unparalleled in U.N. history. The emphasis on changing basic human attitudes is roundly applauded by ecologists, who for a number of years have been saying that the only way to make the environment healthy is to learn to live in harmony with it and to stop trying to conquer it.

32091